# Natural Law

STUDIES IN ETHICS AND ECONOMICS

Series Editor
Samuel Gregg, Acton Institute

Economics as a discipline cannot be detached from a historical background that was, it is increasingly recognized, religious in nature. Adam
Ferguson and Adam Smith drew on the work of sixteenth and seventeenth century Spanish theologians, who strove to understand the process
of exchange and trade in order to better address the moral dilemmas they
saw arising from the spread of commerce in the New World. After a long
period in which economics became detached from theology and ethics,
many economists and theologians now see the benefit of studying economic realities in their full cultural, often religious, context. This new series, Studies in Ethics and Economics, provides an international forum for
exploring the difficult theological and economic questions that arise in the
pursuit of this objective.

Titles in the Series

*Intelligence as a Principle of Public Economy / Del pensiero come principio
d'economia publica,* by Carlo Cattaneo
*And Why Not? Morality and Business,* by François Michelin
*Faith and Liberty: The Economic Thought of the Late Scholastics,* by Alejandro
A. Chafuen
*The Boundaries of Technique: Ordering Positive and Normative Concerns in
Economic Research,* by Andrew Yuengert
*Within the Market Strife: American Economic Thought from* Rerum Novarum
*to* Vatican II, by Kevin E. Schmiesing
*Natural Law: The Foundation of an Orderly Economic System,* by Alberto M.
Piedra
*The Church and the Market: A Catholic Defense of the Free Economy,* by
Thomas E. Woods Jr.

*To Andy with appreciation for his great friendship and assistance in all my endeavours at the Institute.*

*Alberto*

# Natural Law

## The Foundation of an Orderly Economic System

Alberto M. Piedra

LEXINGTON BOOKS
*Lanham • Boulder • New York • Toronto • Oxford*

LEXINGTON BOOKS

Published in the United States of America
by Lexington Books
An imprint of The Rowman & Littlefield Publishing Group, Inc.
4501 Forbes Boulevard, Suite 200, Lanham, Maryland 20706

PO Box 317
Oxford
OX2 9RU, UK

British Library Cataloguing in Publication Information Available

**Library of Congress Cataloging-in-Publication Data**

Piedra, Alberto Martínez, 1926–
  Natural law : the foundation of an orderly economic system / Alberto M.
Piedra.
       p. cm. — (Studies in ethics and economics)
  Includes bibliographical references and index.
  ISBN 0-7391-0934-0 (alk. paper) — ISBN 0-7391-0949-9 (pbk. : alk. paper)
  1. Economics—Religious aspects—Catholic Church. 2. Natural law—Religious
aspects—Catholic Church. I. Title. II. Series.
BX1795.E27P54 2004
330.1—dc22

                                                                    2004012217

Printed in the United States of America

∞™ The paper used in this publication meets the minimum requirements of
American National Standard for Information Sciences—Permanence of Paper for
Printed Library Materials, ANSI/NISO Z39.48–1992.

For my devoted wife, Edita, and my children,
Alberto, Javier, Pedro, Edita Maria, and Conchita

—ᗰ—

# Contents

# Acknowledgments

This book would not have been written without the encouragement and assistance of two prestigious scholars at the Catholic University of America to whom I owe a debt of gratitude: Dr. Jude Dougherty, Dean Emeritus of the School of Philosophy, and Dr. Sophia Aguirre, Associate Professor of Economics. To both, my sincere thanks.

A well-deserved word of thanks must also be given to Dr. Samuel Gregg, Director of Research at the Acton Institute, whose suggestions and recommendations were so useful and enlightening during the final writings of my manuscript.

Last but not least, my deep-felt gratitude and appreciation to Dr. John Lenczowski, Director of the Institute of World Politics, whose warm words of support were, at all times, invaluable.

The patience, encouragement, and love provided to me by my wife, Edita, and my children need not be expressed in writing. They are and will always be kept within the inner depths of my heart.

—〰—

# Introduction

In *A Midsummer Night's Dream*, Demetrius cautions Lysander with the words: "Disparage not the faith thou does not know." For our contemporary world, where there is a tendency to reject the faith and values of our forefathers, Shakespeare's words carry as much meaning today as they did four hundred years ago. Modern man tends to belittle the traditional rich heritage of our Western culture, claiming that the cultural and spiritual principles on which it stands and which, through the centuries, have been transmitted from generation to generation no longer befit his rational mind.

Through all generations and in all civilizations, man has always tended to search for some standard of behavior, a set of principles, that will tell him what is right and what is wrong. This norm of behavior has often been called the Law of Nature but in reality it would be more appropriate to call it the Law of Human Nature because it applies exclusively to man. Among all the various sets of law, the Law of Human Nature is the only one that man is free to obey or disobey. For example, man, like any other object, is not free to disobey the law of gravity. Neither can he, as a living organism, disobey those biological laws which he shares with other animals. However, the only set of laws or principles that man can infringe, if he so chooses, are precisely the ones that distinguish him from all other beings. The fact that man has the possibility of choosing between different alternatives is what differentiates him from all other things.

The idea that there is a law called the Law of Human Nature or a norm of right behavior is so ingrained in men's minds that few, if any, have challenged its existence. Man, from the earliest of times, has always been

1

aware that there must be a power, beyond matter, that directs the universe. This power behind the universe manifests itself in man as a law that tells him that certain types of human behavior are always considered decent while others are not.

Those who deny the existence of Natural Law and contend that this idea of a power beyond matter urging man to do good and avoid evil is unsound, should look back into history and study, for example, the moral teachings of the Greeks and Romans.[1] Greek philosophers, in their search for the source of world order and intelligibility found the explanation for these phenomena in the existence of a Cosmic Reason, an Intelligent Design, or any other transcendental *logos*. Man was not free to disobey the "laws" established by the Intelligent Design without bringing upon him the wrath of the "gods" in the form of some type of punishment.[2]

Aristotle, among others, preached the benefits of a virtuous life in accordance with the Law of Human Nature, stressing at the same time that the man of practical wisdom had to make morally sound judgments. According to him, man's specific nature, different from all other objects, gives him the capacity to make moral judgments; a capacity that is perfected by habit. If he is wise, he must use that capacity properly by practicing virtue and choosing good over evil. However, it is evident from his writings and those of other Greek philosophers that man can disobey the Law of Human Nature because he has the potential to distinguish between right and wrong.

The concept of the transcendental and the belief in man's capacity to do good or evil is not limited to the Greek and Roman moralists and philosophers that populated the shores of the mare nostrum before the advent of Christianity. The Jewish community was the oldest and most outspoken defender of the transcendental as is exemplified in the Torah. In it can be found the entire body of Jewish religious law, including both sacred books and oral tradition. Jewish law spells out in no uncertain terms the ten commandments or norms of behavior given to the Jewish people by the God of Israel.

Islam, together with Judaism and Christianity, practices a faith inherited from Abraham that believes also in one God, the Creator of the universe, provident and active in history. According to Moslem tradition, the laws of the Koran, the sacred book of Islam, were decreed by God and are binding to all faithful Moslems.

The leading religions of the East also recognize the existence of a hidden power that transcends the purely material; a power that inspires men's daily lives with a profound religious meaning. This applies primarily to the Hindu religion, which searches and proposes ways and rules of life that will lead man to the perfect state.[3] Confucianism likewise preaches a system of moral ethics which stresses the moral duties and responsibilities of man. The main goal of Confucius was to help men develop a series of human virtues that would enable them to reach the ideal or what he called the *superior man.*

Christians join the majority of humanity—both in the West and in the East—who believe in the transcendental, in some kind of God—or gods—who transcends the purely material and is not foreign to the fate of man. Christianity maintains that God, the creator of all things, governs the universe by his providence and proclaims the existence of a higher law than the law of man.

For Christians of all denominations the Law of Human Nature or Natural Law is written in the heart of man and can be discovered by him. It is the light of understanding infused in man by God which urges him to do good and avoid evil. It is nothing more than the participation of Divine Law in the rational creature. Thus, man is not morally free to disobey the Natural Law that is derived from Eternal Law and constitutes the basis of the Ten Commandments.

The preceding brief commentary on the various religious faiths that have prevailed through history clearly demonstrates that man has never ceased to believe in the existence of the transcendental. The reality of a transcendental being, external to the universe, that is concerned with the wellbeing of humanity and establishes the rules of morality has rarely been doubted. From the mythological gods of antiquity to the belief in the personal and providential God of Christianity, man has submitted himself to certain norms of behavior or rules of morality that he must not ignore if he wants to reach a state of perfection. Man never went as far as to deny the existence of Natural Law or to claim for himself the exclusive right to establish norms of moral behavior. For man to claim such a right is to usurp God as the source of ethical standards and to place upon himself the cloak of a "god" in order to become the sole arbiter of what is right and what is wrong.

It was not until the seventeenth and eighteenth centuries that the whole concept of the transcendental and the existence of a Law of Human Nature derived from Divine Law began to be seriously challenged; a challenge which has not abated at the dawn of the new millennium. This is precisely the great problem facing the modern Western mind that has denied the transcendental and with it the reality of the Natural Moral Law. Even the possibility of a rational proof of God's existence is totally discarded as an "unproven myth."[4] Carried away with a false interpretation of Natural Law and led by the idea that he is the sole arbiter of what is right and what is wrong, modern man has sacrificed the transcendental in the alter of a false freedom and crass materialism.[5] The idea of God or *logos*, as the center and prime concern of man, has been gradually relegated to a secondary plane.

The newly born science of economics easily fell prey to the bug of immanentism, offering no resistance to the scientific philosophical trends then in vogue. A purely natural, mechanistic and utilitarian approach to economics replaced the belief in free thinking responsible human beings subject to a higher moral order. It discarded any firm metaphysical foundation and accepted the prevailing scientific view of the world. The science of economics soon abandoned the entire notion of the transcendental and replaced it by the "here and now." Utilitarianism, if not outright hedonism, became the prevailing norm of conduct in man's quest for material well-being.

Now, at the dawn of a new century, humanity is witnessing a wave of innovations never before contemplated by man. For the first time in history man is experiencing a transformation of his inner self and has become more convinced than ever before that he has the potential to control his destiny. He has fallen under the spell of his own cognizant power. The tremendous achievements in the fields of science and technology and the latest innovations in information technology seem to give credence to Western man's optimistic expectations about the future of humanity.

Man has become aware that he has the power not only to transform nature and society but man himself. Thus, he can easily become the object of scientific research and manipulation like any other object. A whole new "technology" has developed, particularly in the fields of eugenics and experimental psychology, which can pose a serious threat to man's personal dignity, especially when material gain supersedes all other objectives.

Maximization of output, optimum populations, and the construction of earthly paradises are among the major goals of modern man who assumes that they are within his reach as long as society is "technically" and "efficiently" organized. Man, being in possession of the most advanced scientific knowledge, is capable of attaining these objectives and forge his own destiny. He no longer needs the transcendental and much less a providential God. Through social engineering and organized human selection a "new man" can be created free from the superstitions of past ages; a phenomenon which is fraught with promises and dangers.[6]

With the collapse of communism and the total failure of socialist policies in the former Soviet Union and other centralized economies, capitalism seems to be the system most fitted to carry out the economic objectives of modern man. There is a persistent cry for the implementation of policies based on a capitalism that has its roots in the economic liberalism of the English Classical School. Undoubtedly, economic freedom, contrary to the teachings of Marx, is indispensable for the integral development of man. Credit must be given to Adam Smith for his great contribution to economic theory and the stress he placed on economic freedom. However, to replace the evils of inefficient collectivist economic systems with an economic order that disowns the transcendental and places all its trust in work and "efficiency" can be a serious cause for concern.

It would be ironic that, now that totalitarianism of the Marxist type has lost its luster, a new and more subtle danger would raise its ugly head and threaten not only the innermost dignity of the human being but also the very existence of the free societies of the Western World. In the longer run, this threat could be equally as pernicious to man's freedoms as the more brutal systems of the past. In order to avoid this danger and preserve his freedom and dignity, man must have a better understanding of Natural Law. Without such an understanding, the very concept of Natural Law is distorted to such a degree that man ceases to be considered the most important reality within the social fabric. Consequently, the very dignity of the human person is jeopardized and man may fall prey to the abuses of brute force or the selfish interests of the powerful and mighty. It is precisely this misunderstanding of the true nature of man, together with the prevailing confusion concerning the very concept of Natural Law what lies at the root of the ills of modern society.

It is our belief that to disregard the moral principles derived from Natural Law will only rekindle the baser egotistic appetites of man and give further credence to the critics of a free market system; critics who sponsor collectivist theories under the assumption that they will solve society's multiple problems and bring about a more humane civilization.

Whether capitalism or some other economic system is best fitted to achieve the goal of attaining a more just and benevolent society is open to debate. However, before reaching any tentative conclusions about the material and spiritual benefits to be derived from any economic system certain issues need further clarification.

Can capitalism or any other economic or political system be totally separated from the realm of an ethics based on Natural Law? In other words, can it be said that economics and ethics are so independent from each other that the moral law does not apply within the area of economic activity? Even under the most favorable conditions, can the most efficient political and economic systems devised by the human mind survive if they lack the right moral foundations and a proper understanding of man as a human person? Is it not realistic to believe that any economic or political system void of the notion of the transcendental, no matter how "efficient" it may be, can lead to flagrant abuses of man's dignity by the misuse of science and technology?

The purpose of this book is to review some of these basic issues that are related to man as the principal agent of economic activity and to his role in society: issues which are crucial for the preservation of his freedom and human dignity. We will attempt to demonstrate how the long-run success of an economic system depends on its having a solid ethical foundation.

But, an ethics which is not reduced to the "natural ethics" of the moral philosophers of the seventeenth and eighteenth centuries but with an ethics which is based on transcendental principles and Natural Law. Otherwise, the system will eventually flounder amid a profusion of erroneous interpretations of Natural Law. And, what is even worse, a false assessment of Natural Law eventually will also tear down the philosophical foundations of the Rights of Man. Historically, they are both bound together.[7]

The author is well aware of the complexities involved in the study of these questions and that much has still to be done in the area of economics and its relationship with ethics. But it is to be hoped that the book will stimulate further discussions of a subject which, with few exceptions, does not seem to have received the proper attention by the academic profession.

The book will be divided into nine basic chapters, including an introduction and an epilogue. The first chapter will stress the importance of Natural Law and its relationship with Positive and Eternal Law. The impact of the Cartesian Revolution, the rise of the natural sciences and the views of the philosophers of the Enlightenment will receive special attention because of the great influence they had on the founders of the Classical School of Economics and the development of a natural ethics detached from Natural Law. Comte's materialistic interpretation of history cannot be overlooked as his "positivist" philosophy, discarding Natural Law, became the new arbiter of morality for many of his followers.

Chapter 2 will discuss the dignity of the human person as essentially different from what is generally understood as the individual. It will place emphasis on the harmful consequences of an extreme individualism and how an erroneous interpretation of Natural Law has led to the prevailing misconceptions about freedom, the cornerstone of economic and political liberalism, and to the discrediting of the idea of the Rights of Man.

The Classical School of Economics and the rise of Capitalism will be examined in the third chapter. Adam Smith and his contribution to the development of economic theory and practice will be discussed in the light of the philosophical trends then in vogue. We will focus on the influence of the Enlightenment and the English moral philosophers on his economic thinking. The moral crisis of economic liberalism, the social impact of the Industrial Revolution and the role of the bourgeoisie with its too optimistic reliance on the positive aspects of a utilitarian philosophy will be stressed also.

The fourth chapter will deal with the challenge posed to capitalism by socialism, with special emphasis on Marxism-Socialism, and by the romantic movement that led to the German Historical School. Their basic postulates will be highlighted as possible alternatives to the free market system. The stress placed on Marxism-Socialism is due to the messianic message of its doctrine and its religious faith in the inevitability of progress toward the perfect communist society: a secular objective which in many ways is far from having disappeared. Mention will be made also of American Institutionalism and, in particular, Thorstein Veblen's flagrant criticism of capitalism.

Neoclassicism and other sources of dissent will be the subject of the fifth chapter. In particular, attention will be placed on the Keynesian Revolution and the challenge posed by Chamberlin and others on the traditional concept of perfect competition.

The metaphysical dimension of man—both the individual and the social—will be presented in chapter 6. Special attention will be placed on the human and technical dimensions of capitalism and the need for the development of human virtues in accordance with the traditional concept of Natural Law. A brief summary of Hayek's libertarian approach to the moral foundations of economic liberalism will also be included. The chapter will conclude with some comments on the need to reappraise capitalism after the demise of Marxism.

Chapter 7 will explore the teleological implications of human work. It will stress the true nature and dignity of human work and its place within the context of a just economic order. Focus will be placed on whether man can be treated exclusively as an instrument of production, as is very often the case under an economic system that gives prime importance to the objective dimension of work or, on the contrary, be considered as the effective subject and the true creator and maker of work.

The economic and ethical implications of two basic contemporary issues, population and the environment, will be the subject of chapter 8. The so-called Welfare State and the threat it often poses on the the autonomy of intermediate organizations, in particular the family, will be analyzed briefly in the light of the rights and duties of the state.

The challenge of "globalization" and the need to preserve a healthy diversity within the the growing trend toward greater unity will serve as the basis of chapter 9. Can the rights of man be preserved at the dawn of the new international socioeconomic order that is being created? The attempt will be made to show that, lacking a proper comprehension of Natural Law and the essence of the reality of man, it is highly improbable that human rights can be respected or that any socioeconomic national or international order, including capitalism, can succeed. Both the path of peace and freedom and the one leading to social injustice and continuing conflict are open to contemporary man. The choice is man's to make. It is the author's hope that the thoughts expressed in this book will be helpful to man in his efforts to make the right choice and thus reach a more just socioeconomic order.

## NOTES

1. Professor Jude Dougherty, former Dean of the School of Philosophy at The Catholic University of America, reminds us of the importance natural law had in the ancient world when he writes: "The concept of natural law, of course, is an ancient one. We find it in the Greek poets, in the Athenian philosophers Plato and Aristotle, and in the Roman Stoics, Cicero and Seneca." He further elaborates on the concept of natural law and defines the notion in a rather simple way: "There are laws of nature, some of which we have discovered and articulated for ourselves and for others. A law of nature is simply a report on *what is*. It is a description of a process that under specified conditions remains invariant through time and place." See Jude F. Dougherty, *Western Creed, Western Identity: Essays in Legal and Social Philosophy* (Washington, DC: The Catholic University of America Press, 2000), 101.

2. Heraclitus (533-475) believed that all change is directed by an intelligent law which he called the *logos*. Wisdom consisted, according to him, in understanding the hidden harmony of the *logos*.

3. Buddhism acknowledges the insufficiency of the material world and preaches the need to lead a virtuous life as the only way to a passionless peace of nirvana. Hinduism seeks release from the woes of an earthly life through the practice of asceticism and a loving and trusting refuge in God. It recognizes the inadequacies of this world and teaches men the way by which they can reach the state of absolute freedom or supreme enlightenment through their own efforts or with the help of a higher assistance.

4. The great Dominican philosopher of the thirteenth century, St. Thomas Aquinas, claimed that the existence of God can be proved rationally in five different ways: (1) the argument of motion, (2) the nature of an efficient cause, (3) the difference between a thing that can exist (possibility) and the one that must exist (necessity), (4) the different gradations that exist in things, and (5) the order in the universe. Aquinas, following Aristotle, maintains that man can know God by natural reason and, given his natural inclination to the good of his rational nature, he has a natural inclination to know the truth about God and live in society.

5. C. S. Lewis, *Mere Christianity* (New York: Macmillan, 1952), 43.

6. See Henri de Lubac, *The Drama of Atheistic Humanism* (San Francisco: Ignatius Press, 1995), 406.

7. Jacques Maritain, *Man and the State* (Chicago: University of Chicago Press, 1951), 81.

# 1

—〜〜—

# Natural Law and
# the Age of Reason

## NATURAL LAW AND ITS RELATIONSHIP
## WITH POSITIVE AND ETERNAL LAW

Through the centuries the belief in the existence of an Eternal Law was hardly ever challenged in spite of the philosophical views of some skeptics who doubted everything that cannot be proved by the evidence of the senses.[1] It was defined as the law by which the Creator wishes the world to be governed and was considered the first law and the source of all other laws. Neither was the existence of Natural Law seriously questioned. In fact, the distinction between Natural and Positive Law was clearly delineated. It was generally accepted that Natural Law, *ius naturale*, proceeds from the nature of human reason. The natural law is nothing other than the light of understanding infused in us by God whereby we understand what must be done and what must be avoided. Its precepts are in exact correspondence with our natural inclinations and follow the same order.[2] On the other hand, Positive Law, *ius positivum*, is the result of custom or the will of man. This simply means that there are certain rights that are attributed to man on account of his very nature whilst others are attributed to him by man's decision.[3] The principles of Natural Law, as the English philosopher John Finnis states, "are traced out not only in moral philosophy or ethics and 'individual' conduct but also in political philosophy and jurisprudence, in political action, adjudication' and the life of the citizen."[4]

To acquire a better and fuller understanding of Natural Law it would be beneficial to review some of the writings of the Greek philosophers and

the early Fathers of the Church. For our purpose, it will be sufficient to
limit ourselves to St. Thomas Aquinas, the principal representative of the
scholastic doctors, who summarizes and completes the development of
the concept of Natural Law.[5]

Aquinas emphasizes in all of his writings the rationality of man. He reiterates at all times that man is a rational human being with an intellect
open to all reality. He presupposes that reason performs an instrumental
function or is the means through which, with the cooperation of his cen-
sorial faculties, man is able to know his own nature and that of all beings
that surround him.

According to Thomistic philosophy, law is an obligation founded upon
the demands of reason.[6] However, the imperative order of reason does not
explain in its entirety the existence of a law. It is also necessary that such
an order be directed toward a certain end which is not limited to our individual ends. Thus, to say that law is a prescription of reason that determines what is to be done, implies the existence of practical reason whose
function is to prescribe the acts that are to be performed. But, "this practical reason depends in its turn on a principle which directs it and to
which it must conform; for it prescribes such and such an act only with
the view to guide us to such and such an end, and, if therefore an end exists which is common to all our acts, this latter constitutes the first principle on which all decisions of practical reason depend."[7] The name given
to this first law, by which the Creator wills the universe to be governed, is
called Eternal Law for God Himself is eternal.

In his *Summa Theologiae*, St. Thomas defines Natural Law as the participation of the eternal law in the rational creature. Natural Law is written
in the hearts of each and every man. It is nothing other than the light of
reason infused in us by God, whereby man understands what must be
done and what must be avoided, what is good and what is evil.[8] It is the
highest way of participating in the Eternal Law and has as its main function the ordering of all the forces of human nature toward their proper
ends, particularly the intelligence and the will. Its roots lie in the ordina-
tion of man to God and is not the result of an imperative of practical reason or social disposition. Granted that the world is ruled by Divine Providence, it follows that the whole community of the universe is governed
by Divine Reason; a governance that has the nature of a law and must be
called eternal because it is not subject to time. God orders all things to His
glory and imprints in men a Natural Law or rational command that is
written in their hearts.[9]

St. Thomas stressed the distinction between Natural Law and Positive
Law. For him, Positive Law cannot lay claim to any principle of its own.
It is confined strictly to the definition of the manner of applying the Nat-
ural Law. Once the reality of Natural Law is accepted, it is justifiable to re-

gard certain positive laws as radically defective, *precisely as laws*, for want of conformity to the principles of Natural Law.[10] Gilson reiterates the limitations of positive law when he says, following Aquinas, that "human laws are an obligation only to the extent of their justice, i.e., in so far as they meet the conditions of their own definition."[11]

The "Angelic Doctor" goes to great length to ascertain the power of reason. He concludes that the "natural" light of human reason is sufficient to understand with certainty the existence of God based on the reality of created beings.[12] He did not hesitate to stress man's intellectual capacity to ascertain the existence of God and discover the essence and causes of the world around him. According to St. Thomas, man can arrive to the certitude that God exists through deduction and analogy and not by intuition as some later philosophers have claimed. He cannot reject the simple truth that nature transcends toward God who is the first and last cause of all things and that his intellect and will are subordinated to the will of the Creator. Thus, it is correct to say that the "natural order" is sustained by the Natural Laws imprinted by God on mankind.

The need to have a clear understanding of the true nature of Natural Law and its relationship with Divine Law becomes all the more evident in our confused modern era in view of the various and erroneous interpretations that it has been subjected to since the seventeenth century. Contemporary society must not lose sight of the fact that reason is not independent from Natural Law which, in its turn, draws its own truth authority from Eternal Law. It is precisely because of the reigning confusion concerning the concept of Natural Law and its implications for the well-being of society that it becomes necessary to reemphasize its true meaning and its relationship with Eternal Law. Otherwise, modern man runs the risk of losing all sight of the transcendental and, consequently, distorting the true meaning of the "natural order." It fell on the Cartesians and mainly on the philosophers of the French Enlightenment to challenge the traditional concept of Natural Law, setting themselves as its sole interpreters.

## THE CARTESIAN REVOLUTION AND
## THE RISE OF THE NATURAL SCIENCES

It was the Cartesian revolution, heir to the philosophical methods of Descartes, which opened the gates to pure rationalism.[13] Descartes formulated a new philosophy of pure reason which led to the breaking away from all arguments on authority and initiated a new era in the history of European thought. He was, to a large extent, responsible for the new anthropological approach in philosophy and the development of the social sciences; a trend which became extremely popular in eighteenth century Europe and which has perdured to this day and age.[14]

Descartes' famous dictum "cogito ergo sum" became the cornerstone on which modern rationalism was built. Most of the philosophical work of the last two centuries can be traced to the Cartesian revolution. This applies to Anglo-Saxon philosophical thought just as well as to the works of Kant and Hegel, among others. Descartes, with his reliance on the power of reason, claimed that the mind is not only self-sufficient but can grasp intuitively the primary axioms of mathematics and physics. In his criticism of scholasticism, Hegel went as far as to write in his *Lectures on the History of Philosophy* that the contribution of the scholastics during the Middle Ages was so insignificant that in order to advance in philosophy and science it was necessary to skip the entire period between the sixth and the seventeenth centuries.

The brilliant French philosopher believed that he had discovered a philosophical method which would solve all problems posed by reason no matter to what science they belonged.[15] For him, human thought is prior to being and all things are or exist as long as they are in human consciousness. Ironically, Descartes, by claiming that human thought is the first reality, unlocked the door that led to an outright materialism; a materialism which placed man at the center of the universe and ultimately denied the transcendental nature of the human person.

For Descartes natural phenomena were the result of determined processes, manifestations of a mechanistic design, similar to the very complex automaticity of a clock. He believed that he had found an explanation for the entire universe based on simple material facts without having to rely on any final causes. In other words, a purely mechanistic explanation of the universe.

The contributions of Isaac Newton and John Locke were the ones that effectively established the foundations of the "moral" and natural sciences the rationale of which can already be found in the philosophical ideas that were brewing in the seventeenth century.[16] A. R. Hall, the late professor of History of Science at the University of Cambridge, traced the writings of Newton to Galileo. He claimed that "when Galileo created by abstraction the essential model of the phenomena of motion which he studied, he transformed the pragmatic validity of a generalization appropriate to the world of experience into the absolute validity of the laws of nature in the intellectual model." Newton, he continues, followed Galileo and formulated his laws of nature "as laws of nature having complete applicability within the fabric of mathematical physics, whose conclusions as a whole can be confirmed by direct observation."[17]

It is often said that the scientific approach of Galileo, a contemporary of Descartes, clashed also with the traditional view of nature as understood by the scholastic doctors. It is true that Galileo in his work *Dialogues on the Two New Sciences*, published in 1638, looked at nature as a great book written in mathematics.[18] However, his great scientific contributions did not in any way mean that he rejected the traditional view that nature was also and primarily an intrinsic principle from which all things are born. Galileo never asserted that Natural Law could be limited to pure functional relationships, even though those relationships are, by necessity, the only ones that can be reduced to mathematics. He, therefore, perceived with perfect clarity that the conversion of material beings to pure numerical intelligibility was merely one "method" of study in order to know "one" aspect of reality. To reduce man to this source of knowledge alone would deprive him of having access to the essence of things, to metaphysical discourse and even to truth itself.[19]

Contrary to Descartes, Galileo did not advocate a pure mechanistic approach to the phenomena of nature with its disdain for what is not clearly understood through experience or the science of mathematics. Otherwise, he would have had to deny the reality of anything which cannot be measured or explained in mathematical terms and, thus, exclude any other scientific method which is not purely quantitative.[20] Although Galileo aimed at securing man's dominion over external nature, he did not fall into the error of a mechanism which led to a new scientific interpretation of Natural Law; a Natural Law that was purely practical and rejected or ignored any relationship to the metaphysical order.

Following Descartes' method of analysis, the moral philosophers of the late seventeenth and early eighteenth centuries aimed at securing man's dominion over nature. The new scientific interpretation of Natural Law maintained that the laws of nature were a consequence of design in nature. Natural Law was redefined as a pure deterministic law that could be materially proven. It was based exclusively on a concept of nature which was governed by mechanical causes; causes discovered by pure reason or experimental knowledge, the only ones that could be known mathematically. A separation was de facto established between the natural and the supernatural order. The Deistic philosophy of the period erased the remaining vestiges of a providential God.[21] As the mere discovery of the mechanistic laws of nature implied the absolute dominion of the natural order, the Creator was no longer indispensable. He had no control over life and exerted no influence on natural phenomena. God was reduced to a mere architect who constructs the world and then abandons it to its own mechanical laws.[22] There is no doubt that their interpretation of Natural Law was a total departure from the Greek attitude toward nature and a far cry from the traditional Christian concept of Natural Law.

The empiricism of moral philosophers such as John Locke together with the emphasis placed by modern science on the mechanical interpretation of the universe and the "natural" laws that regulate it have had a tremendous influence on political and economic thought.[23] In economic matters, the ideas of Locke and his followers were the major factors contributing to the classical economists' concept of natural harmony and to the notion identifying the satisfaction of individual interest with the common good of society. The consequences of such mechanistic interpretation of the traditional concept of Natural Law are still being felt today. The well-known French philosopher Etienne Gilson claims that the tremendous success of the applied sciences in industry is proof enough that our contemporary world is still living in the age of Descartes.[24]

But it was Newton's conception of the physical universe that gave so much prestige to the science of observation of facts. His view of the physical universe as a mechanical system that worked automatically, in accordance with existing natural laws, served as a model for the social sciences. As will be shown later, the application of this new interpretation of Natural Law to the affairs of politics and economics, including ethics, constituted the basis of what is known as Utilitarianism or Philosophical Radicalism.[25] The French scholar Elie Halevy in his illuminating work *La Formation du Radicalisme Philosophique* asserts that "in this moral Newtonianism the principle of the association of ideas and the principle of utility take the place of the principle of universal attraction."[26]

It cannot be denied that the explanation of reality in mathematical terms contributed significantly to the science of experimentation. However, it must be accepted also that it was unable to support the late proud affirmation that man had finally found the only way to truth. To affirm that reality and truth are founded exclusively on a scientific concept of nature that can be explained in mathematical terms ignores the fact that the experimental way is subordinated in the pure scientific order to metaphysical knowledge.

Europe's intellectual elites believed that man had finally found in the laws of nature the key to all knowledge and that the future well-being of humanity was at hand. The French prophets of the Enlightenment, following in the footsteps of the English moral philosophers, paved the way for Paris to replace London as the center of intellectual and literary activity. The search for utopia gripped the minds of Europe's prophetic elites.

## THE FRENCH ENLIGHTENMENT
## AND THE SEARCH FOR UTOPIA

In the most influential European intellectual circles of the eighteenth century, particularly in Paris, it was considered an accepted fact that societies, as all mechanical systems, are governed by internal processes that conform to discoverable natural laws whether mechanical or otherwise. They do not need to be artificially ordered by any type of authority, religious or secular, because order already exists naturally. As long as men are free to follow their inner impulses, the natural law of harmony will govern their activities the same way it regulates the celestial bodies in the universe.

The French philosophers of the Enlightenment held firmly to the idea that men, through the power of reason, could discover the mechanical laws of nature. Only by observing these predetermined natural laws could order and harmony prevail.[27] They contended that a world of rational free men was in the making where free and enlightened individuals behaving rationally could reach a new millennium.

Many of these intellectuals of the eighteenth century maintained that the object of reason was not pure reason working without experimental or empirical data but a reason applied to or in analysis of all human experience. As Overton Taylor of Harvard University writes in his book *History of Economic Thought*, "The practiced method of enquiry was tending to become that of 'rational empiricism' rather than that of simple, pure or absolute 'rationalism.'"[28] According to them, the appeals to reason and experience were not adversaries but allies in their efforts to reject all argumentation based on tradition and authority.

One of the most ambitious projects of the philosophes was *L'Encyclopédie*, a monumental work, that had among its many collaborators the prominent minds of Diderot, D'Alembert, and Voltaire.[29] The Harvard economist Joseph Schumpeter does not hide his contempt for many of the philosophes and claims that the best antidote to the compliments they received from a disintegrating French society is to read them. For him, "There are better performances to record than those of Voltaire and Rousseau." Like all disintegrating societies that do not want to face their danger, French society "delighted in protecting its enemies and thus provided a milieu of unique charm for a literature that will attract even those of us who sense a flavor of decay—and sometimes, what is worse, also a flavor of mediocrity—when they turn to these old volumes that harbor so much complacency."[30]

The French historian Paul Hazard reminds us that, according to these lucid thinkers, "the law, in general, is human reason in so far as it governs the peoples of the earth; and the political and civil laws of every nation as nothing more than the various cases where human reason is applied."[31] Greatly influenced by the English moral philosophers, their French counterparts considered as an axiom the existence of a natural order, mechanistically determined. They believed in the natural goodness of man and in his capacity to reach perfect happiness once he discovered the "natural laws" that govern the universe and was free from the bonds of ignorance and superstition.[32]

Even though most of the contributors to the *L'Encyclopédie* professed a vague rationalist Deism, the fact is that they were violently opposed to revealed religion. It did not take long for their vague rationalist Deism to be deluted into crude materialism. An insipid Deism, which had already revealed certain traits of positivism, gradually turned into agnosticism, if not outright atheism. Holbach and Helvetius were outright radical materialists.[33]

Jean-Jacques Rousseau, a firm believer in man's natural goodness, never ceased to claim that "civilization" was the reason for his corruption.[34] In one of the most influential books ever written on education, *Emile*, he advises his readers that the freedom of the "natural" man must be protected from the evils of society through legislation and education.[35] The educator, for Rousseau, must follow the path set by nature. Thus, the most important mission of pedagogy is the development of the natural gifts or tendencies of the child. Everything should be brought into harmony with these natural tendencies. Through education and a proper environment men will flower into something splendid and beautiful. Intelligence must take advantage of their natural instincts and develop them properly.

The French Revolution, the direct heir of the Enlightenment, gave new impetus to the process of rationalization begun in the previous century; a process which was definitely antireligious. Alexis de Tocqueville stresses this point when he writes, "The philosophical conceptions of the eighteenth century have rightly been regarded as one of the chief causes of the Revolution and it is undeniable that our eighteenth century philosophers were fundamentally anti-religious."[36]

The revolutionary movement placed all its efforts in destroying all past religious and secular institutions of the ancien régimes, whether in France or elsewhere. Paul Hazard contends that the eighteenth century was not satisfied with reform. The main objective was to pull down the cross, banish all communication between God and man, and destroy the idea of a providential God, of revelation. A new concept of religion was in the making: a natural religion on which the "city of man" would be built.[37]

Edmund Burke once said that the French Revolution "is one among the revolutions which have given splendor to obscurity and distinction to undiscovered merit."[38] It was, he continues, the most astonishing event that hitherto happened in the world: "Everything seems out of nature in this strange chaos of levity and ferocity, and all sorts of crimes jumbled together with all sorts of follies. In viewing this monstrous tragic-comic scene, the most opposite passions necessarily succeed, and sometimes mix in the mind; alternate contempt and indignation; alternate laughter and tears; alternate scorn and horror."[39]

Europe had never seen, since the classic age of ancient Greek thought, a higher ardent faith in the power of reason and the inevitability of human progress than in the Age of the Enlightenment.[40] Through violence and terror, the French revolutionaries tried to exterminate all former "authoritarian" and "irrational" values, replacing them by the then-popular philosophical notions that predicted the dawn of a new era of progress and happiness for mankind. The French Revolution, claims Christopher Dawson, " . . . was much more than a political revolution: it was a reformation of an even more fundamental kind than the Protestant Reformation of the sixteenth century. The latter, even in its most revolutionary moments, asserted its loyalty to the Gospel and the Christian faith, but the Revolution was more far-reaching and swept away the entire structure of organized Christian institutions so far as it was possible to do so."[41]

In 1794 in the midst of the infamous Reign of Terror, the deification of reason and the hatred toward religion reached such frenzied proportions that the goddess of "reason" was enthroned in a Greek temple placed on the main altar of Notre Dame Cathedral in Paris.[42]

It was an age in which the intellectual elites had an unfounded faith in the ongoing advancement of science. They never doubted that the light of reason would dissipate whatever trace of darkness remained on the surface of the earth and man could reach the millennium by simply obeying the predetermined laws of nature.[43] The power of reason would dissipate all the shadows that covered the earth and men by following the plan of nature would rediscover the happiness that had been lost.

According to Taylor the views of the philosophers of the Enlightenment on man's nature and natural goodness "contributed to the prevailing optimism or utopianism; in a world of potentially, 'naturally', ideally 'rational' human beings, the progress and spread of knowledge and 'enlightenment' would be certain to result in progress toward a realized 'heaven on earth.'"[44] It was the excess reliance on pure reasoning and speculative theorizing that led to the dreams of a golden age where prosperity and happiness would reign in the city of man.

Randall, an ardent admirer of the American philosopher John Dewey, admits that the idea of progress became an obsession for the Western mind.[45] He maintains that "Locke, Helvetius, Bentham laid the foundations for this generous dream: all men of whatever school, save only those who clung like Malthus to the Christian doctrine of original sin believed with all their ardent nature in the perfectibility of the human race. At last mankind held in its own hands the key to its destiny: it could make the future almost what it would. By destroying the foolish errors of the past and returning to a rational cultivation of nature, there was scarcely any limit to human welfare that might not be transcended."[46]

Professor Nisbet of Columbia University in his book *History of the Idea of Progress* claims that "the idea of progress holds that mankind has advanced in the past—from some aboriginal condition of primitiveness, barbarism, or even nullity—and is now advancing, and will continue to advance through the foreseeable future."[47] The great "prophets" of progress were convinced that the very nature of objective knowledge—such as science and technology—was to advance, to improve, to become more perfect. The belief in an unspoiled beginning and the final attainment of the perfect society—advances from a hypothetical state of perfection to a state of restored perfection—is the major trait of all utopian literature.[48]

Only by applying reason to the heap of nonsense inherited from the past would the road be open for the construction of the "city of man," a purely hedonistic and materialistic society. Intellectual Europe wanted to convince itself that it lived in the best of possible worlds and closed its eyes to the evils that surrounded it.[49] Ironically, as Schumpeter reminds us, this wave of religious, political, and economic criticism that swept over Europe was pathetically uncritical of its own dogmatic standards.[50]

## THE REBELLION AGAINST TRADITION AND AUTHORITY: THE NEW MORALITY

The exact sciences had been acquiring levels of increasing prestige since the middle of the sixteenth century. However, the results of the innovative process that was taking place in the eighteenth century convinced the "enlightened" elites that they had found the way to apply to the social sciences the same methods that were used in the natural sciences. Religious issues were not exempt from this "scientific" trend which set the tone for future generations.

As science and technology declared their independence from any submission to an external superior authority, religion in general and ethics in particular began to acquire a new meaning, very different from the traditional Western principles grounded on Natural Law as embodied in the writings of the scholastic doctors and to a large degree in the metaphysics of Aristotle. Schumpeter was a great critic of the philosophers who preached a Natural Law that was based on the science of human nature. According to him, "a Natural Theology as distinct from the sacra doctrina . . . definitely established itself as a separate field of laical social science. Its properly theological contents tended to shrink to an insipid Deism."[51] The abdication of God in favor of the creative power of man's reason over which all superior authority was denied opened the way for "liberated" man to mold his moral laws on a radically new concept of what is good and what is evil. This revolutionary approach to moral conduct turned out to be of such far reaching consequences that even those who subscribed to it were unaware of its long-term implications for the well-being of society.[52]

According to Randall, "the Newtonian world of orderly and harmonious law worked itself out in religion, in the new science of man, in political economy, and in government."[53] The religion of reason believed that the order of nature contained also an order of natural moral law that could be discovered and followed as any other of the rational principles of Newton. This meant, continues Randall, that "the principles of right and wrong, of justice and injustice, were for the eighteenth century incorporated into the scheme of reason and science, and that it was universally admitted that the science of ethics was as independent of any theological or supernatural foundation as any other branch of human knowledge."[54]

The newly "liberated" man of Europe no longer believed in a common destiny. The unifying principle of a common end was shattered in the name of an unrestrained individual freedom that respected no higher authority than its own reason; an authority which was held responsible for the political and social woes that afflicted European societies. The traditional Thomistic view concerning the existence of an objective truth based on Natural and Divine Law was replaced by a subjective conscience which was elevated to the rank of an absolute value.[55]

Montesquieu, for example, did not consider the divine origin of the law.[56] In other words, as Paul Hazard comments, he sanctioned the divorce between Natural Law and Divine Law.[57] Once this divorce was accepted, the moral law was also divorced from its transcendental origin. Thus, it became necessary to find an authority which would serve as the guiding principle for men's actions. That guiding principle was reduced to pure reason. Man became, through the power of his reason, the sole arbiter of what is right and what is wrong in moral matters. It became necessary to redo the concept of morality: a new morality illuminated by the age of the Enlightenment.

The man of the Enlightenment was convinced that the Creator had determined that the fundamental instincts of human nature led toward a harmony of behavior of free men and, thus, to the creation of perfect societies where happiness would finally prevail. Locke, for example, maintained that all men share the same human nature and in justice are entitled to the same rights and liberties. He claimed that all men must act always in a way which is consistant with the rights of all; the rights and liberties they all need to exercise their natural capabilities so as to attain the full satisfaction of their desires.

In his search for an understanding of men's actions Locke admitted that there are innate inclinations of the appetite—principles of action—which are constant. These principles of action lodged in men's hearts are nothing else but a desire for happiness and an aversion to misery; a desire which needs to be checked by rewards and punishments. Moral laws simply act as curbs and restraints to the possible abuses and excesses of man's unchecked desires. However, they cannot be considered as innate moral principles.

Even though Locke's denial of innate moral laws does not imply a denial of any moral law, it is nevertheless true that his new conception of moral law is void of any metaphysical content. He claims that "there is a great deal of difference between an innate law and a law of nature; between something imprinted in on our minds and something that we being ignorant of, may attain to the knowledge of, by the use and due application of our natural faculties. And I think they equally forsake the truth, who running into contrary extremes, either affirm an innate law or deny that there is a law knowable by the light of nature; i.e., without the help of positive revelation."[58]

Perhaps one of the greatest weaknesses in Locke's argument lies in his attempt to establish the morality of economic behavior on the basis of a set of scientific laws; natural moral laws which are observed in the "state of nature."[59] Professor Karen Iversen Vaughn of George Mason University points out that during the Enlightenment—both moral laws and scientific laws "were united by the single common thread: the belief that a Christian God guaranteed the content of both. God gave men a benevolent universe wherein physical things were required to obey scientific laws of nature, and men were expected to obey the dictates of a natural moral law."[60]

Locke always assumed in his economic writings that individuals behaved morally when they followed their own self-interests in their quest for gain. He saw nothing wrong in this attitude. On the contrary, it was the rational thing to do in accordance with the laws of economics which, according to him, were similar to the laws of the physical universe and which man simply had to observe. It was the competitive marketplace, free of government interference, which guaranteed that all participants were treated justly. Thus, as Vaughn tells us, the pursuit of economic gain "is the basis for Locke's emphasis on the limitation of government."[61]

The dilemma in which Locke found himself laid in the obvious fact that oftentimes man transgresses the natural law of nature, which he freely and "naturally" is supposed to follow. As a result, the stability and order of society is threatened and, consequently, it becomes necessary to fall back on an "ordering will" for its enforcement. He tried to solve the problem by claiming that an all-powerful civil society must freely be agreed upon; a governing body that has the power to restrict man's natural inclinations (natural rights). This contrasts sharply with Locke's other statements in which he says that no arbitrary power can be exercised by any government.[62]

C. B. Macpherson, whose Marxist leanings have made him a sharp critic of capitalist morality, claims that it is inconceivable, as Locke suggests, that a free society should give absolute arbitrary power to the government for the following two reasons. First, since individuals by nature do not have arbitrary power over their own lives or over the lives and properties of others, they cannot give arbitrary power to society, and therefore the society does not have it to give to any government. Second, to hand over absolute arbitrary power to the government "would be contrary to the very purpose for which the society was established, that is, the protection of the life, liberty and estate of each member: if they handed over their natural rights and powers to an absolute and arbitrary government they would have less protection than they had in the state of nature where each could at least take protective action for himself."[63] Thus, Macpherson claims, such an ambiguity in Lockes reasoning "allows Locke to argue in the Treatise, both that there must and can be an agreement to establish an all-powerful civil society against which the individual retains no rights, and that no such power can arbitrarily be exercised by any government."[64]

The English philosopher Thomas Hobbes understood very well Locke's dilemma in recognizing the weakness of an argument that relies exclusively on the laws of nature to preserve order in society.[65] He questioned the natural goodness of man and denied that he is naturally a social being, claiming that he was moved only by selfish considerations. It was Hobbes, together with the Dutch jurist Hugo de Groot, better known as Grotius (1583–1645), who established selfishness as a ruling principle of social life.

Hobbes's theory of the social contract, as presented in his work *Leviathan*, justifies the need for an absolute authority to preserve order in society. As freedom had led to chaos in the past, it was in men's self-interest to give up their liberties and place them in the hands of an absolute authority. Hobbes maintained that primitive men lived in a continuous state of war. Under such conditions, civilization was impossible. Thus, it was in men's self-interest to freely join together and establish a social contract for their own protection. This in turn required an absolute authority.

Leaving aside the political implications of Hobbes's theory and the justification of absolute power, his lack of reliance on a natural law of nature to maintain peace and order seems to be more consistent than Locke's reliance on them for the attainment of progress in society. He defined the Right of Nature (*jus naturale*) as "the liberty each man hath, to use his power, as he will himself, for the preservation of his own nature; that is to say, of his own life; and consequently, of doing any thing which in his own judgement, and reason, he shall conceive to be the attest means thereunto."[66] What Hobbes did was to replace the pre-Enlightenment concept of Natural Law, so necessary for a proper ordering of society, with the absolute power of a secular authority, the only one capable of bringing about order and peace in society.[67] For Hobbes, powerful political institutions were the fountain from which flowed all order and justice.

The majority of the self-declared prophets of the Enlightenment, following Locke's idea of the "natural" moral law and the "natural" rights of man, thought that they had discovered a code of conduct—a morality— that was based on a natural order. For them, the "natural ethics," which they claimed to have discovered, prescribed the right conduct for all human societies. They maintained that all men shared the same human nature and were entitled in justice to the same rights and liberties and obliged to act in such a way that their conduct was consistent with the rights of others. They were convinced that the right form of human society, the best adapted to "human nature" was that of a society of free and cooperating individuals following their own interests but at the same time respecting the "natural rights" of others. This "natural ethics" which served as the norm for conduct was supposed to become the "natural" substitute for Christian morality as defined by Natural Law and which they rejected with all other forms of authority.[68]

The misinterpretation or rejection of the traditional concept of Natural Law made it necessary for these enlightened philosophers to find a new moral code of conduct; a different value system. Assuming, as they did, that order should not be imposed artificially by authority, whether religious or political, the question as to how order was established in society became critical. The solution could only be found in the belief that there already exists a naturally ordained order; a natural law of harmony that governs men's actions in a "natural" way as long as there is no external interference. Once they disposed of the canons of external authority they had to replace the vacuum created by their absence with a new faith in a natural law of harmony; a law that can be discovered rationally by man's unaided intellect.

Thus, the self proclaimed liberators of society who had discarded the canons of external authority, as reflected in Natural Law, had no alternative but to replace the vacuum created by their absence with a new faith in a natural law of harmony that could be discovered by their own unaided intellects. The new morality had to be based on a fresh set of values, which they believed was more in accordance with man's natural goodness and which could be enforced through education and legislation.[69]

The influence of the philosophers of the Enlightenment can be clearly seen in the writings of August Comte, the founder of a new religion, a substitute for Catholicism, which he "baptized" with the name of Positivism. Following in the footsteps of his predecessors the new prophet of the Enlightenment rejected the transcendental and confined knowledge to "scientific" knowledge.[70] For him the only positive knowledge is based on the observation of facts and these can only be explained by the facts themselves. Natural Law and all rational explanation of reality were relegated to a place in history without any significance in the modern world.

According to Comte, civilization evolves from a religious or magic stage (theological or fictitious state) to a metaphysical (abstract stage) and then to a scientific one (positive stage). It is an utterly materialistic interpretation of history which is not very different from that of the French philosopher Condorcet.[71] Once man grows up, claimed Comte, he reaches the positive state and rejects all "metaphysical abstractions," the only principle that remains is: "everything is relative." Even though it is true that positivism hardly ever affected the science of law as such, it was only after the nineteenth century, when Positivism began to expand its influence, that it became essential to demonstrate the existence of Natural Law as traditionally interpreted.[72]

The French scholar Henri de Lubac in his critical analysis of Comte's philosophy says the following: "To anyone observing the great spiritual currents of our age from a certain altitude, positivism will seem less the antagonist than the ally of the Marxist and Nietzschean currents. By other methods, in another spirit and in competition with them, it strives for the same essential object. Like them, it is one of the ways in which modern man seeks to escape from any kind of transcendency and to shake off the thing it regards as an unbearable yoke—namely faith in God."[73]

Positivism is primarily a religion of Humanity; a religion that replaces the traditional concept of God by the cult of what Comte calls the benefactors of Humanity. It promotes a new social order in which the new spiritual power, exercised by a regenerative priesthood, will impose upon men a sort of spiritual despotism which will subject all minds to a strict discipline and reorganize Europe by means of education. In establishing his new priesthood, affirms Lubac, Comte "established the harshest and at the same time the most unjustifiable of intellectual tyrannies."[74] The denial of the transcendental and its replacement with a sweeping worship of Humanity, with all the implications that this entails, has placed Positivism at the vanguard of a new morality that claims to be the ultimate determinant of what is right and what is wrong.

## FALSE INTERPRETATIONS OF NATURAL LAW: THEIR IMPACT ON SOCIETY

The entire moral scheme which dominated the European Middle Ages since the time of St. Thomas Aquinas and which included both classical and theistic elements, the structure of which can be found in the *Nicomachean Ethics* of Aristotle, crumbled under the assault of the new secular intellectuals who wanted to shape the attitudes and institutions of society according to their own desires.

They thought that, by rejecting authority, they could solve the problems of society by introducing their own ethical standards of behavior, forgetting that man's integral process of development toward his final end cannot take place if his essential nature is disregarded. In his book *After Virtue* the well-known philosopher Alasdaire MacIntyre reminds us that "within that teleological scheme there is a fundamental contrast between man-as-he-happens-to-be and man-as-he-could-be-if-he-realized-his-essential-nature. Ethics is the science which is to enable men to understand how to make the transition from the former state to the latter."[75] Did the secular philosophers of the Enlightenment meet this challenge or, on the contrary, can they be held responsible for doing exactly the opposite?

Many centuries ago, St. Augustine, the convert of Milan, recognized and placed special emphasis on the power of reason but not to the extent that it could attain all truth through its own powers alone. As he denounced the errors of Manichaeism, and under the influence of St. Ambrose, he soon discovered the value of authority and the limits and pitfalls of human reason. He understood perfectly well that philosophy must not be entirely separate from supernatural knowledge but only separable from it. Thus, the author of the Confessions did not hesitate to claim that "before faith you must understand in order to believe; after faith you must believe in order to understand."[76] He never placed man's power of reason to discover all truth above Natural and Divine Law and much less to separate the moral law from its transcendental source.

To avoid the precepts of ethics from becoming relativized, they must be placed within a framework of theistic beliefs and, thus, understood not only as teleological commands but also as manifestations of a divinely ordained law. That is why man must respect the law of God because the true end of man cannot be completely achieved in this world, but only in another. As MacIntyre emphatically insists, "The threefold structure of untutored human-nature-as it-happens-to-be, human-nature-as-it-could-be-if-it-realized-its-*telos* and the precepts of rational ethics as the means for the transition from one to the other remains central to the theistic understanding of evaluating thought and judgment."[77]

As indicated in chapter 1, God, not man, is the creator of Natural Law. He, by ordering all things to their proper end, is merely showing his providential love for creation. St. Thomas Aquinas states in an unequivocal way that in contrast with beings that are not persons, God demonstrates his care for man "not 'from without,' through the laws of physical nature but 'from within' through reason, which by its natural knowledge of God's eternal law is consequently able to show man the right direction to take in his free actions."[78] Man does not have absolute sovereignty as to what is right and what is wrong. As man is destined to an end which exceeds mankind's natural capacity, it was necessary for him to be directed to this end by a divinely revealed law. Accordingly, "For man to know what he should do and not do without any doubt it was necessary for him to be directed in his actions by a law given by God, for it is certain that such law cannot err."[79] Without a proper understanding of Natural and Divine law, it is very difficult if not impossible for man to avoid falling into the error of believing that he and only he is the final arbiter of what is good and what is evil.

It is important to reemphasize that the philosophical rationalism (*le pouvoir de la raison*) of the seventeenth and eighteenth centuries was distinctly different from the metaphysical rationalism of St. Thomas Aquinas. Aquinas and the scholastics, recognizing and stressing the power of reason, never maintained that human reason was the only admissible source of knowledge, particularly in matters of theology. Schumpeter calls St. Thomas a metaphysical rationalist because "he believed that the existence of God can be logically proved." But not a rationalist in the sense of the seventeenth philosophers who believed that human reason was the only admissible source of knowledge in matters of theology.[80]

The fact that the new theologies of the seventeenth and eighteenth centuries rejected the teleological view of human nature implicitly denied that man has an essence which defines his true end. Since the very concept of ethics consists in enabling man to pass from his present state to his true end, the rejection of the essence of human nature and the repudiation of the idea of a telos, weakened if not destroyed the basis on which morality stands. The only recourse left to them was to accept a set of commands deprived of their teleological content or a certain view of an untutored-human-nature-as-it-is.

As soon as moral precept—designed to correct, improve, and educate human nature— lacked their teleological content, it became very difficult for men to accept them. They no longer would be deduced from true statements about human nature or explained by appealing to some of its basic characteristics. Thus "the eighteenth century moral philosophers engaged in what was an inevitably unsuccessful project; for they did indeed attempt to find a rational basis for their moral beliefs in a particular understanding of human nature, while inheriting a set of moral injunctions on the one hand and a conception of human nature on the other which had been expressly designed to be discrepant with each other. This discrepancy was not removed by their revised beliefs in human nature."[81]

However, the secular philosophers of the Enlightenment were not prepared to do away with all normative standards of conduct and judgment. If, as they claimed, all moral actions were no longer subject to an objective moral order based on Natural Law, they simply had to find another source for their standard of morality. This they found by converting their theory of conduct into a source of norms for conduct. According to them, the new enlightened morality had to be based on man's understanding that the only motives for human action were attractions to pleasure and avoidance of pain. This is especially true of the English philosopher-economist Jeremy Bentham who assigned a new meaning to moral rules and concepts. He, as many of his contemporaries, considered any acceptance of an objective moral order as empty metaphysics.

By rejecting or ignoring the properties of universality and immutability in Natural Law and substituting them by their own moral standards, the philosophers of the Enlightenment set the stage for a relativistic "natural ethics" and jeopardized many of rights and duties derived from the observance of Natural Law. To detach morality from a teleological framework and to "liberate" it from what appeared to the "enlightened" philosophers as the contemptuous external authority of traditional ethics meant "the loss of any authoritative content from the would-be moral utterances of the newly autonomous agent."[82] As a result, nothing impeded each "liberated" moral agent from establishing his own standards of morality free from the externalities of Divine Law, natural teleology or hierarchical authority. Under such circumstances, morality becomes totally relative. On what basis can a person, seeking to protect his moral autonomy, expect others to renounce their principles and points of view in the world of practice in order to follow someone else's generalized pattern of behaviour? Given the frailty of human nature, any permissive society based on liberty for everyone to act in accordance with his own personal value system eventually can only to lead to chaos. This explains to a large degree the anarchy in moral standards which prevails in our contemporary society. The resulting incoherence of men's attitudes toward fundamental principles of behavior are basically the result of the misleading conceptual scheme inherited from the Enlightenment. The rejection of Natural Law led to the present state of grave disorder in the realm of public and private morality. Ironically, man's reliance on a de facto relativistic "natural ethics" has become a major threat to the basic rights of man which the philosophers of the Enlightenment were trying to protect.

To repudiate the Western concept of Natural Law implied a total disregard of man's evil inclinations and to rely exclusively on hedonistic schemes of preferences and benevolent attitudes in the process of creating the perfect society. This is not only utopian but entails a total misunderstanding of the true nature of man. The very concept of authority and orderly behavior is jeopardized when it is believed that there exists in the nature of man, as in that of the stars, an inner impulse to contribute to universal harmony. To believe that man can and must be made free from the "bonds" of authority so that he can have the freedom to follow his inner instincts for the benefit of humanity is not only utopian but counterproductive to the ideals of an ordered society. To suggest that authority, by overriding the dictates of that inner impulse, is destructive not only of liberty but of order as well is extremely dangerous for the future of society.[83]

Both the English and French intellectual elites of the Enlightenment, by detaching themselves from past teleological constraints and declaring their independence from authority and hierarchy, set for themselves their own rules of morality. For them, man is the sole arbiter of the truth and has the moral authority to differentiate good from evil. The inherited rules of morality had found a new expression of "authority" in man himself. He, the good and benevolent creature, was capable of discovering the "ethical" natural laws that prescribed the right patterns of conduct for all human societies. Man's unlimited faith in himself and endowed with full authority over his moral acts, was the best guarantee for his well-being and continuous progress.

The popular writers of the Enlightenment wrongly assumed that all of man's rational actions and behavior would always tend naturally toward the welfare of society. Their views on man's nature and his natural goodness "contributed to the prevailing optimism or utopianism; in a world of potentially, 'naturally', ideally 'rational' human beings, the progress and spread of knowledge and 'enlightenment' would be certain to result in progress toward a realized 'heaven on earth.'"[84]

Their arguments were further strengthened by the then-prevailing Deistic philosophy which, as indicated earlier, claimed that God created a harmonious natural order in the universe with its own self-regulating laws but in which he no longer intervened after its creation. God, like a watch maker after "creating" his masterpiece, is no longer free to interfere in its functioning or its enforcement. It is man's responsibility to discover and study the laws of nature and to have the will to accept and follow them without violating the harmonious natural order established by the Creator. Thus, the "enlightened" philosophers concluded that if scientific research and the study of the laws of nature had contributed so significantly to the huge advances in technology, why couldn't the social sciences conform to similar natural laws?

The candid optimism of the eighteenth century intellectuals had its source primarily in the belief that all sciences had reached the initial stage of an ongoing process which, in the long run, would be conducive to the complete and perfect knowledge of all human nature. The moral law was no exception. It was only after the true nature of the "newly discovered morality"—a natural ethics— was universally understood and observed by all, that the path would be open for the attainment of the "perfect society."

The huge advances in science and technology which have occurred during the last few centuries and, in particular after the Second World War, have strengthened even further the belief in the power of human reason to decide on its own what is right and what is wrong. In many circles, it is widely accepted that rational man, endowed with human freedom and capable of controlling the universe, no longer has to submit to any authority but his own. His far reaching freedom would be elevated to such a degree that truth itself would be considered a creation of freedom. To accept such a position would imply a declaration of total independence from any submission to an objective moral order except the one arrived at by the power of his own reason and, thus, have the primacy over truth. Man would claim for himself a moral authority that would be no different than absolute sovereignty over ethical issues. A complete sovereignty of human reason over ethical issues would mean that man is the exclusive source of morality, of norms that he, in an autonomous manner, would set for himself. The experience of the past two centuries has demonstrated that the "enlightened" philosophers failed to provide a public rational justification for a morality void of a teleological foundation. It is even more lamentable that the significance of that failure has not even been acknowledged either then or now. As a result, instead or reaching the "perfect" society, modern man has opened the door for the spread of tyranny and the abuse of power, a far cry from the prevailing optimism of the eighteenth century.

The main error of the intellectuals of the eighteenth century consisted in believing that reason alone was the final arbiter of all truth; a truth that is free from the possibility of all error. It is true that the existence of God as many other natural truths can be proven by reason alone but this does not mean that all knowledge acquired through reason alone is exempt from doubt or possible error. To avoid such doubts or possible errors, it becomes necessary for man to rely on a higher authority in order to avoid the pitfalls of a weak intelligence. This higher authority gives greater certainty to a frail intelligence and avoids the dangers of a presumptuous rational behavior.[85] They did not realize that man's intellect in its search for truth has its limitations and lacks the capacity to know all truth with absolute certainty; much less the power to decide unequivocally what is right and what is wrong.

Moral ideas do not derive from sense experience or pure reason alone, as Locke claimed and much less that the relations between these ideas are such that "morality is capable of demonstration, as well as mathematics."[86] Moral *good* is not necessarily that which causes pleasure or diminishes pain nor is *evil* that which causes pain or diminishes pleasure. If this were the case, moral good would be defined as that which conforms our actions to a law, the sanctions of which are rewards of pleasure and punishments of pain, an untenable position under Natural and Divine Law.

The new morality became ephemeral and, in the case of the English moral philosophers, merely linked in a subtle way not to a conscious intellectually perceptive reality but to pure sentiment and what is agreeable to the senses and to man's feelings. The consequences of this new interpretation of morality were probably unpredictable at the time Hume wrote his treatise but its consequences are clearly seen in our contemporary world. This leads us to the question of moral law and how, in order to to be effective, it must be based on an objective moral order founded on Natural and Divine Law.

The outright rejection of Natural Law has had disastrous effects in the area of ethics. Moral conduct, no longer based on the existence of objective moral principles of a transcendental nature and evaluated on a purely subjective interpretation of the goodness of an act, lost its original distinctness. MacIntyre claims that the rejection of any theological view of human nature, of any view of man as having an essence which defines his true end had to lead inevitably to the failure of finding a basis for morality.[87] Once the concept of transcendence is rejected and man is limited to the immanent, progress and happiness are reduced to earthly goods and the whole project of morality becomes unintelligible. Detach morality from the teleological framework and "you will no longer have morality; or, at the very best, you will have radically transformed its character."[88] Faith in human progress and earthly happiness becomes the only motivating force of man's actions.

The modern radical, following in the footsteps of his "enlightened" predecessors has become so confident in the moral expression of his stances and consequently in the assertive uses of the rhetoric of a fragmented morality that he criticizes everything in our culture but the language of morality which he wants to maintain just as it is. Ironically, however, in spite of his denunciation of the basic values of Western culture, "he is certain that it still possesses the moral resources which he requires in order to denounce it."[89]

Unfortunately, the language and appearance of morality persists, even though the integral substance of morality has to a large degree been fragmented and in part destroyed. This fragmentation of the concept of morality is still having and will continue to have devastating implications for society as a whole and, unless rectified, it will easily lead, if we are not already there, to "a state so disastrous that there are no large remedies for it."[90] The very dignity of the human person will be jeopardized as the very concept itself would be subjected to the interests and predilections of the authorities in power or to the whims of the majority.

The arbitrariness of our modern culture lies precisely on its exclusive reliance on a natural theology divorced from the *sacra doctrina*; on the power of reason and/or experimentation as the only sources to discover the laws of nature. This assessment runs counter to the belief that there does exist a morality based on Natural Law and Divine Law; a Natural Law which expresses the essential needs of nature and respects the essential order of man's inclinations and of the rights and duties that are derived from them.

No political or economic system can be effective without an ordering will, an external authority which establishes the objective norms of conduct. Otherwise, it will fall into a free-for-all chaos. Social phenomena cannot be explained by law-like generalizations as in the case of the natural sciences. To rely exclusively on natural harmonies as the foundation of an orderly society led, as Taylor reminds us, to "both the ideal-and-theory of liberal democracy in the political sphere, and the ideal-and-theory of the liberal economy—an economic system of free and competitive enterprises and markets."[91] Heimann does not hesitate to mention the hazardous consequences for the future of mankind of a philosophy that turns away from external authority and relies exclusively on natural harmonies and the power of instrumental reason to discover the laws of nature. The fact, he asserts, that the abdication of God in favor of man, presupposed in all modern systems of thought, carries with it the seeds of its own destruction cannot be taken lightly by modern man. Christianity has always maintained that to rely on such godless systems can only lead to catastrophe, "as must all the absolute presumptions of so frail a creature as man, who is always in danger of being unjust, most of all when he claims to be building the kingdom of eternal harmony."[92]

The concept of social science as the provider of law-like generalizations has dominated the philosophy of social science for the last two hundred years, from the Enlightenment to Comte, Mill, and their followers. According to this view, "the aim of the social sciences is to explain specifically social phenomena by supplying law-like generalizations which do not differ in their logical form from those applicable to natural phenomena in general, precisely the law-like generalizations to which the managerial expert would have to appeal."[93] However, MacIntyre contends that this explanation "seems to entail—what is certainly not the case—that the social sciences are almost devoid of achievement. On the contrary, the salient fact about the social sciences is the absence of the discovery of any law-like generalizations whatsoever."[94]

Many of the institutional forms of social life that are generally accepted in our contemporary society follow the Enlightenment's concept of the social sciences and are based on the new "ethics" discovered by the eighteenth century philosophers. Man's actions are no longer explained with reference to an objective moral norm where virtue and vice play the dominant role. His aims, void of a teleological foundation, are now characterized in terms of a scale of goods which provide the basis of behavior but which excludes any reference to the final end of human actions.

Modern managers, not to mention government bureaucrats, very often invoke their own area of competence as scientific managers of social change in order to justify their claims to authority, power, and money. They try to justify their activities by rationally adjusting means to ends

in the most economical and efficient way, appealing to their ability to"
. . . deploy a body of scientific and above all social scientific knowledge,
organized in terms of and understood as comprising a set of universal
law-like generalizations."[95] Value neutrality and the claim to manipula-
tive power is very often proclaimed as the major qualification of managerial skills.

Influenced by the Enlightenment, contemporary man tends to reduce
the whole world of human principles to subjective evaluation, in particular to the sensory and physical demonstrable, not to mention to a pure
utilitarianism as in the case of economics. He often tends to rule out, as
contrary to reason, all that is transcendental and doubts man's intellectual capacity to penetrate the suprasensitive reality of the universe. As a
result, he is implicitly denying man's capacity to reach the truth. His rejection of objective truth and of the transcendent nature of man was one
of the main factors leading to the subjective immanentism and modernism that grips contemporary society and which was expected to bring
about the "perfectly happy" and "harmonious" society free of all past antinomies. But, it was a happiness that had to be obtained at once, today
not tomorrow or the next day. Tomorrow was too late. Happiness was
less of a gift and more of a thing that had to be conquered and found in
the material world. It was a calculated happiness; a far cry from the concept of happiness held by the great minds of the mystics or men such as
Bossuet or Fenelon.

Human actions are no longer related to objective principles of morality
but to the subjective evaluation of man himself which is more than often
guided by his own self interest. This is frequently reflected in the attitudes
of both government and business whose actions are justified by referring
them to their different areas of competence and personal self-interest.
Governments, for example, validate their intervention in society by claiming that they know best what is good for the citizen; they argue that they
have the resources of competence which most citizens do not have.[96] Business often uses similar arguments to foster their own aims, disregarding
their responsibility toward the common good and the dignity of the human person.

The preservation of man's life and dignity, the perpetuation of the human species, which includes the proper education of children and the
pursuit of everything that is good according to the order of reason, are
among some of the basic natural rights that are placed in jeopardy when
man denies the reality of Natural Law. To rely on a relativistic "natural
ethics" that reneges of the transcendental would, for all practical purposes, jeopardize man's basic natural rights. As will be shown in the following chapter, his rights as a human person would be subjected to the
ever changing "moral" standards of history.

## NOTES

1. Pyrrho of Elis (361–270 B.C.), a skeptic, was an ancient Greek philosopher who suspended judgment about truth, right, and wrong. He felt that custom and convention were the only guides to what is just or unjust.

2. Etienne Gilson, *The Philosophy of St. Thomas Aquinas* (New York: Barnes & Noble, 1993), 328. See also *Veritatis Splendor*, para. 40 and para. 50.

3. Javier Hervada, *Introduccion Crítica al Derecho Natural* (Pamplona, Spain: Ediciones Universidad de Navarra, S.A., 1994), 79–80.

4. John Finnis, *Natural Law and Natural Rights* (Oxford: Clarendon Press, 1996), 23.

5. For a brief introduction to the philosophy of St. Thomas Aquinas, see Etienne Gilson, *The Philosophy of St. Thomas Aquinas* (New York: Barnes & Noble, 1993).

6. The following paragraphs are based primarily on Etienne Gilson's work on St. Thomas Aquinas. See Gilson, *The Philosophy of St. Thomas Aquinas*, 324–33.

7. Gilson, *The Philosophy of St. Thomas Aquinas*, 325–26.

8. Etienne Gilson, citing St. Thomas, asserts, "This inclination in us as in all things, which carries us towards certain ends, is the unmistakable mark of what the eternal law imposes on us. Since it is this law that causes us to be what we are, we need but yield to the legitimate tendencies of our nature to obey it." See Gilson, *The Philosophy of St. Thomas Aquinas*, 327.

9. Joseph M. de Torre, *Christian Philosophy* (Manila, Philippines: Vera-Reyes, 1980), 232–35.

10. John Finnis, *Natural Law and Natural Rights*, 24.

11. Gilson, *The Philosophy of St. Thomas Aquinas*, 330.

12. See Vicente Rodriguez Casado, *Origenes del Capitalismo y del Socialismo Contemporaneo* (Madrid: Espasa-Calpe, S.A., 1981), 43.

13. René Descartes (1596–1650) was an intellectually outstanding French philosopher, mathematician, and physicist, who wrote, among other works, his famous *Discours de la Methode*. See René Descartes, *Discours de la Méthode, Texte et commantaires*, 4th ed. (Paris: Librairie philosophique, Vrin, 1967).

14. The inscription on Descarte's grave at St. Germain des Prés in Paris, ignoring the contributions of Aquinas and the scholastics, boasts that he was "the refounder of science (reconditor doctrinae) and the first man to defend the rights of human reason." Not the first man in all history, of course, but the first since the downfall of the ancient world. See Joseph Pieper, *Scholasticism: Personalities and Problems of Medieval Philosophy* (New York: McGraw-Hill, 1964), 15.

15. Carlos Cardona, *René Descartes, Discurso del Método* (Madrid: Editorial Magisterio Espanol, E.M.S.A., 1975), 8.

16. Isaac Newton (1642–1727), a native of England, was a distinguished philosopher and mathematician whose influence was far reaching. He discovered the laws of universal attraction and, at the same time as the German philosopher Leibnitz, set the bases for differential calculus. John Locke (1632–1704), one of the most influential writers of his time, was an English philosopher who considered experience the source of all knowledge. His most acclaimed books were *Essays Concerning Human Understanding* and the *Second Treatise of Government*.

17. See A. R. Hall, *The Scientific Revolution* (London: Longmans Green, 1934), 173.

18. Galileo (1564–1642), an Italian astronomer and physicist, was one of the founders of the experimental method.

19. See Vicente Rodriguez Casado, *Orígenes del Capitalismo y del Socialismo Contemporaneo* (Madrid: Espasa—Calpe S.A., 1981), 193–94.

20. Rodriguez Casado, *Origenes del Capitalismo y del Socialismo Contemporaneo*, 194.

21. Deism asserts the existence of a Creator but rejects the belief in a Providential God. It denies revelation and accepts reason as the only source of truth.

22. Rodriguez Casado, *Orígenes del Capitalismo y del Socialismo Contemporaneo*, 53–54.

23. John Locke (1632–1704) was one of the most influential writers of the seventeenth century. Born in England and educated at Oxford University, he was an empiricist who believed, contrary to Descartes, that man can reach all important conclusions through experience and not by a process of deductive reasoning.

24. Etienne Gilson, *De Aristoteles a Darwin (y Vuelta)* (Pamplona, Spain: Ediciones Universidad de Navarra EUNSA, 1976), 70.

25. As will be shown in chapter 3, English Utilitarianism, also known as Benthamism, was an outgrowth of eighteenth century Enlightenment. The core of Bentham's ideas can be summarized as follows: "to seek pleasure and avoid pain." For example, in economic terms, each individual seeks the greatest financial gain for himself, but in the process, society's wealth increases as well. Harmony can be reached between man's quest for the greatest financial gain and the prosperity of the community. But, Bentham did not limit this idea to economics but extended it to politics and ethics. For him the greatest happiness can be achieved by creating and applying an exact science of ethics by simply using his "felicific calculus" in order to measure the relative quantities of pleasure and pain resulting from men's actions. Jeremy Bentham was an English philosopher, born in London (1748–1832).

26. See Elie Halevy, *The Growth of Philosophical Liberalism* (Boston: Beacon Press, 1955), 6.

27. The Dutch philosopher Baruch Spinoza (1632–1677) had already proclaimed in the seventeenth century that "whatever comes to pass comes to pass according to laws and rules which involve eternal necessity and truth; nature, therefore, always observes laws and rules which involve eternal necessity and truth, although they may not all be known to us, and therefore she keeps a fixed an immutable order." Letter 2, II, 277. As quoted by the late professor of Columbia University John Herman Randall Jr. See John Herman Randall, *The Making of the Modern Mind* (Boston: Houghton Mifflin, 1940), 245.

28. Overton H. Taylor, *A History of Economic Thought* (New York: McGraw-Hill, 1960), 4.

29. Denis Diderot (1713–1784) was a French philosopher who became the editor of the *Encyclopédie*. Jean Le Rond d'Alembert (1717–1783), a total skeptic in matters of religion, was a French philosopher and mathematician. He was a major contributor to the *Encyclopédie* and preached a natural philosophy. François Marie Arouet, better known as Voltaire (1694–1778), was a prolific writer and essayist who became the idol of the anticlerical rising bourgeoisie.

30. Joseph Schumpeter, *History of Economic Analysis* (New York: Oxford University Press, 1963), 123.

31. Paul Hazard, *La Pensée Européenne au XVIIIe Siècle* (Paris: Librairie Arthème Fayard, 1963), 152.

32. See Jose Ocariz-Brana, *Historia Sencilla del Pensamiento Politico* (Madrid: Ediciones Rialp, S.A., 1988), 80.

33. Paul Henri Dietrich, Baron de Holbach (1723–1789) was a materialist and atheist French philosopher who wrote the *Système de la Nature*. Claude Adrian Helvetius was a French philosopher born in Paris. He was the author of *De l'Esprit*, an apology of absolute sensualism.

34. Jean-Jacques Rousseau (1712–1778) based all of his thoughts on the idea that man is naturally good but, being corrupted by society, must return to the original state of natural virtue. Although he did not deny the existence of God, all of his theories implied a rejection of the Christian doctrine of original sin.

35. See Jean-Jacques Rousseau, *Émile ou de l'éducation*, Book 1 (Paris: Garnier-Flammarion, 1966), 35–87.

36. See Alexis de Tocqueville, *The Old Regime and the French Revolution* (New York: Doubleday Anchor Books, 1955), 6.

37. Paul Hazard, *La Pensée Européenne au XVIIIe Siècle*, 8.

38. Edmund Burke, *Reflections on the Revolution in France* (New York: Dolphin Books, 1961), 17.

39. Burke, *Reflections on the Revolution in France*, 21–22.

40. The breakaway of rational knowledge from traditional faith, as occurred in the Western world in the eighteenth century, buttressed the position of those modern philosophers who claim that an opposition exists between faith and reason. In scientific research, this led to a rejection of any metaphysical or moral vision. To deny that faith and reason can stand in harmony endangers the dignity of the human person. Certain scientists emboldened by technological progress can even yield to the temptation of a quasi-divine power over nature and even over the human being. See John Paul II, *Fides et Ratio* #46.

41. Christopher Dawson, *The Dividing of Christendom* (New York: Image Books, 1967), 217.

42. "... Le 10 novembre, la Raison fit son entrée a Notre Dame. ... A l'intérieure de la cathédrale, on a edifié une montagne en carton que couronne un temple grec et que des draperies relient aux bas-cotes. Tout autour des flambeaux et des bustes: Voltaire, Rousseau, Franklin. Il y a eu des discours, des chants, de la musique. Les jeunes filles montèrent sur la montagne et du temple sortit une artiste de l'Opéra qui figurait la Raison. Le danseur Gardel fonctionnait comme maître de ballet." See Pierre Gaxotte, *La Révolution Française* (Paris: Historiques, Editions Complexe, 1988), 337.

43. Paul Hazard has no hesitation in stating that pride fills the pages of many of the writings of the "encyclopédistes." For them, "La raison se suffit a elle même: qui la possède et l'exercice sans prejugés ne se trompe jamais: *neque decipitur ratio, neque decipit unquam* , elle suit infalliblement la route de la verité. Elle n'a besoin ni de l'autorité, dont elle est assez exactement le contraire et qui ne s'est montré qu'une maitresse d'erreur; ni de la tradition; ni des Anciens, ni des Modernes." See Paul Hazard, *La Pense Européenne au XVIIIe Siècle*, 37–38.

44. Taylor, *A History of Economic Thought*, 8.

45. John Dewey (1859–1952) was a radical empiricist. His experimental beliefs had a great influence on the American educational system. They became the basis of what is known as progressive education. Many of his ideas have their roots in the writings of Jean-Jacques Rousseau.

46. Randall, *The Making of the Modern Mind*, 381.

47. Robert Nisbet, *History of the Idea of Progress* (New York: Basic Books, 1980), 4.

48. Leszek Kolakowsky wrote that utopia "is a desperate desire to attain absolute perfection, this desire is a degraded remnant of the religious legacy in non religious minds." Quoted by Nisbet, *History of the Idea of Progress*, 239.

49. Hazard does not waver in affirming the following: " C'est l'histoire éternelle d'une éternelle illusion." See Hazard, *La Pensée Européenne au XVIIIe Siècle*, 27.

50. Schumpeter, *History of Economic Analysis*, 122.

51. Schumpeter, *History of Economic Analysis*, 123.

52. See Eduard Heimann, *History of Economic Doctrines* (New York: Oxford University Press, 1956), 50.

53. John Herman Randall Jr., *The Making of the Modern Mind* (New York: Houghton Mifflin, 1940), 365.

54. Randall, *The Making of the Modern Mind*, 366.

55. Professor Molnar asserts that "the very foundations of the human situation are precisely what utopians would like to uproot. In this case, utopian thinkers fully deserve to be called 'radical' because their reconstruction of society and man demand total rethinking about God and creation." See Thomas Molnar, *Utopia, The Perennial Heresy* (New York: Sheed & Ward, 1967), 9.

56. For an excellent analysis of Montesquieu's writings, see: Pierre Manent, *The City of Man* (Princeton, NJ: Princeton University Press, 1998).

57. Paul Hazard, *La Pensée Européenne au XVIIIe Siècle*, 158.

58. John Locke, *Two Treatises*, Book I, chapter 3, sect. 13. As quoted in, *Second Treatise of Government*, edited, with an introduction by C. B. Macpherson (Indianapolis, IN: Hackett Publishing, 1980), xi. For a more detailed analysis of Macpherson's views, see C. B. Macpherson, *The Political Theory of Possessive Individualism: Hobbes to Locke* (Oxford: Clarendon Press, 1962).

59. For a harsh criticism of Locke's philosophical writings, see Joseph Comte de Maistre, *Les Soirées de St. Petersbourg* (Paris: 1821). Joseph de Maistre (1753–1821) was a French writer and philosopher, very critical of the French Revolution, and a firm defender of the Catholic faith. See especially "La Sixième Soirée" in which, with a great deal of sarcasm, he sharply criticizes the fundamental ideas of Locke.

60. Karen Iversen Vaughn, *John Locke, Economist and Social Scientist* (London: The Athlone Press, 1980), 135.

61. Vaughn, *John Locke*, 134.

62. Locke's stress on man's freedom is unequivocally stated when he affirms that all men are naturally in "a *state of perfect freedom* to order their actions, and dispose of their possessions and persons, as they think fit, within the bounds of the laws of nature, without asking leave, or depending upon the will of any other man." John Locke, Book II, Chapter II, Of the State of Nature.

63. See C. B. Macpherson, ed., *Second Treatise of Government*, xv.

64. Macpherson, ed., *Second Treatise of Government*, xv.

65. Thomas Hobbes (1588–1679) was an English philosopher of the seventeenth century. He was greatly influenced by Galileo and his new system of physics and by the English Civil War and the power of the state.

66. See Hobbes, *Leviathan or the Matter, Forme and Power of a Commonwealth Ecclesiastical and Civil* (New York: Collier Books, 1973), 193.

67. Hobbes asserted like few other political philosophers before him the principle of individual selfishness. He was responsible for basing an ethical and political system on the radically independent individual. For an excellent treatise on Hobbes, see Paul A. Clark, *Hobbes and the Enlightenment*, a dissertation submitted to the Faculty of the School of Philosophy at The Catholic University of America, Washington, DC, 1996.

68. David Hume, for example, claimed that morality was founded on the passions. He excluded the possibility of founding it on reason as Kant had done. Kierkegaard, on the other hand, founded it "on criterionless fundamental choice because of what he takes to be the compelling nature of the considerations which exclude both reason and the passions." See Alasdaire MacIntyre, *After Virtue* (Notre Dame, IN: University of Notre Dame Press, 1984), 49.

69. Greatly influenced by Rousseau, they maintained that education and legislation were crucial to protect man from the corrupting influence of society. New surroundings had to be devised that would permit man from his early childhood to develop fully his natural goodness.

70. August Comte (1798–1857) was a French philosopher born in Montpellier, France. He is considered the founder of positivism and sociology. His most famous work, *Cours de Philosophie Positive* became one of the most widespread treatises of the nineteenth century.

71. Marie-Jean Caritat, Marquis de Condorcet (1743–1794) was a French philosopher and politician who became quite well-known during the French Revolution for his writings and political activities. His most famous work was *Esquises d'un Tableau Historique des Progrès de l'èsprit Humain*. He wrote it while in prison as a Girondin, an enemy of the people. He poisoned himself in order to avoid being executed. See Joseph Schumpeter, *History of Economic Analysis* (New York: Oxford University Press, 1954), 443.

72. August Comte believed that when the human spirit reaches the stage in which it recognizes the impossibility of knowing the existence of absolute values, it no longer accepts the likelihood of knowing the origin and destiny of the universe and of knowing the intimate cause of all phenomena. However, it did not take long for the nineteenth and twentieth centuries to convert into a certainty what previously had been placed in doubt: the total negation of both the existence of God and of any absolute values based on Natural Law and Divine Law. For an excellent study of Natural Law, see Javier Hervada, *Introduccion Critica al Derecho Natural* (Pamplona, Spain: Ediciones Universidad de Navarra, S.A., 1994), 82.

73. See Henri de Lubac, *The Drama of Atheist Humanism* (San Francisco: Ignatius Press, 1944), 136.

74. De Lubac, *The Drama of Atheist Humanism*, 247.

75. Alasdaire MacIntyre, *After Virtue*, 52.

76. H. Daniel-Rops, *The Church in the Dark Ages,* Volume 2 (London: J. M. Dent, 1959), 37.

77. MacIntyre, *After Virtue,* 53.

78. St. Thomas Aquinas, *Summa Theologiae,* I—II, q. 90, a 4, ad lum. As quoted by John Paul II, *Veritatis Splendor,* #43.

79. St. Thomas Aquinas, *Summa Theologiae,* Treatise on Law, Q. 91, #4. As quoted in *St. Thomas Aquinas in Politics and Ethics,* ed. Paul E. Sigmund (New York: W. W. Norton, 1988), 47.

80. See Schumpeter, *History of Economic Analysis,* 113.

81. MacIntyre, *After Virtue,* 55.

82. MacIntyre, *After Virtue,* 68.

83. See Heimann, *History of Economic Doctrines,* 51.

84. Taylor, *A History of Economic Thought,* 8.

85. For an excellent approach to the truths of the natural order, see Joseph M. de Torre, *Christian Philosophy* (Manila, Philippines: Vera-Reyes, 1989), 38–39.

86. See Alasdaire MacIntyre, *A Short History of Ethics* (New York: Touchstone, 1966), 160.

87. MacIntyre, *After Virtue,* 54.

88. MacIntyre, *After Virtue,* 56.

89. MacIntyre, *After Virtue,* 4.

90. MacIntyre, *After Virtue,* 5.

91. Taylor, *A History of Economic Thought,* 10.

92. Taylor, *A History of Economic Thought,* 49.

93. McIntyre, *After Virtue,* 88.

94. McIntyre, *After Virtue,* 88.

95. McIntyre, *After Virtue,* 86.

96. McIntyre, *After Virtue,* 85.

# 2

—⁓—

# Human Nature and the Dignity of the Human Person

## THE HUMAN BEING AS A PERSON

One of the greatest tragedies of the modern era can be traced to a misunderstanding of the true nature of man and his role in society. Intellectuals and politicians, among others, do not cease to write and talk about the rights and dignity of man but, at the same time, rarely in the history of humanity has man experienced such anguish at the sight of so much injustice and suffering that surround him. It is not sufficient to talk and write about a new era of enlightened humanism where man is considered the central fact and final end of the universe. The horrors of two world wars, not to mention the other numerous fratricidal conflicts and acts of terrorism which have characterized the turbulent twentieth century, should be proof enough that a pure anthropocentric approach to life is not sufficient if peace and justice are to prevail. A humanism void of an essential dimension of man's being, the absolute, will not bring about the peace with justice that the world is craving for. On the contrary, as past history has demonstrated, it will only serve to trample the most elemental rights and dignity of the human person. Any attempt to create a "just" order that is neutral, agnostic, or indifferent toward the metaphysical reality of man is doomed to failure.[1]

The general acceptance of the animal nature of man is hardly, if ever, contested. Thus, like any other animal, man is entitled to enjoy the fruits of the earth. However, man cannot be reduced to his animal nature. He is much more than that. What distinguishes him from all other creatures on earth is his power to reason: his intellect. It is precisely the power of reason which

39

makes a human being human and distinguishes him essentially and completely from the brute.[2] Any social theory which disregards this basic truth and ignores the spirituality of man is de facto crippling the very essence of man and opens the door to crass materialism of either the left or the right. To avoid such an outcome, the best antidote to both philosophical and practical materialism is to reassert the reasoning power of human nature—without disregarding its important animal component—and its capacity for reflection or what is more commonly known as conscience.[3]

Our contemporary society seems to be arriving at the crossroads of history. There is an urgent need to protect the most elemental rights of man against an avalanche of juridical and nonjuridical measures which, under the guise of protecting those very rights, are only contributing to denigrate the very dignity of the human person and are threatening freedom itself. The power of the state under the influence of philosophical positivism and its aftermath of other "isms" is greatly responsible for this threatening trend which attempts to give juridical validity to a series of transgressions against the human person under the cover of formal legislation.

Javier Hervada, professor of philosophy at the University of Navarre in Spain, does not hesitate to say that modern man, predisposed by a positivistic ideology to disavow the validity of the true significance of Natural Law, is no longer willing to accept its unique contribution to the advancement of our civilization.[4] To disclaim the true content of Natural Law implies the denial of man as the central reality in society and, consequently, places in jeopardy his dignity as a human being. Man cannot be treated capriciously and disdainfully. On the contrary, he should be respected as a dignified human being endowed with inalienable rights derived from Natural Law. To deny such rights based on Natural Law runs counter to the very objectives that the proponents and defenders of human rights are trying to uphold in our contemporary society.

To the question whether all men are human persons, the juridical positivist, who rejects or ignores Natural Law, might very well answer in the negative. He can argue that the juridical person, being a creation of positive law, can only be considered a person when recognized as such by positive law, the law of the land.[5] Even though all men have been granted juridical personality by Natural Law, it is also true that not all of them have been considered always as human persons. In fact, the nonrecognition by positive law of certain groups or categories of men as human persons has been a frequent occurrence in the history of mankind. Slavery, for example, would not be considered an injustice if positive law, as it often did in the past, would declare that slaves are not human persons but mere objects that can be bought and sold at random by their masters. Other more contemporary examples could be mentioned but, perhaps, the more pertinent one relates to the right to life of the unborn. Not to recognize the personality of the unborn child would "legitimize" the destruction of a human person that had not yet seen the light of day.[6] Positive law, divorced from an ethical foundation based on Natural Law, could not only condone such an act but encourage it under the pretext that it was defending the right (human right?) of a woman to dispose of her body as she pleased.

Hervada, summarizes very well the dire consequences to the very concept of law if juridical positivism is accepted as the general norm. Juridical positivism, he claims, destroys any natural dimension of justice which is reduced simply to a mere legality. The *values*, to which some juridical positivists allude, are not strictly speaking rights because for them the only source of law is positive law and consequently they do not engender a real relation of justice. In addition juridical positivism despoils the human person of all its inherent juridical rights, something which is rigorously impossible. If man were not naturally the subject of rights, a person in a true juridical sense—a natural subject of juridical rights—the juridical phenomenon would not exist because its existence would be impossible.[7]

Thus, Hervada concludes, wherever there is a human being there is also a person in the juridical sense even though not recognized as such by positive law. That is why any natural juridical being, endowed with natural rights and duties, must be respected as a human person. To deny any person his juridical personality as a human being according to Natural Law is a blatant violation of justice.

The foundation of any law or juridical system lies precisely in Natural Law and the dignity of the human person. No matter what its source, the validity of any law and its justice can be questioned when the dignity of the human person is violated and Natural Law infringed. In such cases there is no law but raw power and injustice even though it may have the appearance of law. As we shall see in the following section, jurisprudence may not be created by power or social approval because it emanates from the very nature of the human person.

## THE RIGHTS OF THE HUMAN
## PERSON AND NATURAL LAW

The foundation of any right lies in Natural Law and the dignity of the human person. Without the proper respect for man, for what he is and represents, the very meaning of right is destroyed and in its place raw power, arrogance and injustice make their presence in society even though they may appear under the designation of law. Neither the state nor any particular group or individual in society has the right, in justice, to dictate norms and regulations that run counter to Natural Law and infringe upon the most elementary rights of the human person. Thus, respect for human rights and the dignity of man sets the dividing line between what is legitimate and what is not.[8]

The essence of man lies in his human nature which is his driving principle; principle without which he would cease to be a man. Wherever a man exists there must also be his essence; an essence which cannot be subject to historical change. If it did, it would mean that man as man would also change and this would imply that once the essence had changed, there would be no longer man but a different being. Whether very different or not is not important. What is important is that we would be facing no longer the historicity of man but the evolution of the species. Through time, the human species would have given ground to another species and this one, in its turn, to another and thus successively, something which is contrary to the most elementary experience. History is the *history of man*. Man as a collectivity and man as an individual is a combination of permanent nature and historical change.[9] To shun Natural Law is to discredit the essence of human rights.

The essence of human rights lies in those rights that belong to the human being as such. They are not rights which are conferred by positive law or custom. They are the rights that man is entitled to and not what society, the state or any other international agency is willing to bestow on him. By the mere fact of being a man, man has these inalienable rights which are valid even if society would no longer consider them as legitimate rights. The moral philosophers of the eighteenth century spoke of these inalienable rights as the natural rights of man, though they were not very good at explaining where these came from.

Our own era has bestowed further importance to the concept of human rights. The term itself has been generalized to such a degree that its true meaning has been lost amid the various interpretations given by different people in accordance with their own particular moral point of view. What may be considered a human right from a given person or institution may not be considered as such by another individual or organization who upholds a diverse moral position.

Once man was "liberated" in the eighteenth century from a Natural Law based on Divine Law, the newly autonomous agents were free to interpret human rights in accordance with their own set of moral norms. The proliferation of conflicting "rights" which characterizes our own era is proof enough of the confusion concerning the very concept of human rights. Each newly autonomous agent can demand that his "rights" be respected in accordance with his own moral interpretation of the "rights of man," even though his assessment may openly clash with the "rights" of others.[10] This is often the case in our contemporary society where it is common to see different groups vociferously claiming their own particular "rights" at the expense of the "rights" of others. The consequences of such antagonistic claims for the peace and tranquility of any society are not difficult to visualize.

If the "rights of man" are not clearly defined, why should anyone listen or accept the decision of a self appointed authority—whether individual or group—that has already rejected any external authority besides its own? With reference to human rights in the post-Enlightenment years, MacIntyre maintains that "whether negative or positive and however named they are supposed to attach equally to all individuals, whatever their sex, race, religion, talents or deserts, and to provide a ground for a variety of particular moral stances." The denial of a transcendental moral order has shaken the very foundation of any human right and "de facto" denied that man has rights that are rooted in his God given nature.

F. J. Sheed in his book *Society and Sanity* does not hesitate to state that any understanding of human rights requires a proper grasp of man himself. For Sheed, "The phrase 'rights of man' too often means what it is good, or humane, or socially useful to concede him. But concessions, however liberal, are not rights. Rights are what man is entitled to, not what society is willing to let him have. They belong to man because he is man, and are valid even against society. Unless they are this, they are not rights at all, but only a more or less hopeful expectation of society's kindness. But *has* man rights? Obviously the answer depends on what man is."[11]

In a similar way, the late professor of political philosophy at Georgetown University, Heinrich A. Rommen stresses the personal being of man as the origin of all rights. In his book *The Natural Law* he specifies in no uncertain terms that ". . . the personal being of man exists as a datum prior to all positive law, at least for the formation of the legal community. But this means that it also exists as a datum for the positivist theory of law. For precisely this state of being a person, this state of being an end in oneself, is the first fact, and in it lies the original germ of right."[12] The rights of the person exist prior to the formation of the state. These rights, he continues, are not facts, to which the state attaches legal effects but rather claims that demand recognition. The *suum cuique* is not dependent upon material realization through positive law because there is already a *suum*, a right, that comes into existence with us.[13]

Given the fact that every man is entitled to be respected in his rights as a human being, all institutions, whether political, economic or otherwise, must face the fundamental question as to how man must be treated. To ignore this question would reduce human rights to mere statements without any practical significance. No society can be united or attain peace with justice if there is no common understanding of what man is. This is the major problem facing contemporary man in its efforts to reach peace with justice; a predicament which is clearly reflected in the United Nations and other international organizations. As Sheed points out, "There is neither present agreement in principle as to how man should be treated, nor any agreement in practice flowing out of a long past, for the United Nations has no past, and its constituent members inherit no common attitude to man."[14]

The Spanish philosopher Ortega y Gasset warned us many years ago that peacekeeping efforts in international organizations would not succeed if the main requirement for the attainment of peaceful coexistence were lacking: the acceptance of a higher authority that all members of the international body would be willing to accept.[15] That is why, claims Ortega, the League of Nations of the thirties was destined to total failure. The required higher authority or a generally accepted civil law did not exist, was not accepted or was simply interpreted in different ways by the member countries. There not being common identifiable principles to which the international community can recur to, all efforts to reach a peaceful solution between conflicting parties would ultimately have to fail. New types of organizations may be created in the future but they will all run into the same fate and irremediably fail. Ultimately, continues Ortega, it is not the desire to have peace what is important. What really matters is not to limit the term pacifism to good intentions but to find a new rule of conduct among men so that they can treat each other better.[16]

This general rule of conduct of which Ortega speaks about and which he does not mention specifically is none other but a general acceptance of an accurate account of Natural Law. It is only under the umbrella of a proper understanding of the rule of law (Natural Law) that men can find a refuge in times of conflict and the rights of man properly respected/

The well-known French philosopher Jacques Maritain in his book *Man and the State* writes in no uncertain terms that the philosophical foundation of the rights of man is Natural Law.[17] During the rationalist era, Maritain asserts, jurists and philosophers misused the concept of Natural Law to such a degree "that it is difficult to use it now without awakening distrust and suspicion in many of our contemporaries. They should realize, however that the history of the rights of man is tightly bound to the history of Natural Law, and that the discredit into which for some time positivism brought to the idea of Natural Law inevitably entailed a similar discrediting of the idea of the Rights of Man."[18]

The tragedy of the eighteenth century was to reject God as the supreme source and origin of Natural Law. Instead, Natural Law was deduced from the so-called "autonomy" of the Will and, as a result, the rights of the human person were based "on the claim that man is subject to no law other than that of his own will and freedom."[19] A philosophy built on such a flimsy foundation could not serve as the basis for the rights of the human person because, as Maritain continues, "it led men to conceive them as rights in themselves divine, hence infinite, escaping every objective measure, denying every limitation imposed upon the claims of the ego, and ultimately expressing the absolute independence of the human subject and a so-called absolute right—which supposedly pertains to everything in the human subject by the mere fact that it is in him—to unfold one's cherished possibilities at the expense of all other beings."[20] Sooner or later reality proved how deceptive it is to rely on such a shaky philosophical foundation.

It is man's task at the dawn of the approaching twenty-first century to reestablish his faith in human rights but in order to do this he must realize that the true philosophy of the rights of the human person must be based, as Maritain insists, "upon the true idea of Natural Law, as looked upon in an onto logical perspective and as conveying through the essential structures and requirements of created nature the wisdom of the Author of Being."[21]

By an ontological base Maritain means that man, endowed with intelligence and free will, can act with an understanding of what he is doing. Man's human nature or onto logical structure, which is a locus for intelligible necessities, possesses ends which correspond to his essential constitution. However, he has the power to determine for himself the ends which he wants to pursue but it is man's responsibility to act in accordance with the ends necessarily demanded by his nature. This means, following Maritain, "that there is, by the very virtue of human nature, an order or a disposition which human reason can discover and according to which the human will must act in order to attune itself to the essential and necessary ends of the human being. The unwritten law, or Natural Law, is nothing more than that."[22] It serves as the basis for judging what is right and what is wrong. Without a proper understanding of man's true nature it would be very difficult if not impossible for man to know what he should or should not do. It is Natural Law which lays down the most fundamental rights and duties of man; rights and duties which are grounded or required by the very essence of man.

All beings existing in nature achieve their fulfillment as beings by following their own specific nature and specific ends in accordance with the Natural Law. In other words, the Natural Law of all beings is the proper way in which they achieve their fullness of being. But, once we enter into the specific realm of the human person we enter also into the threshold of human freedom and, as a result, Natural Law cannot be separated from moral law. Quoting again from Maritain: "Natural law for man is *moral law*, because man obeys or disobeys it freely, not necessarily, and because human behaviour pertains to a particular, privileged order which is irreducible to the general order of the cosmos and tends to a final end superior to the immanent common good of the cosmos."[23]

Together with man's intellectual capacity to discover the truth comes the attribute of freedom. Authentic freedom is the best sign that man cannot be reduced to his animal nature. Otherwise, he would not be free. Animals have no power of self-direction and are governed exclusively by two chief instincts: self-preservation and the propagation of the species. These instincts keep their powers alert, move them to use their strength and determine them to action. The brute does not act according to a knowing and free choice.

Unlike animals, man's actions are not the result of blind internal impulses or of mere external pressures. Apart from possessing the full perfection of animal nature—self-preservation and the propagation of the species—man has, in addition, the power of reason and has the freedom to act according to a knowing and free choice. He is personally motivated and prompted from within. This is what makes a human being human. It is precisely in man's authentic freedom—freedom to chose good from evil and thus reach perfection—that lies his supreme dignity and ultimately the reason for respecting the fundamental rights of the human person. Man's dignity demands that man act according to a knowing and free choice.

Natural Law as applied in the area of economics was conceived in a way which resembled very closely the physical sciences. Astronomy shows the harmony that exists in the movement of the heavenly bodies; movement that is not guided by any visible authoritarian authority but by a law which guides them from within their own nature. In the same manner, the economy, because of inner forces implanted in it by nature, can operate better without any external authority. But, these inner forces must operate within the framework of rational free individuals. Thus, for the liberal of the eighteenth century, freedom becomes a fundamental pillar for the "natural" ordering of society and the achievement of its immanent goals.[24] The pertinent question that must now be answered relates to the very concept of freedom itself and the various interpretations that it has been subjected to through the last three centuries. This we will do in the following section.

## MISCONCEPTIONS ABOUT THE NATURE
## OF FREEDOM AND CONSCIENCE

There is probably no other word in common language that has been used and misused so frequently as the concept of freedom. Ever since the beginning of history man has cherished the idea of freedom to the point that, whenever his basic liberties have been threatened, he has not hesitated to fight and offer his life in order to preserve them. Freedom, after all, is the greatest gift given by the Creator to man and, as a result, no one in his right mind is willing to give it up. But, what is true freedom? Can freedom be equated to a person's power to do what he wants as is often interpreted by modern man?

Freedom, let us reaffirm it, is the measure of man's dignity. Genuine freedom is an outstanding manifestation of the creator's image in man. When God created man he gave him the power to be free, to be the master of his own destiny and to rule over all other creatures. There lies the root of true freedom: free will, man's freedom to choose between good and evil. Man is free because he has free will but, until he reaches his full potential as a human being, his freedom is not complete. It is limited. Thus, free will must not be equated with freedom. Perhaps, the mistaken notion that both concepts are synonymous is the cause of much of the confusion prevailing in our contemporary society.

When the word freedom is mentioned there is the tendency to relate the term to the idea of freedom from something: tyranny, oppression, want, and so forth. Man never ceases to claim his natural given right to act freely without constraints and independent from outside interference. He is adamant, and rightly so, about his right to be free from abuse and all sorts of despotic rule. However, when the time is ripe for man to accept the consequences of his freely determined actions, he often shies away from accepting responsibility claiming that his actions have been conditioned by external circumstances over which he has no control.[25] Man wants to be free but, at the same time and paradoxically, he frequently denies free will by avoiding or refusing to accept responsibility for his freely determined acts. This way, he enjoys his freedom whilst, at the same time, denying any responsibility for his free acts, claiming that he is not "free" to choose. His actions, man would claim, would be the product of circumstances, the environment, hereditary factors, and so forth. But, if man's actions are determined by external factors, his choices would no longer be free. De facto, freedom of choice would be denied and, thus, it could no longer be said that man's human nature was different from non rational beings.

There is no doubt that circumstances and other factors influence man's free will. However, no matter how important some of these circumstances may be, they are not the determining factors in the actions of a normal human being. If man is reduced to being a creature of his circumstances, he is no longer free. A free man must have freedom of choice. He cannot claim that he is a creature of circumstances over which he has no control, as some philosophers have maintained. Such a deterministic approach runs counter to the doctrine of free will and denies man's responsibility as a rational human being.

To be free does not mean that man is independent from all constraints and has the right to do what he pleases. In fact, man is dependent from the day he is born, because he is not self sufficient and needs others for his very survival. But, during the very early years of his life, man's dependency is involuntary, as in the case of infancy. It is only later, when he is able to make choices, that he creates for himself new voluntary dependencies that influence his character and tend to be habit forming: dependencies that are very often the result of his own uncontrolled self-interest.

Any man that is guided exclusively by his feelings or passions is not really free. In fact, he is probably very much underdeveloped with respect to freedom. He becomes obsessed with his own instincts and passions and is hardly able to think clearly in order to make the right choices. He can easily become totally dependent on his bad habits or in external things that, although good in themselves, may not be conducive to his full development. Once a man is unable to break away from a given habit, he no longer can be considered a free man. His level of dependence would become so great that it would require a tremendous effort on his part to overcome it. For example, in certain societies corruption and bribery have become so ingrained among the people that to get rid of the habit is extremely difficult. Other evil inclinations may be even more difficult to overcome.

It is important to keep in mind that all of man's choices affect his personality and his total development as a human being. They cannot be considered indifferent in relation to his human development. Poor choices do not help man to be free. Man's dependence on his own inordinate passions does not contribute to his integral development but, on the contrary, make him culturally and spiritually underdeveloped. Man must learn to overcome those dependencies which hinder his development and put obstacles in his path toward true freedom. But to do so, he must become the master of his own choices and this requires time and effort and the will to do it.

Freedom, therefore, does not mean that man is free from all external restrictions. Ironically, a man can be free from external restrictions (i.e., tyranny) and yet not be free when he becomes a slave to his own inner passions. To be genuinely free, man, given his limited human condition, must accept certain self imposed restraints that are indispensable if he is to remain free. For example, he must learn to exercise the power of self control and, when necessary say no to his own passions or inclinations. Otherwise, he will lose his freedom and become a puppet of his lower instincts. In other words, man must not lose control of his own life. He must learn to overcome those self-created dependencies that are an impediment to his integral development.

It is now pertinent to clarify some errors of judgment that have been made in certain intellectual circles concerning the attitude of Christianity and authority in general with respect to the practice of freedom. The Biblical Tradition has never been an enemy of freedom. On the contrary, it has always been the champion of personal freedom as history can easily demonstrate.

Jean-Marie Lustiger in his book *Devenez dignes de la condition humaine* touches upon this important point; a point which has caused much controversy in our contemporary society that is obsessed, and rightly so, with the idea of freedom. According to Lustiger, the very concept of freedom can be traced back to biblical times: the liberation promised and granted by Jehovah to the Jewish people and consummated in the biblical Alliance. A liberal author, such as the great German philosopher Hegel, recognized this truth when he stated that in the despotic regimes of the East only one person was free whilst under Christianity everyone is free.[26]

It was only in later years, as a result of social and political systems which stressed the absolutism of the monarchs and of the religious wars that disseminated Europe in rival political and religious parties, that faith and freedom came increasingly under attack. Many considered kings and religious authorities—often allies—the enemies of freedom and thus, if freedom were to prevail, it became necessary to destroy them both, especially the faith and the Church.

Eighteenth century philosophical liberalism became the champion and defender of freedom. De facto, it became the rallying cry of all those who considered biblical revelation as the quintessence of coercion and division. Ironically, religious freedom in both the public and private areas came under violent attack and often even suppressed or drastically curtailed in the name of that very "freedom" which the new wave of liberalism was trying to implant.

It serves no purpose to try to place the blame for this trend of events that were spreading rapidly all over Europe on any particular person or any particular intellectual movement. As Lustiger quite correctly states, "Can the blame be placed on Voltaire or the Gallicanism of Bossuet, on the *Aufklarung* or on the Pontifical States, on the schism of Henry VIII or the barbarousness of the Catholic soldiery? The accusation will not bring out the truth. But, given the length of time gone by and with the help of memory, it becomes clear that the practice of freedom was inextricably bound to the anti clericalism of the left and right, to a militant laicism, including a deliberate anti Christian and anti Jewish attitude and, frequently, to atheism."[27]

The errors and mistakes of the Christians of past centuries and not the least those of the turbulent eighteenth and nineteenth centuries undoubtedly carry part of the blame for the virulent anticlericalism which characterized many of the liberal movements of the past two hundred years. Pope John Paul II in his letter *Tercio Millennio Adveniente* recognizes the errors of the past when he declares that the Church regrets having used "methods of intolerance, including violence placed at the service of truth."[28] There is a principle in moral law that specifically declares that the end does not justify the means although, at times, this principle may have been sacrificed in the altar of political expediency. The great French philosopher and mathematician Blaise Pascal once wrote that God acts always with gentleness and never uses force to impose religion. On the contrary, it is through grace that He brings religion to the hearts and minds of men. To try to do it with threats and coercion only produces fear, *terrorem potius quam religionem*."[29]

The fact that religious persons committed grave mistakes in the past, and even today, does not affect the credit worthiness of Christianity's teachings on ethical and moral questions, in particular with respect to the proper understanding of the very concept of freedom. But, as mentioned earlier, the love and defense of freedom of expression does not mean an indifference to the truth.

The dynamics of liberalism, and its stress on freedom, undoubtedly had and still can have very positive results as long as it does not separate reason from truth. However, if reason and freedom separate themselves from the principles and values on which their dynamism and proper exercise depend, freedom itself is jeopardized and, sooner or later, license inevitably takes its place. It is erroneous and extremely dangerous, if freedom is to be maintained, to disassociate positive law from moral law and to declare that a justifiable autonomous political power can be totally divorced from any relationship with the absolute and the transcendental. As Lustiger affirms, it is absurd to think that political liberties can only be maintained if they are dispensed from any responsibility toward the common good and that the power of reason can only exercise its control over nature if it ignores the transcendental.[30] The same argument can be applied in the area of economics.

Thus, Christianity, in spite of its human errors, has never shied away from defending freedom and condemning its abuses, independently of its sources. There is no contradiction between legitimate authority and freedom and much less between faith and freedom. The fundamental principles of Christianity are a living testimony of this basic truth. To deny them imperils the very dignity of the human person.

The misguided interpretation of freedom can have destructive consequences on society and the free institutions on which it stands. This applies to all aspects of life, including politics and economics. Perhaps, this erroneous assessment of freedom, to a large extent the result of the philosophers of the French Enlightenment, has been one of the major factors contributing to the abuses of a capitalism void of an ethical foundation.

The founding fathers of liberalism redefined the traditional Christian concept of Natural Law. They exalted their own scheme of principles into an ethical norm of behavior and judged the preferences of other men in accordance with their own set of values. This trend of thought runs through much of the economic literature of the English moralists who did not hesitate to turn their human egotism into an ideal, into a source of norms for conduct.[31] By eliminating all super personal values except the "good of society" they reduced the good of society to the sum total of all satisfactions accruing to all individuals in accordance with their own hedonistic scheme of preferences. Hume and Bentham were primarily the ones who elaborated the fundamental canon of Utilitarian Ethics: good is every action that promotes, bad is every action that impairs, social welfare.[32] As a result, the concept of the human person was reduced to a mere self-centered egotistic individual and, consequently, the rights of man, including freedom, acquired a new significance redefined in terms of a natural ethics divorced from any teleological content.

The ideal-and-theory of a liberal economy composed of self-centered individuals and based on preordained natural harmonies is best exemplified in the writings of the English Classical School and, in particular, in the writings of its founder Adam Smith. Smith was convinced that the self adjusting liberal economy is based on a system of natural liberties for all individuals: a system that is implicit in the nature of the universe and which can lead through men's natural propensities and intelligence to the attainment of the greatest possible happiness. The problems of modern moral theory emerge from the failure of the fallacious rationale promoted by the moral philosophers of the Enlightenment. Their greatest error consisted in believing that the individual moral agent, freed from hierarchy and teleology, could consider himself as sovereign in his moral authority.[33] The toll of this misunderstanding—if not rejection—of Natural Law is still being felt today.

## NOTES

1. José Miguel Ibañez Langlois, *Doctrina Social de la Iglesia* (Pamplona, Spain: Ediciones Universidad de Navarra, S.A., 1987), 75.

2. Leo XIII, *Rerum Novarum*, # 5.

3. Ibanez Langlois, *Doctrina Social de la Iglesia*, 79.

4. See Javier Hervada, *Introducción Crítica al Derecho Natural* (Pamplona, Spain: Ediciones Universidad de Navarra, S.A., 1994), 11.

5. The violations of the basic rights of the human person by ideologies such as those sponsored and ruthlessly carried out by Nazism and communism are too well known to need any further clarification. And, what is even more ironic is that they were enforced under the aegis of the ruling positive law of the land.

6. Hervada, *Introducción Crítica al Derecho Natural*, 121.

7. Hervada, *Introducción Crítica al Derecho Natural*, 119.

8. Hervada, *Introducción Crítica al Derecho Natural*, 11.

9. Hervada, *Introducción Crítica al Derecho Natural*, 99.

10. Very often the call for "women's rights" and the "rights" of certain minorities may clash with other social groups which claim similar rights in defense of their own interests.

11. F. J. Sheed, *Society and Sanity* (New York: Sheed & Ward, 1953), 11.

12. Heinrich A. Rommen, *The Natural Law, A Study in Legal and Social History and Philosophy* (Indianapolis, IN: Liberty Fund, 1998), 205.

13. Rommen, *The Natural Law*, 205.

14. Sheed, *Society and Sanity*, 12.

15. Jose Ortega y Gasset, *La Rebelión de las Masas, Epílogo a los Ingleses* (Madrid: Revista de Occidente en Alianza Editorial, 1983), 225. Ortega in his critique of the pacifist movement stresses the following: "The pacifist needs to realize that he is in the midst of a world where the principle requirement for the organization of peace is either lacking or greatly weakened. People in their treatment of each other can no longer appeal to a higher authority because there is none" (225).

16. Ortega y Gasset, *La Rebelión de las Masas*, 211.

17. Similar views are expressed by other prominent scholars as the following quotes demonstrate: "It is from natural law, and from it alone, that man obtains those rights we refer to as inalienable and inviolable. Man's only right, in the last analysis, is the right to be a man, to live as a human person. Specific human rights, then, are all based on man's right to live as a human person. Some of these rights belong to man simply as a man and therefore are above and beyond the reach of the State. . . . Human rights have no foundation other than natural law. . . . The only foundation for a sound structure of government and of social institutions is natural law." Citations taken from: Neil Thomas, *Weapons for Peace* (Milwaukee, WI: Bruce Publishing, 1945), 155f. See Rommen, *The Natural Law*, 216n50.

18. Jacques Maritain, *Man and the State* (Chicago: University of Chicago Press, 1951), 81.

19. Maritain, *Man and the State*, 83.

20. Maritain, *Man and the State*, 84.

21. Maritain, *Man and the State*, 84.

22. Maritain, *Man and the State*, 86.

23. Maritain, *Man and the State*, 87.

24. See Joseph Hoffner, *Christliche Gesellshaftsehre* (Kevelaer de Renania: Verlag Butzon, 1974).

25. For the Austrian economist Friedrich von Hayek, liberty is inseparable from the concept of responsibility. According to him, "Liberty not only means that the individual has both the opportunity and the burden of choice; it also means that he must bear the consequences of his actions and will receive praise or blame for them. Liberty and responsibility are inseparable." However, he warns that "This belief in individual responsibility, which has always been strong when people firmly believed in individual freedom, has declined, together with the esteem for freedom." See Friedrich A. Hayek, *The Constitution of Liberty* (South Bend, IN: Gateway, 1960), 71.

26. See Jean-Marie Lustiger, *Devenez Dignes de la Condition Humaine* (Paris: Flammarion/Saint Maurice, Switzerland: Saint-Augustin, 1995), 96.

27. Lustiger, *Devenez Dignes de la Condition Humaine*, 97.

28. John Paul II, *Tertio Millennio Adveniente*.

29. See Blaise Pascal, *Pensées* (Paris: Librairie Générale Française, 1972).

30. Lustiger, *Devenez Dignes de la Condition Humaine*, 92.

31. Joseph Schumpeter, *History of Economic Analysis* (New York: Oxford University Press, 1963), 129.

32. Schumpeter, *History of Economic Analysis*, 129.

33. Alasdaire MacIntyre, *After Virtue* (Notre Dame, IN: University of Notre Dame Press, 1984), 62.

# 3

—ꟹ—

# The Classical School
# and the Birth of Capitalism

## ADAM SMITH AND THE
## BRITISH CLASSICAL SCHOOL

The renowned English economist John Maynard Keynes wrote in his influential book *The General Theory of Employment, Interest and Money* that the object of such a title was to contrast his arguments and conclusions with those of the classical theory which had dominated the economic thought, both practical and theoretical, of the governing and academic classes of his generation and of the five generations that preceded him. He included also among the classical economists, not only Adam Smith and David Ricardo but also their followers, including J. S. Mill, and such neoclassical economists as Alfred Marshall, Francis Y. Edgeworth, and Arthur C. Pigou, all of whom believed in the same basic postulates of classical theory.[1]

For the purpose of this book we shall follow Keynes' interpretation of the Classical School and include in its ranks all those economists and political scientists who believe in the automatic self-regulating mechanism of a free competitive market system and the attainment of full employment free from government interference.

Adam Smith, the founder[2] of the Classical School, used the philosophy of the intellectuals of the Enlightenment not only to discredit the theories of the mercantilists but also and primarily to establish the basic principles of a "natural" and rational economic order where the individual reigns supreme. His major contribution to economic theory, as exemplified in his numerous writings, consisted in establishing the foundations of a system of natural liberties that later became known as economic liberalism.

Even though Adam Smith's fame as founder of the Classical School of economics is due to the publication in 1776 of his book *An Inquiry into the Nature and Causes of the Wealth of Nations*, we believe that greater attention should be given to his earlier work *The Theory of Moral Sentiments* written in 1759 and to a series of lectures which he gave at the University of Glasgow.[3] The philosophical basis and the economic applications of economic liberalism were already delineated in these writings and particularly in the latter. Of special interest to us are his views on ethics and the need for moral values.

Credit must be given to such eminent moral philosophers as Lord Shaftesbury and Francis Hutcheson for their contribution to the theoretical basis of the economic liberalism of Adam Smith and the Classical School of economics. Both Shaftesbury and Hutcheson belonged to a group of British moralists that considered ethics as a natural product of human experience. For these scholars, morality no longer consisted of purely rational principles but rather the result of both human emotions and reason. In ethical theory, they departed from pure rationalism; a theoretical departure which greatly influenced eighteenth century economic and political thought.[4]

Shaftesbury and Hutcheson were among the earlier representatives of this new approach to ethics. Their views on the concept of man, self-interest and moral values were significantly different from those of their contemporary moral philosophers. They believed in man's natural goodness and in a wise and benevolent Designer of all nature, including human nature. They were true Deists who rejected Christian Revelation and all religious and moral truths that were not self-evident to natural reason. The concept of original sin was alien to them. But, although they rejected orthodox Christians, they nevertheless did not reject the type of Christianity that was endorsed by the "liberal, enlightenment" philosophers of the eighteenth century.[5]

In many ways, Shaftesbury appears to be a precursor of Rousseau's concept of the natural goodness of man. He anticipated the author of the *Social Contract* in proclaiming the native natural goodness of mankind, ascribing it more to natural emotional dispositions than to reason. Shaftesbury, on his part, did not hesitate to proclaim the high moral capacities of human nature but, at the same time, he believed that mankind could be easily corrupted by the use of reason. This concept of the natural goodness of man ran counter to the pessimistic doctrines of both the somber Calvinists and the oppressive materialism of Thomas Hobbes.

Shaftesbury and Hutcheson challenged the secularism of Thomas Hobbes just as well as the Calvinist exaggeration of the doctrine of original sin and the depravity of human nature. They rejected the puritanical distrust of the free use of freedom and stressed their belief in the perfect goodness of man's natural dispositions. In the case of Hobbes, they repudiated him for having eliminated religion as a source of moral values and for having based ethics on the human urge for self-preservation. This new approach constituted a radical shift from a belief in the natural sinfulness of men to a complete denial of original sin and a confident acceptance of the original goodness of mankind.

Shaftesbury, as most if not all of the moral philosophers of the Enlightenment, assigned a major role to natural self interest in all human activities. For them all unethical behavior or impulses were the result of bad social conditions; behavior that could be overcome only through "enlightened" social reform. Under the appropriate social conditions, malevolent feelings would no longer prevail and there would be sufficient benevolent feelings to counteract and limit man's self-interest. This way man would become a good member of a good society.

John Locke was the chief source of Shaftesbury's ideas and of his empiricist followers, among whom Adam Smith can be included. As we saw in chapter 2, Locke believed that all knowledge was derived from and supported by experience. He claimed that all sense perceptions are mere mental images or copies of the original ones existing in the external world. Although these sense perceptions can be and are useful for the acquisition of data related to all the descriptive sciences, the question remains as to whether they can serve also as the true foundation of a true theory of ethics?

How did the moral philosophers reconcile the views on self interest with the need for moral values? Can ethics within the realm of economics be founded on mere feelings and experiences by simply claiming that they are the ones that engender and support the idea of a "scientific" and "natural" ethics and, by so doing, contribute to the building of a rational economic order? Can the innate benevolent attitude of men be explained in terms of mere feelings and perceptions, as the classical economists claimed?

There is no doubt that these ethical problems occupied the minds of Smith and his predecessors Shaftesbury and Hutcheson. Hutcheson, being a moral philosopher, could not ignore the moral question in economic matters and, consequently, tried to give a satisfactory answer to some of the problems raised above in his book *An Inquiry into the Original of Our Ideas of Beauty and Virtue.*[6] He was not satisfied with Locke's theory that "all knowledge is made up of ideas developed from and supported by sense-perceptions" which are only mental images of their objects in the external world.[7] These ordinary sense perceptions may be used as data for purely descriptive purposes in the natural sciences but not as the basis for the "science" of ethics. The argument that man can be lured to act morally and contribute to the order and harmony of society on the basis of sense perceptions was not convincing.

The problem facing Hutcheson, and later Smith, was to determine what objective items existing in the external world could serve as the originals of those perceptions or experiences which engender or support the ideas of beauty and virtue and, thus, entice man to act benevolently with his competitors. Hutcheson's argument was that, in addition to the familiar five senses, man enjoyed a sixth sense which included both an aesthetic and a sense of virtue. By admitting the existence of this sixth sense—the sense of beauty and virtue—beside the five that permit man to know the physical world around him, he introduced a moral aspect to man's activities which seem to contradict his reliance on practical experience, resulting from impressions and feelings, as the prime motor of man's actions.[8]

Hutcheson, for example, claimed on the one hand that man the scientist, guided by his aesthetic sense, "contributes to *knowledge* of the order and harmony in the variety of nature, *and thereby also contributes unknowingly to later useful inventions* and thus to the welfare and happiness of mankind."[9] On the other hand he states also that "man the (good) citizen, lured on and guided in all good conduct by his moral sense, contributes to *creation and maintenance* of (moral) order and harmony in the variety of his own life and other lives and that of his entire society, and *thereby also contributes, in the main unknowingly, to all useful results* of such order and harmony for the welfare and happiness of all concerned."[10]

Thus, Hutcheson's theory of ethics is linked to both his utilitarian approach to science, in which self interest plays a major role, and to his belief that it is only through man's good actions (virtuous acts) that the happiness of all can be attained. Hutcheson, as later Smith, had to face the problem of combining the utilitarian principle that man's actions are guided by self interest with the obvious fact that man has a conscience and is subject not only to personal rights but also to certain duties toward his neighbour that he cannot ignore if order and harmony are to prevail.

All of these moral philosophers realized that virtuous acts were needed if order, harmony and the attainment of happiness for the greatest number was to be attained. But, they also accepted the fact that the utilitarian criterion (social utility) was not enough to explain the correctness of human actions because "men cannot have or attain enough knowledge and foresight for all the consequences of their possible actions, to be able to choose, deliberately, the actions best calculated to promote universal happiness."[11]

Both Shaftesbury and Hutcheson tried to solve this dilemma by claiming that private and social good coincided. Hutcheson, for example, believed that man by seeking the good of others would also benefit himself.

In his above-mentioned book, *An Inquiry into the Original of Our Ideas of Beauty and Virtue*, he says the following: "That as the AUTHOR of Nature has determined us to receive, by our external Senses, pleasant or disagreeable Ideas of Objects, according as they are useful of hurtful to our Bodys; and to receive from uniform Objects the Pleasures of Beauty and Harmony, to excite us to the Pursuit of Knowledge, and to renew us for it . . . in the same manner he has given us a MORAL SENSE, to discover our Actions, and to give us still *nobler Pleasures*: so that while we are only intending the *Good* of others, we undesignedly promote our own greatest *private Good*."[12]

David Hume, the author of the *Treatise of Human Nature* to whom Smith was greatly indebted, contended also that benevolence or attention to the good of others met social approval and was conducive to equal benevolent acts on the part of their fellow men.[13] According to him, "It may be esteemed, perhaps, a superfluous task to prove, that the benevolence or softer affections are Estimable; and wherever they appear, engage the approbation, and good will of mankind." Thus, he continues, "The happiness of mankind, the order of society, the harmony of families, the mutual support of friends, are always considered as the result of their gentle dominion [i.e., the dominion of the benevolent sentiments] over the breasts of men."[14]

Hume considered moral judgments as simple expressions of passions, such as self-interest. He claimed that they, and not reason, were the ones that moved men into action. Basically, Hume claimed that good and evil acts are not properties of human deeds but simply terms that man uses to convey his approval or disapproval but which include a real concern for others. Thus, the disinterested component of human actions is based on benevolence or mutual sympathies among men; an idea that Smith also used in order to explain the proper functioning of the economic system.

In his *Treatise* Hume tries to build a complete system of moral science by introducing the experimental method of reasoning into moral subjects.[15] As the French scholar Elie Halévy comments in his book *The Growth of Philosophical Liberalism*: "He hoped to do for moral philosophy what Newton had done for natural philosophy, and he thought he had discovered in the principle of association a kind of attraction which in the mental world will be found to have as extraordinary effects as in the natural."[16]

Having denied general and unconditional rules of behavior, he had to invoke the concepts of sympathy and benevolence in order to counteract the obvious defects of a pure self-interest. In other words, Hume and his followers turned human egoism into an ideal, into a normal rule of conduct. As Schumpeter claims, Hume simply modeled the moral world to his own image and, consequently, the scheme of his own preferences became the reasonable scheme.[17]

The belief in the gentleness and goodness of man is reflected in all the above-mentioned English moral philosophers of the seventeenth and early eighteenth centuries. They were convinced that the practice of benevolence and mutual sympathies among men would be sufficient to bring about the harmonious and orderly society that the world was craving for and that past institutions had made impossible to attain. These well-intentioned moral philosophers ingenuously believed that free men led by their self-interest and without the political and religious restraints of previous centuries were capable of building the perfect society.

Adam Smith, in all of his writings appealed to similar arguments to defend his belief in the natural goodness of man and in a harmonious economic system of natural liberties. His main thesis was that there exists a natural identity of interests or rather a spontaneous harmony of egoisms. With very few exceptions there is no explicit denial of the principle of the fusion of interests.

The Scottish-born professor of moral philosophy invoked the idea of man's innate sympathy for others as an explanation for his belief in the spontaneous harmony of interests. To counteract the defects of an argument based on interest and utility, Smith, following Hume, introduced also the concept of benevolence or mutual sympathies. Sympathy and benevolence were supposed to fill the gap when and if the rules of moral behavior, such as justice, did not serve the individual's long-term interests. But, as MacIntyre explains, "the gap of course is logically unbridgeable, and 'sympathy' as used by Hume and Smith is the name of a philosophical fiction."[18]

Smith also believed that private and social good coincided. But, instead of arguing that men benefited themselves from seeking the good of others, he maintained that the maximization of happiness in society would result from men following their own self-interests. Nevertheless, the question was still left unanswered as to how a purely utilitarian criterion guiding men's actions would somehow lead to the happiness of all.

Smith found the "answer" in the notion that there exists a guiding hand of Providence which endowed human nature with certain propensities that led men to take actions—moral decisions—the consequences of which were favorable for social order and harmony and, as a result, conducive to human welfare and happiness.

In the chapter discussing the restraints upon the importation of goods, Smith simply applies to economics the concept of a beneficent Providence using the term *invisible hand*. For example, he mentions the advantages for any individual to employ his capital in the support of domestic industry so that "its produce may be of the greatest value; every individual necessarily labours to render the annual revenue of the society as great as he can. He, generally, indeed neither intends to promote the public interest, nor knows how much he is promoting it. By preferring the support of domestic to that of foreign industry, he intends only his own security; and by directing that industry in such a manner as its produce may be of the greatest value, he intends only his own gain, and he is in this, as in many other cases, led by an *invisible hand* to promote an end which was no part of his intention. Nor is it always the worse for the society that it was no part of it. By pursuing his own interest he frequently promotes that of the society more effectually than when he really intends to promote it."[19]

In their search for the essence of human nature, Smith, and the moral philosophers that preceded him, placed too much trust on the principles of utility and mutual sympathies; principles that, on their own, were fundamental for the growth and development of nations. They considered both of these principles indispensable for a proper understanding of man's human nature and his conduct in society.

Adam Smith tried to combine the principle of utility and self-interest with the obvious fact that man has a conscious and is subject to certain duties or moral obligations that he may not ignore. He realized that his belief in the natural goodness of man together with his reliance on mutual sympathies were not enough to solve this difficulty and explain the moral value of man's actions. Hutcheson, his mentor, had already met with the same difficulty and dismissed the dilemma concerning the spiritual and material nature of man by simply maintaining that although man's actions are guided exclusively by self interest, his actions were not void of any moral value. Smith held that an individual behavior which is both prudent in following his own self-interest and just toward his neighbor would be beneficial not only for himself but also for all other members of society. The only thing that man had to do for the common welfare of all was to let himself be directed by his moral benevolent sentiments and follow the rules of the market.

To Smith's credit it could be argued that, when he wrote about benevolence and mutual sympathies within the context of economic activity, he did not mean to reduce all activity to the attainment of material welfare. He may also have had in mind the common good of all men; the integral development of man as a person and not only his material well-being. As Sophia Aguirre writes, "With this perspective, the idea of *sympathy* and *self-discipline* that play an important role in Smith's concept of good behavior acquire a broader scope to explain and rule economic motivations. No longer can consumption alone be the measure for wellbeing, nor can the benefits of capitalism be reduced to it. In seeking the good of others, man finds his own good and therefore his 'self interest' is fulfilled."[20]

Independently of Smith's ultimate objectives, it is true that he was concerned about general rules of conduct. However, these general rules of conduct, according to him, are "all formed from the experience we have had of the effects which actions of all different kinds naturally produce upon us."[21] When they are universally acknowledged and established by the concurring sentiments of mankind, he continues, "we frequently appeal to them as the standards of 'judgment', in debating concerning the degree of praise or blame that is due to certain actions of a complicated and dubious nature."[22] These norms are commonly cited: "as the ultimate foundations of what is just and unjust in human conduct; and this circumstance seems to have misled several very eminent authors, to draw up their systems in such a manner, as if they had supposed that the original judgments of mankind with regard to right and wrong, were formed like the decision of a court of judicatory, by considering first the general rule, and then, secondly, whether the particular action under consideration fell properly within its comprehension."[23] In fact, these general rules of conduct "are of great use in correcting the misrepresentations of self-love concerning what is fit and proper to be done in our particular situation."[24]

Unless proven otherwise it does seem that Smith's behavioral assumptions of economic theory were based on self-interest and general rules of conduct formed from experience. This description of moral behavior, even though limited by general rules of conduct based on experience, does not provide an adequate answer to the ethical problems faced by the agents of economic activity; problems of moral behavior which may require a significant deviation from the generally accepted model of self-interest rule of conduct as sanctioned in classical economic theory. In his book *On Ethics and Economics*, Amartya Sen correctly states, "Moral acceptance of rights (especially rights that are valued and supported, and not just respected in the form of constraints) may call for systematic departures from self-interested behaviour. Even a partial and limited move in this direction in actual conduct can shake the behavioural foundations of standard economic theory."[25]

Nevertheless, it would be a gross error to believe that Smith was guided exclusively by a purely materialistic self-interest approach to economics and did not realize the injustices that the *homo oeconomicus* was capable of performing. His defense of economic liberalism and the free market system did not imply giving a blank check to the business community. On the contrary, he wrote very harsh words about business when it violated the basic principles of justice and abused the freedom it had been granted.

Smith always maintained that he regarded the pursuit of wealth as an illusion on the part of men. But, at the same time, he believed that this illusion served for a useful purpose because, as the rich could not consume all they earned, they had to apportion some of the acquired wealth to the poor who, as a result, enjoyed their share of the earth's produce.[26] This lack of confidence in the rich, on the part of Smith, is clearly demonstrated when he has no hesitation in affirming in the most categorical manner the following: "The rich only select from the heap what is most precious and agreeable. They consume little more than the poor, and in spite of their natural selfishness and rapacity, though they mean only their own convenience, though the sole end which they propose from the labours of all the thousands whom they employ, be the gratification of their own vain and insatiable desires, they divide with the poor the produce of all their improvements. They are led by an invisible hand to make nearly the same distribution of the necessities of life, which would have been made, had the earth been divided into equal portions among all its inhabitants, and thus without intending it, without knowing it, advance the interest of society, and afford means to the multiplication of the species."[27]

Perhaps, here lies the greatest weakness of Smith's contribution to economic theory. He saw quite clearly the dilemma in which he found himself when trying to combine his basic postulates of freedom, self-interest, profit motivation and competition with the need for ethics as a moral standard for action. His solution, the spontaneous identity of interests and in the last instance the invisible hand of God, was, as mentioned previously, utopian to say the least.[28] It is totally unrealistic to suggest that, given the fallen nature of man, the identity of interests can be achieved spontaneously without the law intervening at all.

The great English economist by placing his emphasis on the goodness of man apparently forgot his fallen nature, with its tendencies toward evil. Without the development of virtue and voluntary moral restraints, it is illusory for man to expect the creation of a perfectly ordered and harmonious society. For example, harmony is definitely not fostered when the producers, following their crude self-interest, promote or maintain scarcities in the market so as to increase their profits at the expense of the consumer. The same can be said of trade union leaders when they apply monopolistic practices in order to foster their own group interests at the expense of other social groups. The self-interest of these powerful groups is placed above the well-being of society. Market forces, per se, will not necessarily bring justice and harmony to the economy. In such cases there is an irreconcilable conflict between the private self-interest of the producers, those of the trade unions and the community at large; a clash of interests that can only be solved by government intervention or voluntary moral restraints. But voluntary moral restraints will not prevail unless grounded on virtuous acts.

Economic liberalism, with its blind faith in the automaticity and harmonious functioning of the economic system, set the stage for a wave of optimism that swept all over Europe. The inevitability of progress, as we shall see in the next section, was accepted by many an intellectual as a dogma of faith. Few voices were heard that dared to challenge this basic premise.

## ECONOMIC LIBERALISM AND THE
## WEAKNESS OF AN EXALTED OPTIMISM

It seems logical to question the "real" origin of the exalted optimism which began in the seventeenth century and swept over large areas of Europe like a tidal wave that shook the continent's very foundations and brought with it a new interpretation of the very meaning of life. Gradually, man abandoned his traditional theocentric approach to his existence and turned to an anthropocentrism which, although in its early stages did not deny the existence of a Creator or Author of all beings, nevertheless, consciously or unconsciously abandoned the belief in the transcendental nature of man and turned to relativism if not outright atheism.

There is no doubt that Adam Smith, a Deist who firmly believed in the existence of God, the Author of all things, fully realized the importance of religion and the need for moral standards. As a humanist of his day and age, he was also convinced that the natural forces of a created universe operated in such a way that man's actions would inevitably lead to the common good of all. But, willingly or not, he set the tone for his followers to preach that an individual, left to himself and permitted to act freely in accordance with his self interest, would always act with ethical correctness and contribute to maximum happiness. Thus, mutual assistance and sympathies among free men is a natural phenomenon that will bring a harmonious and well ordered society. The need for assistance and mutual sympathies is always emphasized by Smith. For example, in *The Theory of Moral Sentiments* he says, "It is thus that man who can subsist only in society, was fitted by nature to that situation for which he was made. All the members of human society stand in need of each other assistance, and are likewise exposed to mutual injuries. Where the necessary assistance is reciprocally afforded from love, from gratitude, from friendship, and esteem, the society flourishes and is happy. All the different members of it are bound together by the agreeable bands of love and affection, and are, as it were, drawn to one common centre of mutual good offices."[29]

To the criticism labeled against Smith that in the *Wealth of Nations* he hardly mentions the moral and ethical values that are highlighted in *The Theory of Moral Sentiments*, Taylor says the following: "Moral control [limitation] of the play of 'self interest' in economic life, by the moral climate and legal framework engendered by men's mutual sympathies in the manner explained in the earlier work, is presupposed in the ideal-and-theory of economic life presented in the *Wealth of Nations*, though it is not discussed in the latter to the same extent."[30]

However, Smith's contention that the existence of mutual sympathies among men is a natural phenomenon which serves as the counterbalancing factor to man's self-interested actions, is not sufficient as an explanation for the moral content of man's actions. His argument, as indicated earlier, is not persuasive, a fact which Smith himself realized and which forced him to find a better explanation for man's moral sense of what is right and what is wrong than a simple reliance on mutual sympathies. His theory of the invisible hand of God and his belief in a providential God, the creator of a natural and harmonious order where man could not go astray and bring about his own destruction, runs counter to practical experience.[31]

It cannot be denied that Smith contributed, without realizing it, to the hyper evaluation of the economic which characterized the liberalism of the nineteenth century and which later became known as *economism*. His faith in the goodness of man, influenced undoubtedly by his deistic approach to life, led him to the naïve conclusion that the free market system, guided by individual self interests, could function effectively and bring about the greatest happiness for the greatest number.

It was Adam Smith and his followers within the Classical school of economics who established the bases of an economic liberalism that was greatly influenced by a rational philosophy which preached the total emancipation of reason from any higher authority than reason itself. As soon as reason refuses to accept any limitations except its own, pride takes hold of man and frustration easily follows. This the case of the rational liberal who believes that he can "construct" the ideal type of economic system based on absolute freedom without taking into consideration human nature with its weaknesses and multiple deficiencies. A liberal of this type would like to convert the economy, built on competition, into a precise mechanical system moved exclusively by man's reason dictating to him the conditions of life. As the famous French philosopher René Pascal would say, reminding us that man is far from being perfect: "L'homme c'est ni ange ni bête, et le malheur veut que qui veut faire l'ange fait la bête."[32]

Nobody can deny the positive aspects of an economic system which is grounded on the very concept of freedom. To liberate man from the errors of a false authoritarianism is worthy of praise. It was the triumphant battle cry of the philosophers of the seventeenth and eighteenth centuries; a battle cry that in the area of economics was carried out successfully by Adam Smith against the abuses of the statist doctrines of mercantilism. As economic oppression and despotism had to be crushed in the name of freedom, a debt of gratitude is due to Adam Smith and the Classical School of economics for having fought the battle against economic rigidity and inefficient government controls, giving men the opportunity to express their freedom in the market place.

However, can real freedom be achieved by trampling on the most fundamental principles of the past? Why was it necessary to accept blindly some of the foremost postulates of the Enlightenment, in particular the idealization of reason, in order to bring about the much desired liberty at the expense of the belief in the transcendental? Are there no limits to economic freedom except those of the marketplace?

Freedom, as we saw in the previous chapter, is not an absolute principle and to think otherwise lends itself to the abuse of the most cherished of all of God's gifts to man, freedom itself. As history has demonstrated once and again, no invisible hand will be able to control man's innate tendencies toward evil as manifested in the numerous wars—including economic wars—bloody revolutions and violent acts of terrorism which have plagued humanity during the last two centuries; centuries which were supposed to bring with them a new era of peace, prosperity and happiness for all.

Liberals, in theory and practice, wanted to pay homage to the fundamental rights inherent in human nature. In many ways, their contribution was undeniably positive. They must be complemented for their desire to build states where the exercise of men's political rights are protected and juridical equality guaranteed by the constitution. These favorable achievements were based on the power of man's reason and not the result of force. But, it must also be recognized that many tragedies and sufferings occurred under the shadow of a liberalism that misused the very concept of freedom. It often forgot the common good by ignoring the need for social justice and stressed a false individualism at the expense of the human person.[33]

History has demonstrated that the deification of rationalism together with the false interpretation of freedom have had very detrimental effects on liberal thinking by perverting many of the original intentions of some its founders. Its negative consequences were especially scandalous during the Industrial Revolution and irresponsible colonialism where the abuses of a blatant capitalism were notorious. This is unfortunate because the essential virtues of economic and political freedoms have been obscured as a result of the misuse and erroneous interpretations of the term.

Roepke, well known for his conservative credentials, does not hesitate to mention the negative effects that an uncontrolled rationalism had on economic liberalism. He recognizes the fruitful effects on society of a liberal economy based on freedom and competition which, in many ways, contributed so much to economic growth and the well-being of society. But, as he asserts, the reputation and greatness of economic liberalism would not have suffered if it would not have fallen under the spell of a rationalism that disregarded the sociological limitations that accompany the free market. It was seriously believed that the free market system, ruled by competition, represented a cosmos in equilibrium, a natural order that only needed to be defended from external threats in order to endure and flourish. It was, after all, regulated by the "invisible hand" mentioned by

Smith or what the deist philosophers called divine reason. Man's mission, within the cosmos, is limited to the elimination of any obstacle that impedes the automatic functioning of a free economic system. Laissez faire-laissez passer was the norm to be accepted in all matters related to economics.[34]

Thus, the market economy was granted immunity from internal error and given full autonomy to operate freely in society without taking into account that, besides self interest, there are other factors of a noneconomic nature that cannot be ignored. In economic literature the assumption has generally been that the maximization of a person's utility function depends exclusively on his own consumption. This implies that a person's behavior is guided by pure self-interest. But this is not necessarily true. Amartya Sen reminds us that a person's goals "may involve objectives other than maximizing his own welfare only."[35] According to him, "The wide use of the extremely narrow assumption of self-interested behaviour has, I have tried to argue, seriously limited the scope of predictive economics, and made it difficult to pursue a number of important economic relationships that operate through behavioural versatility." For example, he continues, "The richness of ethical considerations in welfare-economic evaluations has a direct bearing on personal behaviour."[36]

The belief that the natural goodness of man alone would bring about the desired millennium was so entrenched in the minds of the eighteenth century moral philosophers, including Smith, that it was difficult for them to accept the negative consequences that the malleable tendencies of man could have on the well-being of society if not subject to personal self-control. Future events cast a shadow over the unrealistic optimism of the eighteenth century philosophers. In economics, the need for a greater understanding between the "dismal science" and ethics became increasingly evident.

Roepke, and correctly so, preached incessantly that the free market economy, could not remain really free unless framed within a solid institutional juridical and moral structure which would serve as its fundamental basis. Otherwise, the free market economy would degenerate into a free for all struggle between uncontrolled selfish interests—both individual and group interests—that would destroy the very essence of a free society. No amount of "mutual sympathies," as Smith and his followers proclaimed, would avoid such a nefarious outcome. Competition, for example, could easily turn, using a Darwinian expression, into a struggle for the survival of the fittest.

The economic liberal of the nineteenth century did not realize that competition per se may not be divorced from its moral content; a moral content that should not be ignored if the social organism is to be protected from the abuses of an uncontrolled competitive market. He even went as far as to believe that the market system, based on competition and the division of labour, was an excellent means for the moral education of the people who, by following their own selfish interests, would be stimulated to live in peace and harmony observing all the rules of a bourgeois society. Reality has proven otherwise.

Professor Vicente Rodriguez Casado in an interesting study of the origins of capitalism does not hide his criticism of Smith's contention that economic self-interest and men's mutual sympathies alone would lead to a harmonious and ordered society. The belief in a purely mechanistic and naturalistic conception of society, where the welfare of its members depends on their natural "sympathies," is unrealistic. It is highly utopian to accept that Smith's concept of "mutual sympathies," which according to him is a distinctive characteristic of men's attitudes toward each other, can overcome man's natural tendency towards evil.[37] Apparently, the naïve conception of man and society held by the "liberal" of the nineteenth century did not visualize the rise of a radical socialist ideology which, to a large degree, resulted from the abuses of a supposedly "salutary" and "benevolent" individualism; an individualism which its proponents believed was going to put an end to class struggles and all other social antinomies, bringing with it a new era of continuous progress. However, contrary to the expectations of many a "liberal" thinker, society has had to pay—and is still paying—for a much misunderstood concept of freedom.[38]

To base the economic progress and well-being exclusively on the selfish interests of the isolated individual is not only naïve but runs counter to the reality of life in society which is founded in family ties and other natural social groups such as the community, the professions, the labor unions, and so forth. No wonder the type of liberalism which prevailed in the nineteenth century is discredited and has been the object of so much criticism.

The late professor Goetz Briefs of Georgetown University was certainly correct when he said in his book *Zwischen Kapitalismus und Syndicalismus* that the "real" origin of the excessive optimism of liberalism and its belief in the perfectibility of man must be found "in the transcription of the Christian theology of redemption to the secular plane.[39] For centuries, the Christian has been infused with the notions of sin and redemption, categories that the men of the Enlightenment transferred to the secular plane. As soon as they abandoned the transcendental and transferred these categories to the sphere of time and space, they had to face the reality of men's limitations without recognizing the reality of sin.

Thus, the same way that the Christian believes that the history of salvation begins with the sin of Adam, the secularization of society simply converted his disobedience into a secular sin. For example, according to the Marxist the original sin is private property which he considers responsible for the downfall of the original state of justice prevailing at the beginning of time. For the liberal, the original sin lies in all past institutions such as the monarchy, the aristocracy and religion, whilst for the anarchist it is any type of government or authority. They have all assumed a historical sin and consequently there is a need for a redemption. Whether it comes from the elimination of private property, the destruction of all past institutions or of any type of government, the result is the same: the need for some type of redemption. Most, if not all, modern secularized philosophies of society have not been able to avoid falling into the Christian categories of fall and redemption. They all start from an original state of justice and tend in a secularized way toward the redemption of humanity. Some may expect redemption through the dialectical movement of history whilst others may await it through the power of reason, a return to the natural state of nature, evolution or never ending progress. But, they all expect that once alienation is removed from man and society, redemption in the form of freedom and happiness will necessarily ensue. The optimistic expectations of economic liberalism, undermined by the weight of its own ethical weakness, did not always materialize as its confident proponents had assumed. In the last resort, "the economic liberalism of Adam Smith and Bentham appears to be less an absolute optimism than a doctrine which is perpetually insisting on the difficult and painful conditions to which, by reason of the very constitution of things, we must submit when we apply ourselves to the methodical and calculated realization of our interests."[40]

## THE INDUSTRIAL REVOLUTION, THE BOURGEOISIE, AND THE MOUNTING TIDE OF CRITICISMS

Any study of the rise of capitalism would be incomplete without stressing the importance of the Industrial Revolution.[41] Without the Industrial Revolution, the process of economic growth and development, which characterized the nineteenth century, would not have taken place. The rapidly rising standards of living enjoyed by large sectors of the population was due primarily to the efforts and hard work of the new industrial and commercial classes, the core of the bourgeoisie, who were the ones who gave the initial impetus to the Industrial Revolution.

Even though capitalist enterprise already existed as early as the tenth century, it was not until the fifteenth century that the rise of the commercial, financial and industrial bourgeoisie made its appearance in the European scene as a major force in society. They soon became a powerful force in Europe and, as Schumpeter claims, they eventually shattered the social world of St. Thomas and the still remaining remnants of feudal society. As their power and influence grew, they not only asserted their interests but gradually imparted to society their way of thinking and basic traits. Their mental attitudes in business and at the office slowly spread to all classes of society who were allured by the economic accomplishments of early capitalism.

With the rise of the Industrial Revolution this new and powerful social class, the bourgeoisie, acquired increased importance to the extent that in the nineteenth century its ascendancy in the social structure of society was almost unimpeded.[42] Even though they did not rule politically, most European governments supported the economic interests of the business class and were more than glad to listen to their advice and assistance not only in financial dealings but also in noneconomic matters that could have a bearing on political concerns. They were protected by government officials and received full endorsement for their laissez faire-laissez passer economic policies. The ruling authorities were convinced that the best way to foster economic development was through the mechanism of the free market system without the need for any government interference.[43]

There is no doubt that the free play of market forces performed a decisive role in the economic development of Britain during the nineteenth century; in particular in the area of international trade. England's wealth and power during that century was due in no small matter to the benefits derived from international trade and the competitive spirit of the new commercial classes. Trade became the country's engine of growth. London reigned supreme as the most important commercial and financial centre in Europe. British industry grew at an extraordinarily fast rate and English products were not only known all over the world but also admired for their excellent quality. Little doubt remains as to the advantages Britain derived from the free play of market forces and the application of Ricardos's theory of international trade.

However, criticism of the free market system and in particular of the classical theory of international trade did not take long to appear. Ricardo's argument that trade was beneficial to all countries that participated in it was seriously challenged by many economists. They claimed that the free play of market forces was not always conducive to greater equity in the distribution of wealth. Income disparities tend to appear to the detriment of the weaker less developed countries that depend for their livelihood on basic products for their development. These critics insisted that the free play of market forces did not necessarily bring about equilibrium as suggested by the proponents of the classical trade theory. On the contrary, the incomes of the less developed countries tended to lag behind those of the industrialized nations. Nations endowed with superior human and institutional resources have always had an edge over those that are lagging behind. No matter how important material capital is for the economic growth of the less developed countries, they cannot ignore the even more important role played by the availability of human and adequate institutional resources.

In many cases reality failed to meet the expectations of the proponents of free trade policies. In spite of all the well-known theoretical advantages of free trade, it is nevertheless true that "under its banner" protectionism and other types of trade restraints persisted to the detriment of the less developed countries. Tariffs and other nontariff barriers were applied often whenever it seemed that they would serve the national interests of a particular nation.

The Swedish economist Gunnar Myrdal, a firm critic of the classical theory of international trade, maintained that "contrary to what the equilibrium theory of international trade would seem to suggest, the play of the market forces does not work towards equality in the remunerations to factors of production and, consequently, in incomes."[44] This was also the position taken by the United Nations Economic Commission for Latin America (ECLA) and later by the United Nations Conference on Trade and Development (UNCTAD). The Commission was very influential in recommending policies for development that ran counter to the orthodox, neoclassical theories.[45]

Nevertheless, in spite of the abuses of certain economic policies carried out under the banner of free trade, the fact still remains that the statist and centralized policies endorsed by ECLA and later UNCTAD did not remedy the situation. On the contrary, they only led to inflation and a lack of confidence in the value of money, not to mention the frequent blatant inefficiencies of an expanding bureaucracy. This in its turn brought about the flight of domestic capital in search for safer havens in the more developed countries.

During the 1930s, many prominent economists came to the defense of Ricardo's basic theory of international trade. Among the most renowned the name of Gottfried Haberler can be mentioned.[46] His analysis of the opportunity cost theory which modifies the original comparative cost theory of Ricardo was a major step forward in the development of trade theory. Further modifications came later with the Ohlin-Heckscher theory of trade.[47] They developed an alternative model of comparative cost theory in order to explain the existence of international cost differences.

The vital role played by the bourgeoisie in the economic development of England and in Western societies was the product of a combination of factors, not the least of which were the ideas of the moral philosophers of the Enlightenment with their stress on individual rights and their criticism of any authority not based on pure reason. Mention should also be made of the important part played by utilitarianism in the development of nineteenth century capitalism and its influence on the business class. The utilitarian principles of men such as Bentham, James Mill, and, to a certain extent, John

Stuart Mill, among others, fitted very well with the materialistic rationalism that characterized many aspects of liberalism.[48] As Schumpeter claims, it was only natural for these prominent and militant economists to see themselves "in the role of philosophical patrons of economics and to assume responsibility for an alliance between economics and utilitarianism that was acquiesced in by many later economists."[49] In a certain way they gave the imprimaturs to utilitarianism which they considered the major catalyst for the development of capitalism, even though the philosophical principles on which it stands leave much to be desired.

The bourgeoisie undoubtedly supported an unregulated economic system that allowed the business man to operate freely without, what they claimed, were the "abuses" of government intervention; a system which proved to be extremely efficient, bringing with it wealth and power and gradually increasing standards of living for large sections of the population. It is a historical reality that this frequently maligned bourgeoisie, operating under a free market system, did make it possible for the masses to enjoy gradually the benefits of the free market system. As Roepke has stated, "we have to admit that the market economy has a bourgeois foundation."[50] And the market economy can be credited for the wave of innovations that swept over Europe during the era of the *Pax Britannica*.

The best example of a bourgeois was the individual property owner who either possessed capital of his own or received an income from such a source.[51] He lived in a society which respected and fostered, among other things, such values as individual effort and responsibility, appreciation for the value of work, the need for savings and the courage to personally rely upon himself for his economic needs and not depend on the state to protect him always from the uncertainties of life.[52]

The tremendous achievement of capitalism was due to the profit making entrepreneurial spirit of the bourgeoisie who, through hard work and individual effort, was able to produce the multiplicity of goods and services that the general public was craving for but which it was not able to enjoy in the past.[53] For example, luxuries such as silk stockings, were the exclusive domain of the aristocracy but with the arrival of capitalism and its captains of industry taking advantage of the economies of scale, they gradually became available to the mass of the population.[54]

However, these long-term advances in material well-being that progressively reached the mass of the population did not take place without a high cost in human suffering; a cost which fell squarely upon the shoulders of the laboring poor. The descriptions of the long hours of labor that children had to endure in order to meet the requirements of their masters are well documented and have been the subject of many a novel of well-known literary writers in England and in the continent.

The Industrial Revolution was undoubtedly a tremendous economic success. Economic goods and services were increasingly made available to the masses of the population and, as the years went by, standards of living increased incessantly for larger and larger sections of the population. But at the same time these welcomed achievements were occurring a parallel phenomenon was also taking place, the full consequences of which are still to be seen: the gradual but continuous decline in the cultural and spiritual fabric of society. As the gap between the technological and the cultural advances of mankind grew, the dangers for the survival of a free society increased.

Given the pitiful conditions that prevailed among the laboring poor, criticism of the free market system mounted; a criticism that was not limited to the intellectual elites but which often took the form of violence. Hostility to economic liberalism and its blatant abuses had begun to appear already in the mid-eighteenth century as people became increasingly aware of the squalor in which the laboring poor were forced to live, whilst the new commercial and industrial classes were living in opulence. Confidence in the virtues of laissez faire capitalism were rapidly diminishing and antiliberal forces were gradually gaining strength. The attacks on liberalism and the bourgeoisie came not only from the far left but also from those who no longer believed in the automaticity of the economic system.[55]

The process of industrialization with its consequent inequalities gave rise to the development of trade unions whose initial primary function was to defend the social interests of the workers from the abuses of an unequal bargaining position. However, the labor movement gradually became more aggressive and, as mentioned earlier, began applying monopolistic practices in order to control the supply of labor and have a greater distorting power over the market. Their aggressive tactics in the pursuit of their objectives, which often matched those of their counterparts in the business community, had a negative influence on the healthy development of a market system free of powerful group interests.

In many ways, capitalism itself was responsible for the reaction from socialists and nonsocialists alike. An uncontrolled capitalism ruled by selfish individual or group interests, concerned only in increasing their power and wealth, lent itself perfectly well to the accusations of its enemies whose condemnations were not limited to its abuses but also to the basic foundations on which it stood.[56] The very concepts of classical theory were challenged increasingly. Not only was the theory's methodology criticized but also the system's reliance on the natural harmony of self interests, its automatic functioning without the need for government interference and its stress on the individual to the detriment of the social or national interests.

Economic liberalism's main fault lies in the attempt made by its founders to build a "natural" economic system that relies on ethical values which are founded on "natural" human virtues—that is, benevolence and mutual sympathies—totally disconnected from the transcendental. To rely uniquely on an ideal "virtuous" man, as Adam Smith did, is not sufficient for an economic system to function properly. This is particularly true when the concept of "virtue" is disassociated from the Moral Law, a reflection of Divine Law.[57] To base morality, as was often the case among the typical liberal bourgeois of the nineteenth century, on man's own interpretation of "virtue" and of such concepts as individual decency, rights and duties, courage, the common good, and so forth, may be symptomatic of a certain degree of presumption and, in the end will inevitably lead to overt relativism.[58]

Thus, together with the theoretical and practical objections to classical economic liberalism came a renewed and powerful cry against a social class, the bourgeoisie, which, many of its critics believed, had selfishly constructed for itself a secure and comfortable niche in society with little or no consideration for the needs of others.

Schumpeter was convinced that the bourgeoisie was destined to lose its power and influence over the years. It was incapable of defending itself against the mounting criticism coming from its own ranks, especially from the "intellectuals." Among other things he claimed that "there is surely no trace of any mystic glamour about him [the bourgeois] which is what counts in the ruling of men." He called the bourgeois rationalist and unheroic which is the equivalent of saying that "he can only use rationalist and unheroic means to defend his position or to bend a nation to his will." Furthermore, he also maintains that barring exceptional conditions " the bourgeois class is ill equipped to face the problems, both domestic and international, that have normally to be faced by a country of any importance."[59]

The romantic and socialist movements, as we shall see in the next chapter, were at the vanguard of a powerful antibourgeois movement.

## NOTES

1. See John Maynard Keynes (1883–1946), *The General Theory of Employment, Interest and Money* (London: Macmillan, 1951), 3. Keynes made the classical theory to depend in succession on the following assumptions: "(1) that the real wage is equal to the marginal disutility of the existing employment, (2) that there is no such thing as involuntary unemployment in the strict sense and (3) that supply creates its own demand in the sense that the aggregate demand price is equal to the aggregate supply price for all levels of output and employment" (21–22). For Keynes, therefore, supply does not necessarily create its own demand and, thus, full employment resulting exclusively from the free play of market forces is not the general case but is, in fact, a special case, an exception.

2. The French economists Charles Gide and Charles Rist maintain that the real founders of economics as a social science were the physiocrats. Referring to eco-

nomic science as the new science they claim the following: "La edad de los precursores ha terminado; la de los fundadores comienza con Quesnay y sus discípulos. Este dictado de *fundadores*, que la ingratitud de los economistas franceses, a pesar de ser herederos en linea recta de los Fisiócratas, les habia desconocido, dejándolo que se extinguiera por prescripción, para ser atribuido a Adam Smith, les ha sido restituido mas tarde por economistas extranjeros, y es de suponer que ya lo conservarán definitivamente." See Charles Gide and Charles Rist, *Historia de las Doctrinas Ecónomicas* (Madrid: Editorial Reus S.A., 1927), 3.

3. Smith's book *The Theory of Moral Sentiments*, although less known than the *Wealth of Nations*, is of extreme importance for a proper understanding of his complete system of thought. It is there that he presents his theory of the "natural" basis of ethics and of free societies. See Overton H. Taylor, *A History of Economic Thought* (New York: McGraw-Hill, 1960), 29.

4. The Earl of Shaftesbury (1671–1713) was an English nobleman whose Deist religious beliefs exerted great influence on many of the leading figures of the Enlightenment, including Hutcheson. His major work was *Characteristics of Men's Manners, Opinions, Times*. Francis Hutcheson (1694–1746) was a Scot from Northern Ireland but spent most of his career in Scotland at the University of Glasgow. He was an eminent classicist and moral philosopher and, although a practicing presbyterian, his general view of the world was not basically different from the deistic approach followed by his teacher the Earl of Shaftesbury and the other prominent moral philosophers of his time. His most prominent work was *A System of Moral Philosophy*.

5. Taylor, *A History of Economic Thought*, 31.

6. See Francis Hutcheson, *An Inquiry into the Origins of Our Ideas of Beauty and Virtue*.

7. Taylor, *A History of Economic Thought*, 42.

8. Taylor, *A History of Economic Thought*, 40.

9. Taylor, *A History of Economic Thought*, 42.

10. Taylor, *A History of Economic Thought*, 42.

11. Taylor, *A History of Economic Thought*, 42.

12. Francis Hutcheson, *An Inquiry into the Original of Our Ideas of Beauty and Virtue: II, Concerning Moral Good and Evil*, 127–29.

13. Adam Smith opined that David Hume was "by far the most illustrious philosopher and historian of the present age." See Adam Smith, *An Inquiry into the Nature and Causes of the Wealth of Nations* (Indianapolis, IN: Liberty Classics, 1981), 790.

14. David Hume, *Essays and Treatises on Several Subjects, Volume 2, An Enquiry Concerning the Principles of Morals*, sect. 2, 239–41 as quoted by Edmund Whittaker in *A History of Economic Ideas* (New York: Longmans, Green, 1940), 145.

15. For a more comprehensive understanding of Hume's views on the role of passions and morals, see David Hume, *Treatise on Human Nature* (London: Penguin Books, 1985), Books II and III.

16. Elie Halévy, *The Growth of Philosophical Liberalism* (Boston: Beacon Press, 1955), 9.

17. Joseph Schumpeter, *History of Economic Analysis* (New York: Oxford University Press, 1963), 129.

18. Alasdaire MacIntyre, *After Virtue* (Notre Dame, IN: University of Notre Dame Press, 1984), 49.

19. Smith, *The Wealth of Nations*, vol. 1, Book IV, Chapter II, 456.

20. See Sophia Aguirre, "The Wealth of the Nations, Sympathy and Their Relation to Economic Behavior," *Economics and Philosophy* 8, no. 2 (October 1992), 259–71.

21. Adam Smith, *The Theory of Moral Sentiments* (Indianapolis, IN: Liberty Classics, 1982), 160.

22. Smith, *The Theory of Moral Sentiments*, 160.

23. Smith, *The Theory of Moral Sentiments*, 160.

24. Smith, *The Theory of Moral Sentiments*, 160.

25. Amartya Sen, *On Ethics and Economics* (Oxford: Blackwell, 1987), 57.

26. According to Smith, the pleasures of wealth and greatness may strike the imagination as something grand and noble but in reality it is a deception that nature imposes on us. It is this deception which rouses and keeps in continual motion the industry of mankind. See Smith, *The Theory of Moral Sentiments*, 183.

27. Smith, *The Theory of Moral Sentiments*, 184–85.

28. According to the German scholar Walther Eckstein, Smith was probably influenced by the Stoic concept of social harmony and their opinion that every single event can be considered as a necessary part of the plan of the universe and tended to promote the general order and happiness of the whole. This stoic concept of harmony, as Eckstein indicates, "anticipates the better-known statement of Smith's own opinion that the rich 'are led by an invisible hand' to help the poor and to serve the interest of society at large." The German scholar is quite correct in saying that "the famous phrase may have sprung from an uneasiness about the reconciliation of selfishness with the perfection of the system." See introduction and notes to Walther Eckstein's translation into German of the *Theory of Moral Sentiments*. Smith, *The Theory of Moral Sentiments*, 7–8.

29. Smith, *The Theory of Moral Sentiments*, 85.

30. See Taylor, *A History of Economic Thought*, 78.

31. See in footnote 28, Walther Eckstein's interpretation of the famous phrase the "invisible hand" of God.

32. Man is neither an angel nor a beast, the tragedy is that when he pretends to be an angel he acts as a beast.

33. See Jean-Marie Lustiger, *Devenez Dignes de la Condition Humaine* (Paris: Flammarion/Saint Maurice, Switzerland: Saint-Augustin, 1995), 95.

34. Wilhelm Roepke, *La Crísis Social de Nuestro Tiempo* (Madrid: Biblioteca de la Ciencia Economica, 1942), 65.

35. Sen, *On Ethics and Economics*, 81.

36. Sen, *On Ethics and Economics*, 79.

37. Vicente Rodríguez Casado, *Orígenes del Capitalismo y Socialismo Contemporaneo* (Madrid: Espasa- Calpe, S.A., 1981), 208.

38. For an excellent book detailing the atrocities committed by the communist regimes of this century, see Stephane Courtois, Nicolas Werth, Jean-Lois Panne, Andrzej Paczkowski, Karel Bartosek, and Jean-Louis Margolin, *Le Livre Noir du Communisme, Crimes, Terreur, Repression* (Paris: Robert Laffont, 1997).

39. See Goetz Briefs, *Zwischen Kapitalismus und Syndicalismus* (Bern: Franclie Ag. Verlag, 1952), introduction, 30.

40. Halévy, *Growth of Philosophical Liberalism*, 120.

41. For an interesting approach to the Industrial Revolution, see Paul Mantoux, *The Industrial Revolution in the Eighteenth Century* (New York: Macmillan, 1961).

42. However, socially speaking, there was still a clear distinction between the upper bourgeoisie and the aristocracy. Britain was probably the only country in Europe where businessmen could be absorbed into the aristocracy and almost uniquely in the case of bankers and financiers. See E. J. Hobsbawn, *The Age of Capital, 1848–1875* (New York: Penguin Books, 1979), 266–74.

43. See Joseph Schumpeter, *History of Economic Analysis* (New York: Oxford University Press, 1954), 393–94.

44. Gunnar Myrdal, "Development and Underdevelopment." National Bank of Egypt, Fiftieth Anniversary Commemoration Lectures, Cairo, Egypt, 1956, 47–51. For a more complete analysis of his theory of international trade, see Gunnar Myrdal, *An International Economy* (New York: Harper & Brothers, 1956).

45. See Raul Prebisch, *Towards a Dynamic Development Policy for Latin America*. (New York: United Nations, 1963). For a more comprehensive view of Prebisch's theory on development, see *Change and Development: Latin America's Great Task* (Washington, DC: Inter-American Development Bank, 1970). For a sharp criticism of Prebisch's approach to development and the policies of UNCTAD, see Jacob Viner, *International Trade and Economic Development* (Glencoe, IL: The Free Press, 1952) and T. Bauer, *Dissent on Development* (Cambridge, MA: Harvard University Press, 1972). An approach very critical of classical international theory was the so-called dependency theory. Among its most important representatives the following works can be mentioned: Paul Baran, *The Political Economy of Growth* (New York: Monthly Review Press, 1957); Celso Furtado, *Economic Development of Latin America: A Survey from Colonial Times to the Cuban Revolution* (Cambridge: Cambridge University Press, 1970); Gunder Frank, *Latin America: Underdevelopment or Revolution?* (New York: Monthly Review Press, 1959); Oswaldo Sunkel, *El Subdesarrollo Latinoamericano y la Teoria del Desarrollo* (Mexico: Siglo Veintiuno Editores, 1970); and Theotonio Dos Santos, "Socialismo o Fascismo, Dilemma dell America Latina" in *Il Nuovo Marxismo Latino Americano* (Milan: Feltinelli Editore, 1970).

46. For an excellent analysis of classical trade theory, see Gottfried Haberler, *The Theory of International Trade* (London: William Hodge, 1954).

47. For a more complete assessment of the Heckscher-Ohlin theorem, see Bertil Ohlin, *Interregional and International Trade* (Cambridge, MA: Harvard University Press, 1933). A very recent study on international trade in a globalized economy refutes once again the arguments in favor of protectionism. See *Globaphobia: Confronting Fears about Open Trade* (Washington, DC: Brookings Institution, 1998).

48. Jeremy Bentham (1748–1832) defined utility the following way: "By utility is meant that property in any object, whereby it tends to produce benefit, advantage, pleasure, good or happiness (all this in the present case comes to the same thing) or (what comes again to the same thing) to prevent the happening of mischief, pain, evil or unhappiness to the party whose interest is considered; if that party be the community in general then the happiness of the community: if a particular individual, then the happiness of that individual." See Jeremy Bentham, *An Introduction to the Principles of Morals and Legislation*, 3–4. James Mill (1773–1836)

was a British economist and philosopher who applied to the moral sciences the positivist method. He was a follower of Bentham. John Stuart Mill (1806–1873), the son of James Mill was an English economist and philosopher who is well known for his book *Principles of Political Economy*.

49. Schumpeter, *History of Economic Analysis*, 408.

50. Wilhelm Roepke, *A Humane Economy* (Chicago: Henry Regnery, 1960), 98.

51. When comparing the French and the English bourgeoisies during the eighteenth century, Henri See, the late French professor of the University of Rennes, is not very complimentary of the French. He says the following: "Cette classe de rentiers, de bourgeois 'vivant' noblement est bien l'un des traits carectéristiques de la société française du XVIIIe siècle. Les familles riches tendent au repos, repugnant a l'effort. En Angleterre, cette tendance n'existe guère: les fils des riches bourgeois et de *gentlemen* n'hésitent pas a travailler, a se livrer au negoce. Le contraste est intéressant a signaler, surtout a une époque ou le droit d'ainesse existait en France, comme en Angleterre." See Henri See, *La France Économique et Sociale au XVIIIe Siècle* (Paris: Librairie Armand Colin, 1952), 162.

52. Roepke attests that the bourgeois philosophy "taught us that there is nothing shameful in the self reliance and self assertion of the individual taking care of himself and his family, and it led us to assign their due place to the corresponding virtues of diligence, alertness, thrift, sense of duty, reliability, punctuality, and reasonableness." Roepke, *A Humane Economy*, 119. See also Lord Acton, *The History of Freedom and Other Essays*, (London: 1907), 28.

53. Late Professor of economics Frank H. Knight of the University of Chicago gave an excellent explanation for the need for profits. He stated correctly that profits are the result of the impossibility of predicting the future. The results of human activity can not be predicted with any degree of certainty. See Frank H. Knight, *Risk, Uncertainty and Profit*. (Chicago Hart, Schaffne & Marx, 1946), chapter 7. See also Frank H. Knight, *On the History and Method of Economics* (Chicago: University of Chicago Press, 1956), 23–24.

54. Schumpeter asserts the following: "The capitalist achievement does not typically consist in providing more silk stockings for queens but in bringing them within the reach of factory girls in return for steady decreasing amounts of effort." See Joseph Schumpeter, *Capitalism, Socialism and Democracy* (London: George Allen and Unwin, 1952), 67.

55. For an excellent defense of the free enterprise system and how the teachings of the Catholic Church have resulted in a more humane type of capitalism, see Michael Novak, *The Catholic Ethic and the Spirit of Capitalism* (New York: The Free Press, 1993). For another powerful argument in support of political and economic freedom, see Richard John Neuhaus, *Doing Well and Doing Good* (New York: Doubleday, 1992).

56. Even such a traditional French writer as François René Vicomte de Châteaubriand (1768–1848) expressed his indignation at what he called the excessive inequality of conditions and fortunes which prevailed at the time of the Industrial Revolution. As if predicting the oncoming Marxist revolution, he warned Europeans about the dangers posed to society by an abused proletariat. See his literery masterpiece, *Mémoires d'Outre-Tombe* (Paris: Gallimard, 1952), volumes I and II. It is interesting to note the high opinion that Châteaubriand had of the

American Founding Fathers in contrast to what had happened in France since the French Revolution. He wrote the following in *Mémoires d'Outre-Tombe*: "Les anciens présidents de la république ont un caractère religieux, simple, élève, calme, dont on ne trouve aucune trace dans nos fracas sanglants de la République et de l'Empire. La solitude dont les Americains étaient environnes a réagir sur leur nature; ils ont accompli en silence leur liberté." *Mémoires d'Outre-Tombe*, Volume I, 272.

57. Virtue, according to the German philosopher Joseph Pieper "is not the tame 'respectability' and 'uprightness' of the philistine but the enhancement of the human person in a way befitting his nature." It is the orientation toward the realization of his nature, that is, the common good. See Joseph Pieper, *Faith, Hope, Love* (San Francisco: Ignatius Press, 1997), 99.

58. Analyzing the concept of presumption and its perverse anticipation of fulfillment, Pieper says the following concerning liberalism: "Associated with it [presumption] is the typically liberal bourgeois moralism that, for no apparent reason, is antagonistic not only to dogma per se but also to the sacramental reality of the Church: solely on the basis of his own moral 'performance', an 'upright' and 'decent' individual who 'does his duty' will be able to 'stand the test before God as well'" (Pieper, *Faith, Hope, Love*, 126).

59. See Schumpeter, *Capitalism, Socialism and Democracy*, 137–38. Max Weber seems to have a similar opinion of the bourgeoisie as a class when he comments about the German bourgeoisie in the following way: "The political immaturity of broad strata of the German bourgeoisie does not have economic causes, nor is it due to the frequently cited 'politics of interest' which affects other nations just as much as it does the Germans. The reason is to be found in its unpolitical past, in the fact that it was not possible to catch up on a century of missed political education in a single decade, and in fact that rule by a great man is not always a means of educating the people politically. The vital question for the political future of the German bourgeoisie now is whether it is too *late* for it to make up the lost ground. No *economic* factor can substitute for such education." Max Weber, *Political Writings*, ed. Peter Lassman and Ronald Speirs (New York: Cambridge University Press, 1994), 25. Neither did Oswald Spengler, writing in the mid-twenties, have a very high opinion of a social class who looks only for economic gain. Although perhaps somewhat biased, he wrote the following in his classical book *The Decline of the West*: "He who is out for purely economic advantage—as the Carthaginians were in Roman times and, in a far greater degree still, the Americans in ours—is correspondingly incapable of purely poltical *thinking*. In the decisions of high politics he is ever deceived and made a tool of, as the case of Wilson shows—especially when the absence of statesmanlike instinct leaves a chair vacant for moral sentiments." See Oswald Spengler, *The Decline of the West* (New York: Alfred A. Knopf, 1999), 475.

# 4

—◊—

# The Romantic and Socialist Reactions to the Industrial Revolution

## THE ROMANTIC REACTION TO THE CRASS INDIVIDUALISM OF THE NINETEENTH CENTURY

The Romantic movement represents a strong current of opposition to the rationalist and progressive world of the nineteenth century; precisely the century in which the bourgeoisie played such a prominent role. Romanticists were certainly opposed to the rationalist individualism of the utilitarians but, on the other hand, they also glorified individual intuitive feelings. The Romantics were not interested so much in finding universal truths but in experiencing reality as they saw it. For this reason, they put so much stress on feelings, imagination, and passion. They rejected the classical view which was based on an objective, rational order where a balanced harmony prevailed. To the Romantic, the world and life are dissolved into an infinitude of stimuli, opportunities, and challenges. He discarded the idea held by the early rationalists that in spite of the individual method of searching for truth there still exists an objective truth, corresponding to God's divine will or derived from the power of reason. As professor of history J. L. Talmon writes, "This type of individualism was no longer enough for the Romantics. It came to mean to them no more than individually bowing to the same 'fixities' and 'definities'. And the Romantic craved not to find the same universal truth, but to experience reality in a way wholly his own."[1]

The romanticists gave a tremendous impulse to historical research, in particular in the area of economics.[2] They set the tone for what later became known as the Historical School, a school of thought that achieved wide influence in Germany where English political economy was greatly criticized.[3]

Contrary to the English Classical School of economics, the origins of which, can be traced to the Enlightenment, the German Historical School is a direct descendent of nineteenth century Romanticism. It was greatly influenced by the romantic fervor of an irrational and organicist weltanschauung and rejected totally the basic postulates of economics.

The idea of the English Classical School that the greatest social good was the maximum individual happiness had no great appeal in Germany and much less the hedonistic views of men such as Hutcheson, Hume, and Bentham. The German Historical School of political economy denied that universal economic laws could be established, much less that the economic laws envisaged by Smith and his followers could be equated with natural laws. Its supporters repudiated the idea that there exists an autonomous economic science.

For the German Historical School, self-interest was not the ruling motivation force in society. Its advocates believed that the motives of human conduct were many and rather complex. To suggest otherwise is misleading and leads to the wrong conclusions. Following the ideas of Kant, Fichte and Hegel, they tended to subordinate individual self-interest and personal wants to social and national ends.[4] Stress was placed on the priority of collective over individual goals.

The German Historical School posed a serious challenge to the philosophy of capitalism. Its promoters criticized the classical belief that the free market system leads to the harmonious resolution of economic forces without the need for government interference.

Georg Friedrich List, an early exponent of the Historical School, accepted many of the analytical premises of classical theory but, at the same time, he was a firm believer in a national political economy and the superiority of the nation's interests over those of individual citizens.[5] For List, economics, as all social sciences, should use a historically based methodology and not attempt to imitate the methodology of the physical sciences.

List denied the assumption that identified social good with individual wealth. He was mainly concerned with the welfare of the state and favored mercantilist policies over free trade. As the forerunner of the infant industry argument, he believed that protectionism would foster economic growth and give new vigour to German capitalism. For List, economic "laws" and ideas were related to their environment and did not have universal validity, as the English Classical School maintained. For example, an economic policy that could be very reasonable for England during Ricardo's time might not be suitable for Germany and the United States in the mid-nineteenth century.[6]

Wilhelm Roscher who some consider the leader of the German Historical School claimed that the science of national or political economy deals primarily with the material interests of nations. In his book *System der Volkswirtschaft*, he states that political economy is "the science which has to do with the laws of the development of the economy of a nation or with its economic national life."[7]

Some years later, the Romanticist Othmar Spann of the University of Vienna repeats on the fly leaf of his work *The History of Economics* a theme which is very dear to the German Historical School: "Political Economy is not a Science of Business but a Science of Life."[8] Political economy, the historicists insist, cannot ignore the realities of the social environment. In many respects, they echo the words of the English writer and social reformer, John Ruskin, who claimed, "Among the delusions which at different periods have possessed themselves of the minds of large masses of the human race, perhaps the most curious—certainly the least credible— is the modern *soi-disant* science of political economy, based on the idea that an advantageous code of social action may be determined irrespective of the influence of social affection."[9]

The principal exponent of what is known as the Young Historical School was Gustav von Schmoller who was highly critical of the automatic-deductive approach of the classical economists. He was a firm supporter of an interdisciplinary approach and, as Schumpeter asserts, it can be generally said that the sum total of his work "meant a tremendous advance in accuracy of knowledge about the social process."[10]

It is interesting to note that Schmoller did not call his school of thought simply historical but historical-ethical because he wanted to express his protest "against the whole imaginary advocacy of the hunt for private profit of which the English 'classics' were supposed to have been guilty."[11] Schmoller with the entire German Historical School joined the forces of all those economists and social reformers who for various reasons were critical of the crude and harsh individualism of laissez-faire economics and what they considered the lack of social consciousness which characterized many aspects of the Industrial Revolution.

The British economist Eric Roll has some harsh words concerning the romantic movement in economic thought. He believes that it produced work "of an altogether inferior theoretical level because its purpose was not the understanding of reality and its representation in a consistent academic system." Its "science," he insists, rejected logical analysis and, as a result, "any kind of economic and political thought produced on such a basis has no place in the history of the development of economic science."[12]

Romantic social thought began to lose its luster in Germany toward the end of the nineteenth century when the process of industrialization accelerated and the basic premises of English capitalism were generally accepted. As Germany's political and social structure was liberalized, the new institutional environment that developed made it increasingly possible to analyze rationally the economic processes. The realities of economic life gradually did away with the ill-conceived illusions of the early romantics. However, the idea of a powerful national state was not forgotten among many an intellectual who saw in some of the basic postulates of the Historical School the best way to foster their own power objectives; objectives that were not only economic but primarily political. Roll maintains that the general tenor of the ideas of the Historical School "is particularly suited to any kind of political movement which needs to rely on obscurantism in intellectual matters and on totalitarian methods in government. These ideas are, therefore, unfortunately not without relevance to the modern world."[13]

We now turn to socialism that, although in many ways dissimlar to the basic postulates of the German Historical School, does have some points of contact with it, especially in relation to the role of the state as a powerful force in social matters. In fact, in Britain the members of the Manchester School called the followers of the Historical School "socialists of the chair," a name which they proudly accepted.

However, before doing that, it is pertinent to point out that the Romantic movement and the German Historical School constituted only a small portion of the European nonsocialist response to the abuses of the Industrial Revolution. Since 1872 there took place a very strong reaction on the part of the "Ethical School," the "Verein für Socialpolitik," and other Christian thinkers in Germany, Austria, France, and Italy. The well-known German scholar Anton Rauscher has often stated that Christians contributed very significantly to social policy in the Bismarck era and also after the First World War and during the Weimar Republic. The same can be said of the years of recovery following the Second World War.[14]

## THE SOCIALIST "SOLUTION"

Probably the greatest challenge to laissez-faire capitalism has come from the socialist idea that collectivism in any of its various forms, rather than individualism, can better foster the general well-being of society. This is not a new idea which only emerged during the last two centuries. In fact, ever since early antiquity, philosophers and other intellectuals have relied on the state or some other form of authority for the establishment of an "ideal" society where justice and equality would prevail and the fruits of the earth could be shared equally among all of its members. This desire to attain absolute perfection in this world, whether social or individual, is nothing else but a secular perversion of the Christian legacy that man's final end is the beatific vision. Thus, it would be wrong to state that the utopian vision of the world was a phenomenon which surged with the socialist and revolutionary movements of the eighteenth and nineteenth centuries.

The possibility of creating the "ideal" society is closely connected with the very concept of utopia. For centuries man has dreamed about the possibility of developing a millennialist doctrine that would eventually lead to the perfect society. The belief in an unfolding linear progress through history assumes that all change is for the better and that, as professor Leszek Kolakowsky claims, "there is a radical discontinuity between the world as it is and as it will be, a violent leap is needed to do away with the past, a new time will start."[15] During the French Revolution, claims Nisbet, *revolutionistes* such as Saint-Just and Babeuf "were able to combine belief in the necessity of a period of catastrophic violence to usher in the golden age on earth with a philosophy of cumulative stage-by-stage progress from the past to the future."[16]

The optimism and utopian tendencies of the utilitarian-liberal philosophy of Bentham and his followers, so characteristic of the late eighteenth and early nineteenth centuries, soon gave way to the more pessimistic realism of Malthus and Ricardo. The gloomy economic situation that prevailed among large sectors of the population during the early parts of the nineteenth century did away with the high expectations of the philosophers of the Enlightenment. The harsh realities of everyday life seemed to contradict the belief in the attainment in a not too distant future of a happily ordered free and harmonious society. As a result, laissez-faire competitive capitalism, with its reliance on individual initiative and competition came increasingly under attack. The distress experienced by the laboring poor during the early stages of the Industrial Revolution bred a deep hatred of capitalism and became fertile ground for the development of more radical socialist philosophies.

Sismondi can be counted among the earlier critics of the abstract reasoning of the English Classical School and its belief in a self-regulating economic system. He belonged to the intellectual circle of the famous Madame de Stael in the outskirts of Geneva and was probably one of the most outspoken critics of Ricardo. In his book *Nouveaux Principes d'Économie Politique*, he challenged Ricardo's abstract reasoning on which the English economist based his analysis without regard to the specifics of time and place. The economy, argued Sismondi, is a social science and cannot be based on generalizations that have as their foundation a Natural Law which is opposed to the natural rights of the human person. To believe in the automaticity of the economic system to bring about order in society is a grave error that can lead to great injustice. It simply gives the authorities the excuse not to interfere in times of crisis. That is why Sismondi believed in the need to introduce ethical values into economic thinking.[17]

In his writings, Sismondi refuted the theory that classical economics would lead to a harmonious society. On the contrary, he was concerned that the conflicts in society would lead to a greater polarization between the capitalists and the proletariat. As the Italian economists Screpanti and Zamagni assert, "Without advocating violent revolutions and without demanding the abolition of private property, Sismondi's socialism aspired to construct a society dominated by small agricultural and craft producers, with an industry which distributed its profits also to the workers, land divided up into small plots, an efficient and extensive social-security system, and sharply progressive death duties."[18] Whether he was a socialist, as some critics claim, or not is a debatable question. He simply called himself a petit bourgeois socialist.

It was primarily in the early nineteenth century when there rose a more organized collectivist movements, such as socialism, denouncing individualism with its emphasis on personal liberty. The socialist movement blamed capitalism for the actual or presumed injustices which, they claimed, resulted from the application of utilitarian liberal policies that ignored the fate of labor and the common good.

Although a distinction can be made between the English and continental versions of socialism, they both shared the same antipathy toward capitalism and, in particular, against the social conditions created by the Industrial Revolution. They both repelled the bourgeois type of society which they considered responsible for the penury in which the laboring poor found themselves as a result of the process of industrialization. According to Rodríguez Casado, the sociopolitical order created by the selfish interests of the bourgeoisie was in great part responsible for the collectivist criticism of the nineteenth century socialists, especially in the case of the French Utopian socialists.[19]

The socialist frontal attack on capitalism that gave rise to various radical revolutionary movements reached its climax with the Marxist-Leninist revolution of 1917 that took over Russia through violence and deceit and brought with it one of the most ruthless and totalitarian regimes that the world has ever known. A revolution that not only created economic chaos and brought political tyranny to the people of Russia but threatened the peace and stability of the rest of the world.

Karl Marx was the intellectual genius behind the Russian communist revolution, the repercussions of which were felt around the globe. As all utopians, he converted the idea of progress into the new god of future generations and predicted the arrival of the "Golden Age." But, what really gave Marx's theory its special characteristic was his authentic "religious" conviction that the construction of the perfect communist society was not only feasible but a certainty.

Marx was highly critical of the socialists of the past. He called them sarcastically "utopian" socialists. For him what was utopian was not the socialist vision of a future perfectly harmonious society but the ways and methods that his predecessors used in order to arrive at such a goal. It was precisely the revolutionary and violent character of Marx's theory what distinguished him from the Utopian socialists that preceded him.[20]

The pitiless and brutal reaction of Marx's scientific socialism against the bourgeois class, which he considered the cornerstone of capitalism, can best be exemplified by quoting directly from the Communist Manifesto that he wrote together with his close friend Friedrich Engels.[21] In it, both authors express their well-known radical pronouncement concerning the future of capitalism and of the bourgeoisie: "The communists disdain to conceal their views and aims. They openly declare that their ends can be attained only by the forcible overthrow of all existing social conditions. Let the ruling classes tremble at a Communist revolution. The proletarians have nothing to lose but their chains. They have a world to win."[22]

Marx gave a philosophical and scientific base to his social revolution. Contrary to the socialist movements of the past, he made socialist thought scientific. He tried to found a science of all human history. In opposition to what he considered the impractical ideas of the "utopian" socialists, Marx and Engels presented a revolutionary doctrine that tried to demonstrate that capitalism with its innate contradictions carried within it the seeds of its own destruction. However, the fall of capitalism and the establishment of communism could be hastened through the violent overthrow of all existing institutions.

To protect ourselves from the possible application in the future of doctrines similar to the one held by Marx and his followers, it becomes clear that we should have better understanding of the basic philosophical and methodological foundations on which Marx's theory stands.

The Chilean philosopher Miguel Ibañez Langlois maintains that from an analytical point of view, Marxism is primarily the result of the following basic elements: (1) the dialectics of Hegel, (2) the materialistic interpretation of history and the class struggle, (3) the economics of the English classical school, in particular Smith and Ricardo, and (4) the atheistic humanism of Feuerbach.[23]

1. There is no doubt that Hegel's philosophy of history played a dominant role in Marx's approach to capitalism. Hegel maintained that history advanced progressively by the interaction of a series of ideological forces that he called thesis, antithesis, and synthesis. Once an idea exists it is soon contradicted by its opposite, its antithesis and, as a result of the ensuing conflict, a synthesis is created that represents a higher form of truth. This new and higher truth becomes a new thesis. which in its turn is opposed by an antithesis that later transforms itself into a new and superior idea, its synthesis. The historical process proceeds by means of a continuous

conflict of ideas which eventually will lead to a harmonious universe of perfect beings. Hegel called this process dialectic.

For Hegel humanity transcends man. Each historical period is nothing more than a transitory stage in the endless development of human society that advances continuously from the inferior to the superior. Here lies the key to progress. Through the dialectical process, death becomes the creator. It generates new life. All being contains within itself, not only the seed of its own destruction but also the seed of a new and superior being. Becoming, proclaims Hegel, is the first concrete idea and, thus, the first notion, whilst being and nothingness are empty abstractions. Contradiction is the source of all life. The old principle of identity is replaced by the principle of creative contradiction. In a similar dialectical way political and social institutions and systems evolve over time: theocracies are replaced by monarchies and, eventually, monarchies become democracies, a superior form of political system.

2. Marx retained Hegel's dialectical method of analysis but at the same time he reacted against his "idealism" in the philosophical sense. Applying Feuerbach's materialism to Hegel's dialectic, Marx constructed his own dialectical materialism which he used as the basis for his materialistic interpretation of history.[24] Marx opposed his own "materialism" to Hegel's "idealism."

It would have been better for Marx to have called the materialistic interpretation of history by the more appropriate name of the economic interpretation of history. For Marx, production is the primary human activity and history is nothing more than the history of the economic process. He defines economics as the sum of the forces of production, capital resources and material

According to Marx, the whole nature of society is determined by the particular form of production prevailing at any given moment in time. He believed that all social, political and intellectual relations, all religious and legal systems, all the theoretical outlooks which emerge in the course of history are derived from the material conditions of life.

As modes of production change, so does society. Economics is the dominant factor in the historical process. All other motives are subordinated to it and de facto are ineffective and will not change the eventual outcome of the process. Ideas, beliefs, and attitudes depend on existing social systems and conditions and not the reverse. He claimed that he had found Hegel standing on his head and turned him over and set him upright on his feet.[25]

Thus, applying Hegel's dialectics, Marx stated categorically that the dynamic process of social change is determined by the forces of production.[26] He claimed that as the dynamic *forces of production* come into conflict with the static *relations of production*, the conflict of interests becomes more acute bringing with it a new set of relations. The class struggle is the mechanism through which the new set of relations comes into existence.[27]

The dialectical theory of the class struggle, which is one of the key concepts of Marx is not new to him. What is new is the union of the idea of the class struggle with Hegel's dialectics. In each historical stage one class dominates and exploits the others for its own advantage. This is the result, not of pure chance, but of the inevitable laws of history.

In accordance with the dialectical process the dominant class will necessarily develop its opposite, the class that will eventually destroy it. The new class that arises will, in its turn, create an opposition, an opposition that ultimately will overthrow it also and become the dominant force. The process will continue until it reaches its final stage.

It is the triumphant working class or proletariat who, in their struggle against the oppression of the bourgeoisie, will bring about the downfall of capitalism and the eventual establishment of a society of free and equal men: the communist ideal. But prior to the communist ideal there will be a transition period in which the dictatorship of the proletariat will be established and all classes abolished.

However, in order to accelerate the final outcome, the proletariat must carry the struggle at three different levels: the ideological, the economic, and the political. The practical consequences of such a philosophy are obvious. The dictatorship of the proletariat cannot come about through peaceful means. It can arise only through violence and the smashing of the bourgeois state machine, the army and the police. Concerning the task of the proletariat, Marx wrote to Kugelman in 1871, "No longer as before, to transfer the bureaucratic military machine from one hand to another, but to smash it, and that is a preliminary condition for every real people's revolution in the continent."[28] Lenin on his part claimed that "the dictatorship of the proletariat is the rule—unrestricted by law and based on force—of the proletariat over the bourgeoisie, a rule enjoying the sympathy and support of the labouring and exploited masses."[29] The final victory of the proletariat is inevitable and in accordance with the laws of nature.

3. The same way that Marx used Hegel's dialectics and placed it at the service of his own particular objectives, he also used the labor theory of the English Classical School to condemn economic liberalism. It is precisely on the basis of the fundamental postulate of the liberal economists that he builds the corner stone of his theory: the thesis of surplus value.[30] Marx's theory of surplus value is simply the corollary of his labor theory of value.

Marx considered labor as the only source of value. Being a materialist, he did not accept purely subjective valuations and held that all values are determined exclusively by material relations. Labor is the only property common to all commodities. This is not an idea which pertains exclusively to Marx. It is to be found also among the founders of economic liberalism, in particular Smith and Ricardo.

Smith later abandoned his labor theory of value and maintained that the "natural" competitive, equilibrium price is equal to the total cost of production which includes wages, profits, and rents, all of which must be included in the final price.[31] Ricardo tried to revive Smith's labor theory of value in order to apply it to capitalism. He argued that in the equilibrium state of the competitive system the relative values of the different products would tend to be approximately or nearly proportional to the total amounts of labor time needed (per unit of output ) to produce them.[32] But Ricardo's doctrine, unlike Marx's labor theory of value, did not assert that the values of all commodities were directly equivalent to the labor time embodied in them.[33] Thus, to say that the Marxian theory of value is the same as that of Ricardo's is incorrect. Ricardo did not say that the value of all output is created entirely by labor and that all non-wage income is the result of exploitation. The real exploitation of the laboring may occur through the abuse of monopoly or bargaining power in the product or labor markets. This type of exploitation is, of course, unethical and must of course be condemned. But, as Taylor, stresses, "All this has little to do with the different, far more extreme, and non sensical Marxian dogma, that *all* income or value of output is due exclusively to the wage-earning workers, and as long as *any* of it goes to anyone else, they are being 'exploited.'"[34]

Marx sustains that the main reason for class conflict and the final demise of capitalism lies precisely in the existence of surplus *value*. It occurs because labor is not paid in accordance with his contribution to production. The extra value, surplus value, contributed by the laborer and expropriated by the capitalist, becomes the major cause of the alienation and polarization of classes.

Capitalism, therefore, is presented by Marx as a system of inevitable and necessary exploitation. Without it, capitalism could not survive. No capitalist can remain in business if he does not have before him the expectation of profits, of surplus value. And what is worse, he is totally unable and incapable of changing the very essence of capitalism which, according to Marx, is reduced to the exploitation and alienation of the worker and the inevitability of class conflict. The dynamic materialistic dialectics of capitalism must necessarily lead to the creation of an atheistic society free of all antinomies: "perfect communism."

4. The atheistic nature of Marx's ideology can be traced to many of the liberal intellectuals of the eighteenth century. He shares with them the belief in the unlimited power of instrumental reason, faith in the progressive evolution of nature and history, and the perfectness of the human being. For Marx there is only one reality and that is matter. This matter, submit-

ted to the blind forces of nature, evolves in due time into more advanced types of existence, such as plants, animals and finally man. It is by a law of inexorable necessity and through perpetual conflict that matter moves towards the final synthesis of a classless society, communism.

Marxism-Leninism does not recognize the existence of any supernatural or creative force. It is based exclusively on the real world and insists that this life is the only life. Man must be liberated from the idea that there is a Supreme Being and reject the superstitions and spiritual slavery of the past. Marx himself observed that "criticism of religion constitutes the premise for all criticism."[35] In such a doctrine, Pope Pius XI affirms, "there's no room for the idea of God; there is no difference between matter and spirit, between soul and body; there is neither survival of the soul after death nor any hope in a future life."[36]

The theory and praxis of the Marxism-Leninism, with its torturous "religious twist," reemphasizes Marx's atheistic foundation which denies with forcefulness the existence of the transcendental. The strength of Marxism-Leninism lies precisely in its having placed the spiritual force of the soul at the service of an atheistic messianic doctrine. It is precisely the messianic message that it conveys, carried out with tremendous apostolic zeal, what makes Marxism and other similar ideologies or "isms" so dangerous for the future of mankind.

Religion, according to Marx, constitutes the prototype of all alienations. It is "pure misery," "abjection," "the radical loss of oneself." He goes on to say that it is "the fantasy of human nature," "the cry of the overwhelmed creature," "the heart of a world without a heart," "the spirit of an existence without a spirit," and finally, it is the "opium of the people." Furthermore, he maintains that the Christian state or any confessional state for that matter is contradictory because politically it depends on secular norms for its existence, whilst at the same time it betrays its secular character by discriminating in favor of religion. Such a dilemma cannot be solved by the separation of church and state because, insists Marx, that will only transfer the contradiction to the interior of the individual who will be torn between his political existence as a citizen and his religious commitment. He would lead two different lives: a transcendental one and a secular one.

The practical consequences of Marx's views on religion are perfectly clear: its ultimate elimination. Religion, however, does not need to be crushed during early stages of the revolution. First, it is necessary to suppress the secular, political and social alienation from which religion emanates. This does not mean that Marx renounces his intellectual criticism of religion, just as much as his disciples do not give up their struggle against religion. For example, Marx claims that the disappearance of religion as an illusory happiness of the people is absolutely necessary for their ultimate real happiness. For people to give up their illusions about religion requires that they abandon the economic condition of penury in which they find themselves; condition which creates the need for religion. Religion is nothing more than an illusion which serves as a palliative for the misery resulting from the exploitation of the proletariat by the capitalists. His criticism of religion boils down to a criticism of the Christian belief in "the vale of tears."

All of this means that in a communist dominated world there is no place for religion because all contradictions and antinomies would disappear. For Marx, nothing in religion can be saved because its very raison d'être depends on the existence of misfortune, misery, and alienation. Religion exhales a spiritual aroma that only a world politically and socially alienated can exhale. Once the misery and alienation brought about by the exploitation of capitalism is eliminated, there will be no longer need for religion.

It has been said that to understand Marxism, one has to be a Christian. Maybe the reason for this is that, as Miguel Ibanez Langlois claims, only he who possesses the model can understand the copy: the model being Christianity, the copy Marxism. According to him, "The Marxist theory and praxis, in spite of their originality, have an intrinsically derived character. They essentially depend of the original—Christianity—whose order they invert. Both the theory and praxis can only become fully comprehensible if they are taken for what they are: a Christian heresy, a parasitical development of Christianity."[37] Even Toynbee, the British historian, once said that "Marxism is a Judeo-Christian heresy." The Catholic Church has rejected Marxism totally and unequivocally not because it is opposed to an original and "new truth" but simply because it recognizes in Marxism a heresy which has sprouted from a distorted understanding of Christian faith.

Thus, it is possible to perceive in Marxism, just as in most utopian theories, a strange and distorted "twin" of Christian faith, a precise transposition of all of Christianity's essential mysteries, from the creation of man and the world to man's final end: the vision of God. The mystery of Christ is prolonged into history as the movement of all temporal realities toward their total fulfillment. In a similar way, Marx's secularized concept of human progress was a rational transposition of the Christians' efforts to reach their final goal: salvation. However, in the case of Marxism it is much more than a simple process of secularization. Marx believed that he was the prophet of a new era. He condemned this sinful world—capitalism—and announced a new messianic message: communism. His message, therefore, is the total inversion of the Christian message of salvation.

Mao Tse-Tung in Communist China followed this same line of thought. In a speech on the role of the Communist Party in October 1938, he stated categorically the following: "1) the individual is subordinated to to the organization, 2) the minority is subordinated to the majority, 3) the lower level is subordinated to the higher level and 4) the entire membership is subordinated to the Central Committee of the Communist Party." The cultural revolution which took place more than twenty years later constituted the epitome of communist rejection of all past traditional values. Totalitarianism, in any of its forms, follows a similar pattern: the total subordination of the human person to the prevalent ideology imposed by the state.

Marx's belief in the creation of a future communist society in which the "new man" would live free of contradictions places him squarely in the ranks of his utopian predecessors. In many ways Marx is a descendant of a line of thought which began with the nominalism of the fourteenth century and which continued with the purely humanistic and anthropocentric approach to life of the fifteenth and sixteenth centuries. This trend later led to the Deism of the Enlightenment and finally to Marx himself.

Marx, like most utopian thinkers, was convinced that the perfect society could be reached. He acknowledged the desirability and the possibility of creating an ideal society and had no hesitation in recommending the use of whatever means were necessary to bring it about as soon as possible. Like most utopian perfectionists, Marx believed in what is actually a conscious and concentrated form of being godlike. As he believed in an initial state of justice, which was stained by the original sin of private property, the solution to man's ills lay in the destruction and elimination of all those structures and institutions which supported it. Lenin described this ideal state of affairs as the moment "when all members of society, or even only the overwhelming majority, have learned how to govern the state *themselves*, have taken this business into their own hands, have 'established' control over the insignificant minority of capitalists, over the gentry with capitalist leanings and the workers thoroughly demoralized by capitalism—from this moment the need for any government begins to disappear."[38] The door would then be open to the complete withering away of the state and the creation of the perfect society free of all alienations.

The utopian beliefs of Mao Tse-Tung and other totalitarian tyrants were not much different from those of Marx. In a speech Mao gave in 1937, the Chinese leader claimed that "in the present epoch of the development of society, China had already reached a historic and unprecedented moment, that is, the moment of for completely banishing darkness from the world and for changing the world into a world of light such as never previously existed."[39]

The most serious problem of all utopians, who believe in the possibility of constructing the perfect society here on earth, is their tendency to identify themselves with God. This applies to modern utopians just as well as to those of the past. As the British author H. G. Wells once said, "Modern utopianism is kinetic: it dreams of mankind on the way to becoming God;

it envisions individuals as indefinitely mobile, expanding, cosmic and godlike."[40] Marx was no exception.

Events have proven Marx's theory false. The creation of a utopian classless society where equality and justice would prevail never materialized. On the contrary, the former Soviet Union and its socialist satellites were plagued with social injustices and a "new class" came into the foreground who enjoyed the few benefits that an inefficient and corrupt system was able to provide. The abuses and privileges of the "nomenclature" of the communist regime were no different and probably much worse than that of past Russian autocratic regimes.

Even though Marxism-Leninism—including his economic theory and policy—has been totally discredited as a result of the collapse of the former Soviet Union and its satellite states, the negation of a providential God and the belief in man as the sole artifice of his own glory still permeates large sectors of our deistic if not agnostic and relativistic society. Materialistic and hedonistic principles still abound in our communities even though they may appear under a different form or name.

Marx's doctrine and praxis reveals an enormous level of intellectual pride which, probably, had never been known before in the history of mankind. It is only this consummated pride—the one that lies at the root of all sin: You will become like gods, with the knowledge of good and evil—that is able to obscure the eyes of man in such a way that he can only see truth in the theory and praxis of Marxism-Leninism.[41] But this pride can also be found in the very principle of modernism and its intellectual expressions: rationalism, liberalism, pantheism, and idealism. The doctrine and praxis of Marxism is the quintessence of an agnostic and active movement, which as mentioned earlier, began with the dawn of modern times and which under different forms and in spite of the demise of communism, is still very much alive today.

We have discussed Marxism-Leninism to a large extent because the seeds of pride and the belief in earthly paradises, so characteristic of his teachings, have not disappeared in our contemporary world. Communism seems to have lost its luster and influence after the collapse of the Berlin Wall but a secularist mentality void of any ethical or religious foundation still lies at the root of many of our contemporary problems. This applies just as much to politics as to economics. The atheistic economic theories of Marxian socialism undoubtedly have been discredited and capitalism, because of its much greater efficiency, has been declared the winner against the collectivist theories of Marxian socialism. But, the secularist mentality that lies at the very roots of Marxism is not absent from the consumer society that predominates in our modern Western type of capitalism.

We shall now turn to another type of criticism of capitalism that occurred in America under the banner of institutionalism.

## AMERICAN "INSTITUTIONALISM"

The American economist Thorstein Veblen is considered by many the founder of institutionalism, a "school" of economic thinking that was highly critical of neoclassicism and its defense of a harmonious natural order.[42] He maintained that the basic assumptions of the classical and neoclassical method of analysis were unscientific.[43] Veblen rejected the whole concept of the "invisible hand" claiming that there is no natural harmony in the system. For him the orthodox idea that there are natural laws in the economy similar to those in the physical sciences lacked a rational basis. To suggest that, with the help of the "invisible hand," private vices would turn to public benefits was not only false but also arrogant. The its own ranks; a criticism which is not always valid and which is the result of the egotistic interests of powerful individuals or economic groups.

Veblen's rebuke of orthodox theory was really directed at the the very core of capitalism rather than at the flaws of neoclassical economic theory. Although not being a Marxist, Veblen did stress the idea of conflict in society. He claimed that within the capitalist system there is always a permanent clash of interests between the changes in technology, the most powerful force of changes in institutions, and the existing habits or modes of thought (institutions) which, as a result of the technological changes, soon become obsolete and new ones are created.[44] Thus, man's individual conduct varies in accordance with the changes in the institutional framework. His wants and desires, inasmuch as his aims and means to attain them, become a function of institutional variables.

According to Veblen, the conflict of interests in our contemporary society is best exemplified by the opposition between "industry," that produces the goods, and "business," whose primary concern is making money. The engineers, professionals, and workers, not the merchants and rentiers who typify the business class, are the real active agents of progress. The hedonistic spirit of the businessman, geared toward making money, makes him indifferent to the needs and well-being of his fellow men. Eventually, the conflict of interests between the engineers and workers and the captains of industry and absentee owners will lead to the fall of capitalism.

The clash between advancing technology and the structure of business organization will create conditions that eventually will lead to the concentration of power and high profits in the hands of the business community together with an underutilization of resources. This process will make the crisis of the capitalist system inevitable. But, the crisis will not occur, as Marx had predicted, because the poor are getting poorer and the rich richer but because the working classes are under the impression that they are "relatively" poorer. Contrary to Marx, Veblen was mainly concerned with human motives in general.

Darwin's theory of evolution greatly influenced Veblen's thinking.[45] He believed that the economy evolved over time with no specific purpose, contrary to the orthodox teleological view that the economy was moving towards a set goal: a long-run equilibrium that could not be proven empirically but assumed from the onset. The economy was always changing and could be considered as a mechanical process where people developed in accordance with environmental changes. It had no specific design or purpose. Orthodox theory, which had a pre-Darwinian teleological preconception of economics, was lagging behind developments in the physical sciences.

Probably the better known of Veblen's work was *The Theory of the Leisure Class*. It is in this book that he introduced the concept "conspicuous consumption." By that he meant that businessmen compete with each other in the production of goods that do not satisfy the real needs of the population. They simply try to foster the consumption of products that satisfy the vanity and snobbery of the consumer.[46] His contempt and bias against the upper classes is clearly reflected in the book clouding whatever objectivity he tries to demonstrate in his otherwise interesting work.

Veblen attempted to construct a new social science which would not be limited to economics. For Veblen, man's economic behavior cannot be divorced from his other activities. Economics must be integrated to the other social sciences, including ethics, psychology and history. He did not endorse a particular type of ethics but what cannot be denied is that he expressed in all of his writings a strong ethical dissent of what he called the hedonistic conception of man guided exclusively by calculations of pleasure and pain. He rejected the *homo oeconomicus* as the basic datum of economic activity. His scientific and ethical views played an important role in the development of heterodox thinking in America.

Even though Veblen does not offer a serious alternative to orthodox economic theory, he did object and vehemently criticized the perfectly competitive market and the assumptions of a harmonious and self-regulating economic system as endorsed by the Classical School. Perhaps, his most important contribution was the stress he placed on normative economics. Many of his ideas were used by his followers as a justification for a greater degree of government intervention so as to curtail the abuses of a hedonistic money minded culture.

The three most important American economists who are generally classified as institutionalists are Wesley Clair Mitchell,[47] John Roger Commons,[48] and Clarence Edwin Ayres.[49] The three of them were very critical of orthodox economics and its assumption of the static nature of the concept of equilibrium. Although they deviated from many of Veblen's ideas, they still accepted many of his criticisms of the capitalist system.[50]

The institutionalists of the 1930s were largely responsible for implementing significant policy changes. In most of their writings there prevails an ethical dissent from capitalism in addition to their scientific research. They stressed the need for government planning to avoid the violent fluctuations of economic activity and their negative impact on society. Commons, in particular, maintained close relationships with government agencies and contributed greatly to the enactment of social legislation. This relationship between the academic and the political worlds acquired national significance during President Roosevelt's New Deal policy. A new era of government intervention was in the making. According to Kenneth Boulding, Commons has been described as "the intellectual origin of the movement toward the welfare state."[51]

John Kenneth Galbraith is probably the best representative of the line of thought started by Veblen.[52] He is a sharp critic of neoclassical economic thinking, rejecting the concept of a self-regulating economic system. Laissez-faire economics with its reliance on Smith's "invisible hand" will only bring about greater income inequalities and the impoverishment of the less privileged sectors of society. Economic planning should play the leading role in the process of economic development.

In his book *American Capitalism*, Galbraith introduces the concept of countervailing power. According to this theory, the best way to keep a social system in equilibrium is to balance the excess of power in the hands of certain interest groups by permitting the creation of other power groups with opposing interests. Countervailing power, claims Galbraith, develops as a response to the economic power concentrated in the hands of certain dominant groups and which is the result of the breakdown of competition. This the way he explains the development of trade unions and other powerful groups.

In many ways Galbraith's criticism of capitalism is similar to that of Veblen. Both have very disparaging things to say about American society. An affluent society, such as the one in the United States, has been able to solve the problem of scarcity and is now able to provide the consumer with goods that are no longer absolutely necessary. For him the American consumer is no longer sovereign. His wants are manipulated by the producer through the process of advertisement. Consequently, his needs are artificially created independently of whether the goods purchased are necessary unnecessary. The consumer no longer determines how resources are to be allocated in order to meet his needs.

Galbraith calls the process, through which the consumer becomes dependent on the producer, the "dependence effect." As Professors Ekelund and Hebert have commented, "With scholarly impertinence, Galbraith asserted that consumer sovereignty is a myth and that in modern times the chain of cause and effect runs from production to consumption. In order to maintain an affluent society, one in which production and income are growing, new wants must be manufactured."[53] Obviously Galbraith's approach to demand theory runs counter to the orthodox theory of demand with its reliance on scarcities, given prices, and marginal utility.

Galbraith is an ardent critic of capitalism and a defender of a more equal distribution of income. He advocates planning and state regulation of the economy, as if governments were the only entities capable of providing social goods. Nobody doubts the need that all societies have for social goods, but those who defend the neoclassical theory of markets "are at least as interested as Galbraith in the problem of the provision of social goods. The debatable point, of course, is the method of provision and the theory and philosophy behind it."[54]

In the following chapter we will discuss briefly the neoclassical counterattack against the surge of interventionist policies which were undermining the basic postulates of a natural self-regulating economic system based on "natural" laws. The "Keynesian Revolution" and other voices of dissent, which opened the doors of the so-called Welfare State, will also be included.

## NOTES

1. See J. L.Talmon, *Romanticism and Revolt* (New York: Norton, 1967), 139. See also Maurrice Cranston, *The Romantic Movement* (Oxford: Blackwell, 1994) and Nicholas V. Riasanovsky, *The Emergence of Romanticism* (New York, Oxford University Press, 1992).

2. Schumpeter, when writing about the contribution of Romantic movement to historical truth, says the following: "It taught us better understanding of civilizations other than our own—the Middle Ages, for example, and extra-European cultural worlds as well. This meant new vistas, wider horizons, fresh problems, and, above all, the end of the stupid contempt that Voltarians and utilitarians professed for everything that preceded 'this enlightened age.'" See Joseph Schumpeter, *History of Economic Analysis* (New York: Oxford University Press, 1963), 422–23.

3. In Germany, the Romantic movement had a great impact on economic thinking. "In economics it grew together with the first aristocratic and reactionary opposition to capitalist development, and with Fichte, Gentz, and Muller it opposed *laissez-faire* economics and political liberalism, both for the political consequences they implied and for the philosophical premises from which they came. The individualist and rationalist connotations of those premises were thoroughly rejected." See Ernesto Screpanti and Stefano Zamagni, *An Outline of the History of Economic Thought* (New York: Oxford University Press, 1993), 93.

4. See Edmund Whittaker, *A History of Economic Ideas* (New York: Longmans, Green, 1940), 732–33.

5. Screpanti and Zamagni remind us that "the famous infant-industry protection strategy was brought to Europe by List who, as a political exile in the United States, had been the secretary of Henry Clay, the true inventor of that strategy." See Screpanti and Zamagni, *An Outline of the History of Economic Thought*, 92.

6. List recommended protection and tariffs for the development of the United States. Free trade could be beneficial for an England that was already in an advanced state of industry but not for countries in the process of building an industrial base. His influence was great in the United States where he spent a number of years in the mid-1980s. His book *The National System of Political Economy* was warmly received in America and his protectionist policies received such a wide acclaim that he was often called the father of American protectionism.

7. Roscher, *System der Wolkswirtschaft* (Stuttgart, 1854). Quoted by Whittaker, *A History of Economic Ideas*, 734.

8. Othmar Spann, *The History of Economic Thought*. As quoted by Whittaker, *A History of Economic Ideas*, 736.

9. As quoted by Whittaker, *A History of Economic Ideas*, 736. John Ruskin (1819–1900), an English art critic and social reformer, applied his interest in art to social life. He believed that the artistic side of human nature was being sacrificed in the altar of material wealth.

10. Schumpeter, *History of Economic Analysis*, 810.

11. Schumpeter, *History of Economic Analysis*, 812.

12. Eric Roll, *History of Economic Thought* (London: Faber & Faber, 1953), 212.

13. Roll, *History of Economic Thought*, 212.

14. Through the years, Christians and in particular the Catholic Church have been very much concerned with the social problems of our time, especially after the rise of Marxism. The social teachings of the Catholic Church have always stressed the need for a better understanding of the relationship between economics and ethics, something which the main body of economic theory has tended to avoid. Among the original contributors to Catholic social thought the following can be mentioned: Joseph Ritter von Buss, Bishop Wilhelm von Ketteler, and Heinrich Pesch. Also can be mentioned Oswald Nell-Breuning S.J., Goetz Briefs, Anton Rauscher, and Heinrich Rommen. Among the many French contributions to the social teachings of the Catholic Church—although sometimes controversial—the following three can be mentioned: Albert de Mun and his *Oeuvres des Cercles Catholiques d'Ouvriers*, René de la Tour du Pin author of *Vers un Ordre Sociale Chrétien*, and finally Cardinal Pie. For a closer understanding of his views, see Chanoine Étienne Catta in *La Doctrine Politique et Sociale du Cardinal Pie*. Anton Rauscher has recently published in three volumes a comprehensive study of the role of the Church in the world. See Anton Rauscher, *Kirche in der Welt* (Wurtzburg: Echter, 1998).

15. Statement quoted by Robert A. Nisbet, in his book *History of the Idea of Progress* (New York: Basic Books, 1970), 239.

16. Nisbet, *History of the Idea of Progress*, 239. Louis de Saint-Just (1767–1794) was a member of the Committee on Public Safety in Paris and was the theoretician of the French revolutionary government during the Reign of Terror. He was executed together with Robespierre. Francois Noel Babeuf (1760–1797) was a French revolutionary who conspired against the *Directoire*, was denounced and executed during the latter years of the French Revolution. The doctrine that he preached was very similar to communism.

17. Leonard Sismonde de Sismondi (1773–1842) was a Swiss historian and economist considered by some as a socialist but not by others who see him rather

as a critic of economic liberalism, not to be included in the socialist camp. Marx, however, claimed that he belonged to a group of petit-bourgeois socialists who criticized liberal practices not only in France but also in England. See Vicente Rodriguez Casado, *Origenes del Capitalismo y del Socialismo Contemporaneo* (Madrid: Espasa-Calpe, S.A., 1981), 395.

18. Screpanti and Zamagni, *An Outline of the History of Economic Thought*, 124.

19. Rodriguez Casado, *Orígenes del Capitalismo y del Socialismo Contemporaneo*, 385–88.

20. Much can be said about the socialist movements in the eighteenth and nineteenth centuries which Marx classified under the name of Utopian socialists and were the object of his bitter criticism. He claimed that they were discrediting the entire social movement. Under this category he included, among others, Robert Owen (1772–1837), Charles Fourier (1772–1837), and Claude-Henri de Rouvroy, Comte de Saint Simon (1760–1825).

21. Friedrich Engels (1820–1895), together with Marx, was the most important German theorist and organizer of the Marxist movement. He was born in Barmen, Germany, of a wealthy industrial family that owned a textile factory in the Rhine land. His strict background soon made him a natural rebel and once in Berlin, as a brilliant student, he was easily converted to communism. Most of his early writings were already very satirical of religion. However, it did not take long for his rebellious attitude toward religion to be turned into social rebellion.

22. Karl Marx and Friedrich Engels, *Manifesto of the Communist Party*, ed. Samuel H. Beer (Arlington Heights, IL: Harlan Davidson, 1955), 46.

23. Miguel Ibañez Langlois, *El Marxismo: Visión Crítica* (Madrid: Rialp, 1973), 32.

24. Ludwig Feuerbach (1804–1872) was a German philosopher who studied in Berlin under Hegel. His major work was the *Essence of Christianity*. He was one of the patrons of "atheistic humanism." According to Feuerbach, it was not God who created man but man who created God. Man created an imaginary god, an ideal heaven into which he projected all that is best in him. God is only an idealized figure of man himself. The religious man is presented by Feuerbach as a self-alienated being who no longer belongs to himself but to a fictional god, oppressor of human thought.

25. See Overton H. Taylor, *A History of Economic Thought* (New York: McGraw-Hill, 1960), 291.

26. For Marx, "The mode of production of material life determines the character of the social, political and spiritual processes of life. It is not the consciousness of men that determines their existence but, on the contrary, their social existence that determines their consciousness." See Karl Marx, *A Contribution to the Critique of Political Economy* (Moscow: Progress, 1970), 20.

27. The dynamic changing forces of production consist of land, labor, and capital, but above all, new technological developments. The static relations of production were personal and social relations, including property relations. They are the thesis of Marxian dialectics whilst the changing forces of production are the antithesis. The legal, political, and religious superstructure is superimposed on the sum total of these relations. The superstructure corresponds to specific forms of social consciousness. Initially there is harmony between the forces and relations of production (thesis and antithesis) but as the historical process advances con-

tradictions and violent revolutionary movements occur bringing with them a new synthesis. As a result a new set of relations of production appear which soon become the new thesis. More than a theory of economics, it is a theory of history.

28. Joseph Stalin, *Foundations of Leninism* (New York: International Publishers, 1939), 55.

29. V. I. Lenin, *State and Revolution* (New York: International Publishers, 1939), 55.

30. Marx takes from Ricardo his labor value theory and introduces the modifications that he considers appropriate to justify his own surplus value theory, For example, with reference to Ricardo's analysis of the magnitude of value, he says, "As regards values in general , it is the weak point of the classical school of political economy that it nowhere, expressly and with full consciousness, distinguishes between labour, as it appears in the value of a product and the same labour, as it appears in the use-value of the product." See Karl Marx, *Capital* (New York: Modern Library, 1906), footnote 2, 92.

31. According to Smith, the labor theory of value applied only to a primitive economy. Nevertheless, even there, the market mechanism would eventually bring about a correspondence of relative values with labor time requirements.

32. See Taylor, *A History of Economic Thought*, 303.

33. Taylor, *A History of Economic Thought*, 303.

34. Taylor, *A History of Economic Thought*, 304.

35. Robert C. Tucker, ed., *The Marx-Engel Reader*, second edition (New York: Norton, 1978), 53.

36. Pius XI, *On Atheistic Communism*, no. 2.

37. Ibañez Langlois, *El Marxismo: Visión Crítica*, 278.

38. Lenin, *State and Revolution*, 53.

39. Mao Tse-Tung, "On the Relation between Knowledge and Practice" in *Selected Readings from the Works of Mao Tse-Tung* (Peking: Foreign Language Press, 1971), 81.

40. Thomas Molnar, *The Perennial Utopia* (New York: Sheed & Ward, 1967), 152.

41. Ibañez Langlois, *El Marxismo: Visión Crítica*, 298.

42. Thorstein Veblen (1857–1929), an American economist, was a fierce critic of capitalism. He was highly caustic in his criticism of the social waste incurred by the wealthy class. Eric Roll classifies him the following way: "If by some system of proportional representation, in which originality, not to say uniqueness of contribution, was the decisive quality , an American had to be chosen for inclusion among the great economists, there are few who would be so well qualified for this purpose as Veblen." See Roll, *History of Economic Thought*, 440. Schumpeter, on the other hand, has less regard for him as an economist. He considers that Veblen's work was practically all in economic sociology. Perhaps the only exception was his popular book, *The Theory of the Leisure Class*, written in 1899. See Schumpeter, *History of Economic Analysis*, 795.

43. Veblen did not create an institutional school of thought—in the sense of a classical or a Keynesian school of thought—even though he did have a significant influence on American political and social ideas at the turn of the century. His institutionalist interpretation of social development, stressing the importance of legal forms and modes of thought as the essential areas of economic study, was not

always followed by those economists who followed or acknowledge their debt to him. Veblen defined institutions as principles of action about which men have no doubts, that is, religious, aesthetic, and other preconditioned ideas.

44. For an excellent summary of Veblen's theory see Roll, *History of Economic Thought*, pp. 439–54.

45. Charles Darwin (1809–1881) was an English naturalist who wrote the well-known book *On the Origin of the Species by Means of Natural Selection, or the Preservation of Favoured Races in the Struggle for Life*. His revolutionary theory of evolution through natural selection caused an uproar in biological science.

46. Thorstein Veblen, *The Theory of the Leisure Class* (New York: Mentor, 1953), 50.

47. Mitchell (1874–1948) was a student of Veblen. He is better known for his work in founding the National Bureau of Economic Research and his magnus opus *Business Cycles*.

48. Commons (1862–1945) was a social reformer who was very instrumental in formulating labor legislation.

49. Ayres (1891–1972) supported liberal modifications of capitalism. Even though he rejected communism, he favored economic planning as a remedy for the abuses of capitalism.

50. Mitchell wrote the following about Veblen: "A heretic needs a high heart, though sustained by faith that he is everlastingly right and sure of his reward hereafter. The heretic who views his own ideas as but tomorrow's fashion in thought needs still firmer courage. Such courage Veblen had." See Wesley C. Mitchell, *What Veblen Taught* (New York: Viking, 1936).

51. Kenneth Boulding, "A New Look at Institutionalism," *American Economic Review* 48 (May 1957), 7. As quoted by Harry Landreth and David C. Colander, *History of Economic Thought* (Boston: Houghton Mifflin, 1994), 345.

52. John Kenneth Galbraith (1908–) is a professor of economics at Harvard University and former president of the American Economic Association. He is a prolific writer. Among his works the following can be mentioned: *American Capitalism, The Affluent Society*, and *The New Industrial State*.

53. Robert B. Ekelund Jr. and Robert E. Hebert, *A History of Economic Theory and Method* (New York: McGraw-Hill, 1997), 431.

54. Ekelund and Hebert, *A History of Economic Theory and Method*, 433.

# 5

—ᴍ—

# Neoclassicism, the Keynesian Revolution, and Other Sources of Dissent

## THE NEOCLASSICAL APPROACH

The neoclassical economists—contrary to Marx, the mercantilists, and their classical predecessors—largely ignored macroeconomic problems, in particular the forces responsible for economic growth and development. They dealt mainly with microeconomic theory and were mainly concerned with the study of a static equilibrium system, stressing the problems related to the allocation of given resources among alternative uses. The major difference between classical and neoclassical economics lies primarily in the area of methodology and in the use of abstract model building.

The transition from classical to neoclassical economics expresses both continuity and change. On the one hand, neoclassical economists did not deviate from the fundamental idea that the free play of market forces would guarantee the full utilization of resources without the need for government interference. All of them tended to recognize that equilibrium at full employment was the normal state of the economy, given price and wage flexibility. Aggregate equilibrium was synonymous with full employment.[1]

On the other hand, they developed a new tool of analysis—marginalism—which they used to explain the price mechanism. According to them, demand plays the primary role and not supply in the determination of value as the classicals up to John Stuart Mill had alleged. They replaced the objective theory of value by a subjective one.

However, it is fair to say that the acceptance of the concept of marginal analysis and its application to the theory of demand developed gradually during the middle and late nineteenth century. It had already been presented in a more rudimentary form by Herman H. Gossen but his writings were neglected until they were rediscovered by the British economist Stanley Jevons.[2] It was only Alfred Marshall who, a few years later, stated in no unclear terms that prices are determined by both supply and demand. By stressing the dual determination of prices, he, de facto, invalidated the classical labor theory of value.[3]

As Professors Screpanti and Zamagni assert, "The most important theoretical contribution of Jevons, Menger, and Walras lies, still more than in their complete and coherent reformulation of the utility theory of value and in the hypothesis of decreasing marginal utility, in the way they modified the utilitarian foundation of political economy. Their marginalism gave credit to a special version of utilitarian philosophy, one for which human behaviour is exclusively reduced to rational calculation aimed at the maximum utility."[4]

Utilitarianism became the cornerstone of the neoclassical approach to economics. According to this philosophy, the agent of economic activity is reduced to the individual. The economic man reigns supreme in the market and is guided in his decision-making process by the goal of maximizing his utility or profits. In our contemporary society the same utilitarian principle applies to the various groups and associations that are trying to maximize their own self interests. Collective or social goals cease to play a significant role in the neoclassical system. The common good of society will result automatically from the free play of individual or group interests, following their own self interests and operating within a free market system.

An important point that needs to be restressed is the neoclassical's belief in the universal validity of economic laws. They like, the classical economists, assumed that economic laws were similar to the laws in the physical sciences and, thus, had the same absolute and objective characteristics. But, as Screpanti and Zamagni claim, "for this to make sense, it is necessary to remove social relations from the field of economics, exorcising them as a superstition, a waste of time, a subject not in line with the new acquisitions of the science of the period."[5] This simply means that, in accordance with neoclassical thinking, economics is limited in its research to technical relationships. Ethics, at least as it was traditionally understood before the age of the Enlightenment, had become, for all practical purposes, superfluous.

## THE KEYNESIAN REVOLUTION

It would be wrong to assume that the Keynesian Revolution had no antecedents or that it constituted a total departure from the accepted classical theory. Sismondi was among the early critics of capitalism. He rejected the automatic functioning of the liberal economic system, demanding a greater role for government in the belief that the free play of market forces alone were insufficient to bring about the full employment of resources.[6]

Nonsocialist critics of laissez-faire capitalism can already be found in the writings of Malthus in the early nineteenth century. He discovered weaknesses and contradictions in the system and presented some remedies which years later were picked up by Keynes.[7] The Keynesian innovations were mainly a refinement or extension of a system of thought which had already been established by the Classical School.[8] The principal divergence consisted in the fact that the majority of the classical and neoclassical economists tended to share the same basic belief in a self-regulating automatic system, a belief that Keynes and his followers rejected. In spite of their methodological differences, both classical and neoclassical economists accepted Ricardo's view that there is an underlying assumption that the economy functions at full capacity and that any disturbance to employment must be transitory.

Keynes revolutionized classical economics by claiming that production does not depend on supply. Rather, he argued, production is a function of "effective demand." This "new" concept delivered a strong blow to the optimism of the English Classical School and its belief in an automatic self regulating economic system. He challenged this assumption and claimed that the normal situation under laissez-faire capitalism is a fluctuating state of economic activity which may range from full employment to widespread unemployment. It is a theory of shifting equilibrium rather than the stationary envisaged by the classicals.

On many occasion, Keynes attacked the basic postulates of the classical school. For him, these postulates were applicable only in special cases. For example he stated categorically the following: "I shall argue that the postulates of the classical theory are applicable to a special case only and not to the general case. . . . Moreover, the characteristics of the special case assumed by the classical theory happen not to be those of the economic society in which we actually live, with the result that its teaching is misleading and disastrous if we attempt to apply it to the facts of experience."[9] Obviously, it must be remembered that when Keynes wrote these words, the industrial nations were in the midst of a depression.

Keynes argued forcefully in defense of the role of government in the economy as an antidote to liberalism's blind faith in the ability of the system's natural tendencies to restore full employment of resources in an automatic manner. He maintained, as was the case during the depression of the thirties, that a capitalist economy could remain in a high level of unemployment unless some force exogenous to the system were used to lessen it. Demand, insisted Keynes, does not necessarily absorb the existing supply. Say's Law does not always work as the Classical School had assumed. The required flexibility of prices, wages and interest rates may not occur and, as a result, the economy can remain for a long period of time in a state of unemployment equilibrium. Government expenditure must be the exogenous force that brings back the economy to the full employment level. The private sector alone cannot do it. The serious flaws in the inner mechanism of the English Classical School could not be solved automatically by the laws of supply and demand.[10]

Even though people may disagree with Keynes' approach to economics and his criticism of the English Classical School, no one can deny that his contribution to economics was impressive.[11] He was one of the most influential economic thinkers of the twentieth century and his ideas have greatly influenced the ideological and political trends particularly, in Western Europe and the United States. The followers of Keynes have expanded and developed his theory, setting the trend for policies which have a heavy welfare content. The defenders of the "Welfare State" must be greatly indebted to the interventionist ideas of Keynes.

However, a word of caution is needed when some of his critics accuse Keynes of being a socialist. In his later years he began to be concerned about the negative impact his ideas might have on the younger generation of economists. Thus, he gave a word of warning to the younger "revolutionaries" who were willing to throw away the entire classical tradition. In an article published after his death in 1946 he said, "I find myself moved, not for the first time, to remind contemporary economists that the classical teaching embodied some permanent truths of great significance, which we are liable to-day to overlook because we associate them with other doctrines which we cannot now accept without much qualification. . . . It shows how much modernist stuff, gone wrong and turned sour and silly, is circulating in our system."[12]

What is undeniable is that Keynes opened a breach in the classical system and left the doors wide opened for the interventionists to take a firm hold and lead the way toward the establishment of the so-called Welfare State. He was a source of inspiration for policy makers and his ideas were felt around the globe but not always with positive results, especially in the countries in the process of development. More than once his policy of government expenditures gave way to runaway inflation with disastrous consequences for the economy.

## COMPETITION RECONSIDERED

Two major works which grew out of Marshallian economics but who were also critical of some of the British economist's traditional classical assumptions were *The Economics of Imperfect Competition* by Joan Robinson[13] and *The Theory of Monopolistic Competition* by Edward H. Chamberlin.[14] Contrary to classical economic theory, both of these authors challenged the assumption of a perfectly competitive economy.[15] They emphasized the importance of "market imperfections" and the "monopoly power" of the individual firms and industries.[16] For them, firms, through their actions, can affect significantly market conditions and influence the supply and price of a given product. Each single firm no longer has to consider the price as a datum over which it has no control. Chamberlin, for example, asserted that most firms practiced both price and nonprice competition. According to him, the competitive element in monopolistic competition permitted each firm to have a particular product or advantage that gave it some control over the price. Through advertising and packaging, a firm can easily differentiate its product from that of his rivals and, thus, charge a higher price than the normal competitive one.

Chamberlin was concerned with dynamic market phenomena such as product differentiation and advertising.[17] He attempted to develop a theory of competition where product quality, information, and other elements played an important role in appraising market performance. He no longer identified competition with large number of competitors but rather in terms of the "competitive rivalry" that characterizes the modern firm.[18.]

Under conditions of monopolistic or imperfect competition, advertising can be a very successful way of manipulating the desires of the consumer so that he will acquire a given product. Modern businessmen use advertising to "differentiate" their products from those of their competitors with the aim of increasing their sales. They use all sorts of means in order to convince the consumer of the superiority of their product. Whether advertising within a monopolistic-competitive free enterprise system is ethical or not will depend on the type of advertising used by the firm or industry. Obviously, the use of fraudulent, deceptive or misleading types of advertising cannot be accepted on ethical grounds. Concerning the effects of advertising on the efficiency of production there are differences of opinion but Taylor is right when he says that "the purely economic case against advertising, or charge that it is economically unproductive or wasteful, remains unproved; its results in this regard are so mixed or complex that the full net sum of them all cannot be known."[19]

The important question that arises in relation to Keynes' theory of "effective demand" and the theory of "monopolistic competition" is whether they have contributed to the gradual loss of faith in the classical competitive markets as exemplified by the English Classical School. Have their theories contributed to the demise of economic liberalism and the need for a greater level of government regulation in business matters? Taylor correctly poses the following crucial question: "How far, if at all, do these new discoveries logically oblige the modern political economist to move away from adherence to the old economic liberalism into advocacy of new public controls, in the place of reliance on market competition, to promote the public interest?"[20]

We shall not analyze in greater detail Chamberlin's theory of "monopolistic competition" nor Keynes' economic theory of "effective demand" and the adjustments that he proposed to capitalism, a capitalism that he admired and merely wanted to "fine tune" so that it could function more effectively. We shall rather deal with a more subtle assault that very often comes from those sectors of society that are supposed to be the most firm defenders of economic freedom. I am referring to those businessmen and executives of large corporations who, claiming to be firm defenders of the free enterprise system, nevertheless ask for government intervention when their interests are affected.

## OTHER VOICES OF DISSENT

It is ironic that the demand for government regulation in the economy should come not only from socialists sources of the left or by the more radical neo-Keynesians but by powerful individual or group interests within the capitalist camp who feel that their profits are threatened by the free play of market forces. They often place their own self-interests above the common good of society and, what is even more surprising, above the basic postulates of capitalism and the free market system on which they thrive. Many an industrial group in its search for profits is more than willing to ask for government protection or subsidies when its interests are at stake or, if necessary, petition the authorities to interfere directly with the free operation of the market system in order to foster their own objectives.

It is quite evident that the business community has not always agreed or followed the basic premises of classical liberalism. Quite correctly, businessmen and corporations have not hesitated to demand freedom to carry out their economic activities but when their interests are at stake they have not wavered to reject what they consider an encroachment on their private field of operations. Although in general they tend to support the economic liberalism of the English Classical School, very often they dismiss as irrelevant some of its basic premises if they run counter to their own private self interest. It is not uncommon for businessmen, in spite of their calls for nongovernment interference, to be the first to support and even demand from the government assistance in order to foster their commercial interests.

It is a well-known historical fact that public policies geared toward the establishment of free competitive markets have not always been endorsed by the business community. Particularly in the area of free competition the business community's understanding of economic liberalism has digressed frequently from the traditional way of thinking of the liberal political economists. As Taylor mentions with reference to the attitude of the business community in the post mercantilist era: "In short, they [businessmen] really wanted the state to be active in all the ways seen as helpful to their own business interest; and *laissez faire* to them meant only a ban against all the kinds of reform legislation or state intervention that were beginning to be demanded by spokesmen for labor, social service workers and reformers, discontented agrarian groups, etc."[21]

The extensive list of requests for the government to intervene in the free play of market forces by precisely those individuals and groups that are benefiting the most from economic freedom is no secret. When things get tough and profits are endangered, these powerful individual or group interests are the first to ask for government assistance in order to bail them out of their predicament. For them, the state should interfere only when their own business interests are at stake. This applies just as much to the area of foreign trade as to any other part of the economy.

However, in other cases, the business community wants the government to stay out of their field of operations. It claims that the government has no role to play in the economic system and should not get involved in the free play of market forces. This is very often the case when large businesses want to maintain certain types of monopolistic practices that tend to place obstacles in the way of their competitors. Government regulations are not welcomed.

The case of advertising is an interesting one because it shows clearly how very often businesses claim their right to use whatever type of promotion that will foster their own sales and increase their profits. As long as the consumer accepts it there is no need for the public authorities to intervene. The acceptance of such a conclusion would imply that the responsibility would fall entirely on the consumer. Can or should the government impose restrictions on certain types of advertisements in order to foster the common good? Is it justified to intervene and even suppress the business practice of misleading the public through advertisements and other debatable methods with the sole objective of increasing sales, even though often they violate the most elementary conventional moral standards? Can intervention be justified also when there takes place a crass violation of the most elemental ethical principles; principles which have traditionally characterized our Western culture?

Business practices such as these only give ground for increased attacks on the free market system by its critics and for more regulatory measures on the part of the authorities. The reaction against such abuses is unavoidable in a free society, a reaction which results from a public that feels betrayed by a system on which it has placed its trust and has not met its high expectations.

The great error of liberalism was to believe that the free market system would, by its own inner mechanisms, create the necessary "moral" conditions that would permit the system to operate efficiently for the benefit of all. Such blind faith in the automaticity of the market to operate freely without restrains of any type turned out to be unrealistic, as history has amply demonstrated. To assume that the stimuli of self-interest and competition were sufficient to bring about peace and harmony to society implied a total ignorance of human nature. On the contrary, it is a well-known fact that a morally unrestrained competition can undermine and eventually destroy the most rudimentary principles of morality unless sufficient moral reserves are in existence that can counteract its negative effects. Morality cannot be learned by simply having a competitive spirit and/or practicing the "virtue" of self-interest. Competition is not a source of moral principles. These have to come from exogenous sources; they are not endogenous to the system. The belief in an uninhibited individualism, fruit of an exaggerated rationalism, has become the Trojan horse of a true liberal economy based on free responsible agents.

Economic liberalism as the legitimate son of rationalism tried to found economics on the isolated individual as if the various social groupings, including the family, did not play a significant role in society. As a result, the individual became isolated from society, self-centered and so engrossed in his own self-interest that he played little or no attention to society as a whole. Lacking moral restraints of any kind, except the laws of the market, there was no limit to his ambitions and material desires. It is quite evident that such egotistic attitudes were not propitious for the development of a harmonious and orderly society. The events in recent history have demonstrated the error of believing that the market economy, regulated by competition, represents a cosmos in equilibrium, a natural order that for its proper functioning only needs to be defended from external threats. To abandon ethics and to rely exclusively on market forces can only lead to increasing restrictions on personal freedom and further cries for government intervention.

Credit must be given to those critics of economic liberalism for their awareness that a totally self-regulating economic system, free from all government interference and guided exclusively by self-interest and the laws of supply and demand is not necessarily conducive to the common good of society. The German Historical School did not have a significant influence on economic thought outside Germany but some of its basic criticisms of economic liberalism cannot be discarded lightly. They constituted a powerful salvo aimed at the eighteenth century liberal's unquestionable belief in an automatic functioning economic system of natural harmonies that has universal applicability both in time and space. The German Historical School fully realized that a totally unregulated laissez-faire economic system, guided exclusively by individual self-interest is not conducive to the well-being of society. Economic laws cannot be equated with natural laws. It would be foolish to believe that an economic system based on such assumptions would have universal validity, especially when applied in different cultural and economic backgrounds.

Unfortunately some of the postulates of the German Historical School lent themselves to all sorts of abuses that eventually led to the centralization of economic policies and threatened the very essence of personal freedom. The subordination of personal liberties to the collectivist policies of a centralized state is the first step toward totalitarianism, examples of which abound in history.

The principles of socialism represented also a reaction against the basic assumptions of capitalism but, in most cases, of a much more violent nature. The socialist ideal constituted a popular platform against the abuses of early capitalism even though from the economic point of view its economic theory had little to offer. Marx's economic theory, as presented in *Das Kapital*, the bible of Marxism-Leninism, has been totally discredited and remains only as a nonworkable relic . The same can be said of his theory of surplus value the importance of which is limited to its historical merit.

However, the same cannot be said of Marx's philosophical "humanistic" concept of man. His interpretation of history, his dialectical materialism, and his belief in an ideal equalitarian society free of antinomies may still have an appeal to the downtrodden and dissatisfied sectors of society but reality has proven them to be totally false. The irony is that, in spite of its flagrant fallacies, there are still those who believe in some type of communist ideal even though it make take a different form and carry a different designation.

Keynes's *General Theory* was published at a time when people were disappointed with orthodox economic theory. As the world depression worsened and unemployment reached unbearable proportions, criticism of capitalism mounted. The ground was fertile for the development of new ideas and Keynes was ready to provide a remedy for the public's frustration over the prevailing economic policies.

Schumpeter, in his book *Ten Great Economists*, commenting on the role of savings in Keynes's *General Theory*, claims that "here, at last, was a doctrine that may not actually say but can easily be made to say both that 'who tries to save destroys real capital' and that *via* saving, 'the unequal distribution of income is the ultimate cause of unemployment. *This* is what the Keynesian Revolution amounts to."[22] One of his last comments on Keynes that appears in that same book is the following: "As with Marx, it is possible to admire Keynes even though one may consider his social vision to be wrong and every one of his propositions to be misleading."[23]

The modern theory of competition, as the one introduced by Chamberlin, is mainly a revision of traditional orthodox theory. However, to a certain extent it helped undermine the belief in the "natural" functioning of the economy. Private businesses, operating within a competitive market, do not necessarily harmonize their interests with the common good of society. The automatic functioning of a laissez-faire economic system does not always serve the public interest as the classical economists had assumed. The very fact that some of the flaws of the liberal economic system were presented with such clarity by the advocates of the new theory of "monopolistic competition," tended "to suggest that there may be needs for some new departure from *laissez faire* i.e., reforms and public control policies of some kind or kinds to cause the economy and all the unit-actors in it to serve the public better than it is being served in consequence, merely, of the existing forms of competition."[24]

The criticisms labeled against economic liberalism tends to indicate that there is a decreasing trust in the automaticity of the system to work in a harmonious manner for the benefit of all sectors of society. In most cases, the belief in "natural harmonies" is no longer being accepted by friends and foes of liberalism. Governments, it is often said, have to play an increasing role in economic affairs. But how far can it be said that government intervention is legitimate and serves the public good without violating individual freedoms?

Policies of government intervention leading to the Welfare State have often had negative results as the experience of many countries amply demonstrate. Nevertheless there are still those who maintain that individual decision making, the cornerstone of liberalism, must be replaced by collective action, which is the equivalent of socialism. A proper balance between individual freedom and the role of the state is necessary if the wellbeing of society is to be attained.

In the following chapter we will deal with some of these problems and how, if the liberal economic system or any other social or political organization is to survive, man's dignity as a human person must be respected. For capitalism to remain efficient and productive both its human and technical aspects must be taken into account but first it is essential that man acquire a full understanding of his metaphysical dimension.

## NOTES

1. Some of the more prominent economists of the neoclassical school in England were Alfred Marshall (1842–1924), Francis Edgeworth (1845–1926), and Arthur Pigou (1877–1959). In Austria the following can be mentioned: Karl Menger (1840–1921), Friedrich von Wieser (1851–1926), and Eugen von Bohm-Bawerk (1851–1914). Among others, the names of Stanley Jevons (1835–1882) in

England and Marie-Esprit Leon Walras (1834–1910) in France can also be added. Vilfredo Pareto (1848–1923) of Italy is an interesting case because, although he maintained the strict and pure concept of economics, his interests turned increasingly to general social problems. It was alleged by some of his critics that during the later years of his life he became an intellectual supporter of Fascism. However, he never embraced Fascism nor did he identify himself with any other "ism."

2. Herman Heinrich Gossen (1810–1858) was a German economist and a forerunner of neoclassical theory. He developed the principle of diminishing marginal utility and believed that the goal of economics was to obtain the greatest amount of pleasure. From the philosophical point of view Gossen can be classified as an utilitarian. J. H. von Thunen (1783–1850) is another German economist who has been given credit for anticipating such concepts as diminishing returns and the marginal productivity theory of wages. However, his most famous book was *Der Isolierte Staat* in which he developed an economic theory of location based on the notion of opportunity cost.

3. Alfred Marshall (1842–1924). He was a brilliant English economist whose main contribution to economics lies primarily in his method of partial equilibrium analysis. He was mainly interested in the theory of the firm and industry.

4. Screpanti and Zamagni, *An Outline of the History of Economic Thought*, 148.

5. Screpanti and Zamagni, *An Outline of the History of Economic Thought*, 149.

6. J. C. L. Sismonde (1773–1842), better known as Sismondi, was a Swiss social reformer who in his later years rejected Say's Law asserting that both Smith and Ricardo had overestimated the benefits of laissez-faire economics. He repudiated the harmony of classical liberalism and was convinced that society was become more polarized as a result of industrialization. As the poorer sectors of society were not receiving the benefits from capitalism, the end result would be an increase in class conflict. In certain ways he was a predecessor of Marx.

7. See John Maynard Keynes, *The General Theory*, 32, 362–64. See also John Maynard Keynes, *Essays in Biography* (New York: Harcourt, Brace, 1933), 122–49.

8. The distinguished British economist Lionel Robbins claimed that "the Keynesian innovations were not without antecedents, and although the extent of the divergence of their conclusions from the then accepted theory was capable of considerable exaggeration, their impact on thought was not of this nature. I personally think that, in the verdict of history, their ultimate influence will be found to reside much more in the realm of the theory of policy than in pure economic analysis. But even in this latter sphere the influence has been conspicuous." See Lord Robbins, *The Evolution of Modern Economic Theory* (Chicago: Aldine Publishing Company, 1970), 37.

9. Keynes, *The General Theory*, 3.

10. As mentioned earlier, Keynes challenges Say's and Ricardo's assumptions that supply creates its own demand. In other words, there may be times when the aggregate demand price is not equal to the aggregate supply price for all levels of output and employment. Equilibrium at full employment level does not have to occur necessarily. See Keynes, *The General Theory*, 18–22.

11. Schumpeter has this to say about Keynes with reference to his *General Theory*: "As a prominent American economist put it in a letter to me: 'It [the

*General Theory*] did, and does, have something which supplements what our thinking and methods of analysis would otherwise have been. It does not make us Keynesians, it makes us better economists.' Whether we agree or not, this expresses the essential point about Keyne's achievement extremely well. In particular, it explains why hostile criticism, even if successful in its attack upon individual assumptions or propositions, is yet powerless to inflict fatal injury upon the structure as a whole. As with Marx, it is possible to admire Keynes even though one may consider his social vision to be wrong and every one of his propositions to be misleading." See Joseph A. Schumpeter, *The Great Economists* (London: George Allen & Unwin, 1951), 291.

12. "The Balance of Payments of the United States," *The Economic Journal* 56, no. 222 (June 1946), 185–86.

13. Joan Robinson, *The Economics of Imperfect Competition* (London: Macmillan, 1954).

14. Edward H. Chamberlin, *The Theory of Monopolistic Competition* (Cambridge, MA: Harvard University Press, 1950).

15. Marshall was perfectly aware that in the midst of the two extremes of perfect competition and perfect monopoly, there existed a middle ground between the two but, with few exceptions, he did not analyze output equilibrium of firms operating under conditions of imperfect competition.

16. Chamberlin and Robinson were not the first to analyze an imperfect market. Years before, the economists Cournot and Edgeworth had already analyzed the behavior of a duopoly, how their profit maximizing behavior depended on each believing that the other's output would remain the same. Antoine Augustin Cournot (1801–1877) was a French social philosopher and economist who used marginal theory to develop a fairly thorough analysis of the firm, including the case of duopoly. The Englishman Francis Y. Edgeworth (1845–1926) refined Cournot's theory of duopoly.

17. In spite of Chamberlin's dynamic market concerns, his analysis can be classified as static because he was mainly interested in the process of adjustment towards equilibrium under given conditions in the economy.

18. Chamberlin was a pioneer in the development of industrial organization. His assertions about quality variability and advertising greatly influenced the Chicago tradition in industrial organization. The University of Chicago, led by the late Professor Frank Knight and later by George Stigler and others, made a great contribution to the new and expanded notions of competition.

19. Overton H. Taylor, *A History of Economic Thought* (McGraw-Hill, 1960), 463–64.

20. Taylor, *A History of Economic Thought*, 466.

21. Taylor, *A History of Economic Thought*, 320.

22. Schumpeter, *Ten Great Economists*, 290.

23. Schumpeter, *Ten Great Economists*, 291.

24. Taylor, *A History of Economic Thought*, 447.

# 6

—⚋—

# The Metaphysical
# Dimensions of Man:
# Their Ethical Implications

## THE TWO DIMENSIONS OF MAN:
## THE INDIVIDUAL AND THE SOCIAL

In the previous chapters we discussed briefly the basic postulates of philosophical liberalism and two of its main branches: individualism and collectivism. With respect to economic liberalism we emphasized its belief in the automatic regulation of the market without government interference and its reliance on individual initiative for the attainment of the common good of society. Competition and self-interest were sufficient regulators for the proper functioning of an economic system of natural harmonies and "mutual sympathies." At most there was a need for a "natural" ethics which implied that if there prevailed in a country the correct liberal institutions and public policies, the self-interest of each individual would somehow bring about decisions and actions which would lead towards the greater wealth of the nation to the benefit of all. In other words, the "natural" moral law of equal freedom and justice for all would automatically secure the welfare of every member of society. At least, there was an implicit rejection of the traditional concept of Natural Law.

Thus, the fundamental theory of Adam Smith and of the Classical School of economics was based on the natural identity of interests of each and every individual or as Elie Halevy states on "the spontaneous harmony of egoisms."[1] But this principle of the identity of interests, continues Halévy, "is not perhaps a principle which is true to the exclusion of all others, but it is a principle which can always be applied, in a general if not in a universal way, in the sphere of political economy."[2]

We also discussed the reactions to capitalism from the German Historical School and the socialist movement, in particular Marxism-Socialism.
They both had in common their rejection of the "spontaneous harmony of
interests" and placed the power of the State above individual interests.
For them, the interests of society were above those of the individual.

In spite of the importance of the German Historical School for a proper
understanding of the evolution of economic ideas, we do not consider it
necessary to dwell on it any longer. It was a phenomenon which affected
primarily the German nation and was, to a large degree, supported by the
German elites of the nineteenth century. It is rarely presented as a possible alternative in our present day and age, although one cannot totally
discard it in the future.

For many economists, the German Historical School and the various interpretations of socialism were not acceptable alternatives to the economic
liberalism of the English Classical School and its followers, the economists
of the distinguished Austrian School. They did not prove to be a viable alternative to the often quoted abuses of a liberal economic system as they
were described by the critics of the Industrial Revolution. On the contrary,
by fostering the creation of an all powerful State and negating the importance of the individual and private initiative they threatened the foundations of freedom itself.

The total failure of the socialist collectivist policies in the Soviet Union
brought out into public light the inefficiencies of the regime. It demonstrated that an economic system based on free individual actions which
limits the role of the State is much more efficient and serves better the interests of society. A free market that relies on the operation of the laws of
supply and demand is much more conducive to growth and development
than a regulated economy that is subject to the whims of a socialist State
bureaucracy.

Nevertheless, even after the fall of Soviet communism and the total discrediting of its centralized economic system, socialism is still presented as
an alternative to economic liberalism or what is generally understood as
capitalism. Leaving aside the proven economic inefficiencies of an unmitigated socialist system, the fundamental error of socialism lies in its denial
of human freedom and its lack of respect for the dignity of the human being. It considers man as a mere part or element of the social order. The
good of the individual, no longer being the autonomous subject of moral
decisions, is subordinated to the inner mechanism of the socioeconomic
order and, as a result, can no longer be considered a person. Man becomes
totally dependent on the arbitrary decisions of the State and of those who
control it.

Thus, in a pure unadulterated socialist system the social dimension of
man is not only stressed but so overpowers and exploits the very individu-

ality of man, that it makes him a caricature of a human person. All intermediate associations, lying between the individual and the State, are forced to forfeit their inalienable rights under the all encroaching power of the State; a power that it later uses in the name of "society" to destroy them. The so-called people's democracies are a prime example of this type of socialism.

On the other hand, economic liberalism is not exempt from some of these errors. There is little doubt that economic liberalism with its reliance on individual freedom made man the master of his own future. With its claim that the only singular and concrete being is the *homo oeconomicus* who, endowed with freedom, has the capacity to determine for himself what is best suited for his self interest, economic liberalism paid little attention, if at all, to man's social dimension. As the individual is sovereign in the administration of his private "economy," as long as he does not interfere with the correlative sovereignty of all other individuals, society is reduced to the sum of individuals operating individually in the market system.[3] The social dimension of man and his responsibility toward the common good is drowned in an ocean of autonomous individuals who accept a preestablished harmonious order under the assumption that it would bring about automatically the well-being of all members of society.

After so many abuses of centralized power, it seemed only logical that the men of the eighteenth century rejected the idea that the State was the only arbiter of what is best for the well-being of man. They relied on man's freedom in his search for happiness. The history of past totalitarianisms is sufficient proof that liberalism's stress on man's prerogative to determine his own destiny was more than justified. But, on the other hand, the emphasis placed on the individual did not justify its indifference and, at times, even scorn for the common good nor the subjection of the interests of the weak to the interests of the strong and powerful. The liberal State disqualified itself when, by omission, it often permitted power to be used by the rich to the detriment of the poor.

As mentioned in chapter 2, perhaps the greatest error of liberalism—and socialism alike—was to ignore the distinction between individual and person. Liberalism by reducing man to a strict individualism tended to forget that he is also a human person. Man must be considered not only as an individual but also as a person with social responsibilities. As an individual—*indivisum in se, divisum ab aliis*—man is undivided in himself, distinct from others, incommunicable, self-centered and autonomous. As a person—*rationalis naturae individua substantia*—he is an individual endowed with an intelligent nature, and through intelligence and love, communicable, sociable and self-transcending.[4]

The philosopher Joseph de Torres, following St. Thomas Aquinas, reminds us that "a man has two metaphysical dimensions; the individual and the social, *distinct but not separated*: one conditions the other."[5] Liberalism stresses the first dimension whilst socialism, on the other hand, emphasizes the second one by placing society above the individual or any other intermediate organization, such as the family, if it considers that it stands in the way of the State's preestablished goals.

The main error of liberalism lies in the emphasis it places on individuality (egotism) to the detriment of personality (self-transcending love of what is good). This can easily lead to depersonalization and a process of "massification" or "standardization" and to outright materialism, given the fact that individuality is rooted in matter.[6] Under socialism, on the other hand, man loses his individuality and consequently is forced to forfeit his personality. Man's social dimension is stressed to such a degree that man has no room to develop his own personality. Once man's personality is destroyed, the roots of which are in the spirit, he is no longer free and master of his own destiny. Liberty simply becomes a word with no real meaning.

Both types of societies, unrestrained liberalism and socialism, pose a threat to the dignity of the human person. For a proper order in society man needs to keep a correct balance between an autonomous individual and the coercive power of authority. The greater the level of responsible personal freedom, the less the need for the coercive power of authority. To ignore such a balance between freedom and coercion can have devastating effects on the autonomy of the various intermediate organizations which constitute the chore of a healthy society.

In a strict individualistic economic system, intermediate organizations such as the family tend to lose their significance and run the danger of no longer being considered indispensable for the welfare of society. Priority is given to the individual even at the expense of destroying the family unit. Attacks against the family as an institution become more frequent and questions such as abortion and other issues that have moral implications are left exclusively to individual choice with little regard—if any— toward the well-being of society as a whole.

Under Marxist socialism the family, like all other intermediary associations, is de facto absorbed by a State that repudiates any institution which can challenge its total control. Man loses his individuality and becomes part of an anonymous mass that follows the dictates of the state. The family is a reflex of economic structures and is subject to the same laws of evolution. According to Hegel, the initial state of history was characterized by the communal family and it was only with private property that monogamy came into existence. But, continues Hegel, this bourgeois family leads to the *alienation* of women and to their subordination to men's domination. It reduces marriage to a question of money and converts the woman into the first servant of the household whilst man is the sole contributor to the social product.[7] It is only when women become ordinary workers on an equal footing with all other citizens, as communism promotes, that all the contradictions of the past will be solved. By making them producers like men, they will be "liberated" from the inferior position they had under capitalism. Thus, women's "liberation" would have as a first condition *the participation of the entire feminine sex in public industry* and this condition demands the suppression of the individual family as an economic unit of society.[8] Once all women participate in the labor force, the private domestic economy is transformed into social industry and the care and education that must be provided to children becomes a public obligation. Society will take care of all children whether legitimate or not. As a result, women are "liberated" from submission to men and matrimony as an institution will no longer be needed. "Love" will become the only determinant factor in any union between man and woman. Free love will be the best expression of freedom, equality and fraternity in the new communist society.[9]

The ultimate phase of communism presumes the same conclusion with respect to the State, the economy or the family: the complete rejection of past customs and traditions. It basically follows Rousseau's concept that evil is not found in man but in the structure of society. As the predecessor of modern socialism, the author of the *Contrat Sociale*, propagated the idea that once the structure of society is changed, man will change also.

Ironically both liberalism and socialism stem from the same philosophical background, a philosophy which lost touch with reality. Truth is no longer the adjustment of man to reality. As de Torre mentions, it is something purely subjective, whatever each man feels in his own ego. This, he asserts "leads to either the 'rat race' of liberalism or the 'class struggle' of Marxism: callous egoism on an individual scale or active hatred on a collective scale."[10]

It was a gross error for man, the agent of political and economic activities, to brush aside as obsolete the principles of general ethics based on Natural Law or a moral philosophy that deals with man's final destiny which is God, the creator of all beings.[11] Even though all created things have man as their end, they are ordained, through him, toward God who is the transcendent common good of the entire universe.[12] Friedrich von Hayek, one of the major representatives of contemporary liberalism, seems to reject in his last work, *The Fatal Conceit: The Errors of Socialism*, the reality of an objective moral order.[13] He sustains the evolutionary character of ethical norms, a theory that runs counter to the traditional concept of moral philosophy.

## HAYEK'S ETHICAL APPROACH
## TO ECONOMIC LIBERALISM

Since the time of Adam Smith, liberalism has often made efforts to find a moral justification for its economic principles. Leaving aside past attempts to do so, it is perhaps the Austrian economist Friedrich von Hayek who has tried to construct a theory of justice and ethics in accordance with the economic principles that he has so ardently sustained.

Hayek can rightly be considered one of the greatest economists of our modern era and deserves to be recognized as a standard bearer in the defense of economic and political freedoms: freedoms unabashedly threatened by a wave of collectivist policies which the Austrian-born economist so ardently opposed.

As is well known, economic liberalism, in the classical sense, is based on individual freedom and the all important premise that the role of government should be reduced to a minimum. Efficiency is better served through the free actions of individuals in the market place. An economic order that relies on the operation of the laws of supply and demand in a free market is more conducive to growth and development than a regulated economy that is subject to the whims of a State bureaucracy.

*The Fatal Conceit* constitutes the crowning effort of his extraordinary career. In it he shows once again how "one of the most influential political movements of our time, socialism, is based on demonstrable false premises, and despite being inspired by good intentions and led by some of the most intelligent representatives of our time, endangers the standard of living and the life of a larger part of existing population."[14] The total failure of the Soviet socialist experiment has demonstrated the correctness of Hayek's arguments concerning the ineffectiveness and gross inefficiencies of socialism.

But, the errors of socialism are not limited to the former Soviet Union and its satellites in Eastern Europe. In spite of the total debacle of Marxism-Socialism, socialist principles and collectivist policies still threaten the well-being of Western societies. In many instances, well intentioned people are led to believe that the government, as a deus ex machina, will solve the "economic problem" and will bring about an era of sustained economic growth and prosperity. The utopian ideal that an equalitarian society can be constructed under the aegis of a so called Welfare State is still very much alive even though the merit of economic policies based on liberal principles seem to have been generally recognized by many academicians and politicians. The path leading toward the *Road to Serfdom* has been reversed, thanks, in no small way, to Hayek's valiant stand in defense of economic freedom.[15]

Although an eminent economist, many of Hayek's works (*The Road to Serfdom, Essays on Liberty*, etc.) dealt with philosophical, historical and political problems just to mention a few of the many topics he so brilliantly discussed. He placed his profound knowledge of the methodology of the sciences, the history of ideas, and so forth, and his great interest in justice and ethics at the service of economic liberalism. He strived to give a philosophical foundation to economic theory.

Hayek can only be praised for his successful defense of the free market system against the corroding influence of a too-powerful State which totally disregards the principle of subsidiarity. He put into relief the arrogance of the constructivist solution preached by the collectivists; a solution which only led to a loss of freedom and a sharp decline in economic development.

Hayek's *The Fatal Conceit*, reflects even more than the *Constitution of Liberty* and *Law, Legislation and Liberty* his thought provoking works an attempt to find an ethical foundation to economic liberalism. However, his main theory gives ground for concern. Following David Hume, he makes the following statement concerning morality: "The starting point for my endeavour might well be David Hume's insight that 'the rules of morality' are not conclusions of our reason' (*Treatise*, 1739/1886:II:235). This insight will play a central role in this volume since it frames the basic question it tries to answer—which is *how does our morality emerge, and what implications may its mode of coming into being have for our economic and political life?*"[16]

In his aversion to contractivism, Hayek rejects as a source of morality the constructivist contention that an adequate morality can be designed by instrumental reason. He considers also unsatisfactory the innate morality of our instincts (solidarity, altruism, group decision, and such like), the practices flowing from which, he claims, "are not sufficient to sustain our present extended order and its population."[17] For Hayek, the origin of the moral norms necessary for the extended society is "the evolved morality (savings, several property, honesty, and so on) that created and sustains the extended order." "Morality," continues Hayek, "stands *between* instinct and reason, a position that has been obscured by the false dichotomy of instinct versus reason." The extended order depends on this morality "in the sense that it came into being through the fact that those groups following its underlying rules increased in numbers and in wealth relative to other groups."[18]

In brief, Hayek believes that what characterizes man is not the power to reason but the incidence of the cultural restrictions on innate responses. Indeed, he admits that the basic point of his argument—that morals, including, especially, our institutions of property, freedom and justice, are not a creation of man's reason but a distinct endowment conferred on him by cultural evolution—runs counter to the main intellectual outlook of the twentieth century."[19] In fact, it runs counter to the Aristotelian concept of ethics.

Hayek, correctly, maintains that human reason is incapable of fully understanding the complexity of the extended social order. Thus, it is not only preposterous but arrogant for man to try to construct a better and more efficient extensive social order through central planning or other centralized devices than through the knowledge acquired from the free inter play of market forces. But, the fact that human reason cannot "invent" or create the extensive social order does not mean that reason in abstract or that each man in particular cannot look for and find the spontaneous order and once found look for ways to improve it. Given the imperfections of human nature, there is always the possibility of improvement, but it will not be through government intervention in the productive process that these improvements will take place. Rather, the changes should take place through reforms in the institutional structures of society, primarily ethical and cultural.[20]

Hayek's criticism of reason as the essential and distinctive faculty of man can lead to unacceptable consequences. But, in my opinion, what is even worse is that his criticism is totally unnecessary in order to justify the benefits of a spontaneous free economic order. De facto, Hayek seems to deny free will and tends to fall into some type of determinism or what he calls "social evolutionism." The rules of conduct are subjected to a selective evolutionary process in which only the more efficient endure. Furthermore, the fact that Hayek repeatedly denies that justice should be sought does not impede him from referring to the ideal of a better society. For him justice is not related directly to man but rather to the system of with he forms part. This seems to contradict not only the fundamental principle of individualism but also the fact that, in spite of his criticism of constructivism, he himself is a theoretician of politics and politics is by necessity constructivist.

To give a solid foundation to the free spontaneous economic order, there was no need to deny reason or man's freedom to improve institutions and foster greater social justice. The free enterprise system and the spontaneity of the market forces does not need an evolutionist foundation to prove its superior efficiency over socialism. It is sufficient for it to be based on a philosophy that maintains that man, through the power of reason, can choose freely between different alternatives. The technical dimension of the free enterprise system can stand by itself. There is no better judge of its performance than its economic successes. It is in its human dimension where it has sometimes failed.

Hayek's contribution to economic thought will be difficult to surpass. At a time when Keynesian economics was in vogue, Hayek always had the courage to defend economic freedom and the basic principles of a spontaneous economic order in the face of a rising tide of collectivist policies. One cannot help but express admiration for a man who, at all times, was committed to the principles of freedom in a world plagued by equivocal socialist ideologies.

The above comments are in no way meant to reduce von Hayek's brilliant contribution to economic thinking. On the contrary, he will always be remembered as one of the greatest economists of our time. But, being a person who adheres to teleological morality and is both rational and a firm defender of freedom, there seems to be a lack of consistency in the moral system that Hayek proposes and the "social evolutionism" that he endorses in *The Fatal Conceit*. As Professor Argandona of the Business School of the University of Navarra (IESE) writes, "We must redeem Hayek's rich contribution, emptying it of its evolutionist adherences, which it does not need."[21] But, we repeat, Hayek's greatness is not in the least diminished by his attempts to give an evolutionist foundation, which we find unnecessary, to a spontaneous extended economic order.

## A REAPPRAISAL OF CAPITALISM AT THE TWILIGHT OF SOCIALISM

It would be an error to believe that the demise of Marxism-Leninism in the former Soviet Union and its satellite nations guarantees the success of economic liberalism in the Western World and in the countries in the process of development. Residues of collectivism together with the tensions resulting from unrestrained economic freedom have demonstrated that the market economy, if it is to succeed, must be based on responsible freedom and a solid ethical foundation. Otherwise, it is destined to failure and the specter of collectivism in any of its many forms will rise again and destroy the freedom that has been won at so heavy a price.

Hayek and his libertarian followers are absolutely correct in asserting the total practical failure of socialism. The arrogance of its entrenched bureaucracy has demonstrated better than anything else the need to restore free and spontaneous markets around the world. The importance of competition and the price mechanism as regulators of an economic system can hardly be denied. Individual self interest must be encouraged but that, in itself, is not enough. The eminent conservative German economist Wilhelm Roepke as early as the 1940s was already shocked by the process of dechristianization and secularization that was taking place in our culture. To the question, Is it enough to appeal to people's "enlightened self interest to make them realize that they serve their own best advantage by submitting to the discipline of the market and of competition?" his answer was decidedly in the negative.[22] At this point is where he draws the line between himself and the nineteenth century liberal utilitarianism and immanentism, whose traces, he believes are still with us. The market, competition and economic rationality, stresses Roepke, do not provide a sufficient answer to the question of the ethical foundations of our economic system. To reject the transcendental nature of an objective moral order can only lead to the destruction of a free economic system.

The error of the early theorists of the market was precisely to consider the market economy as a process which relies exclusively on itself and operates automatically. It ignored the fact that the market economy is only one part of man's social life. The early theorists forgot the economy's intimate relationship with other parts of man's social life where men and women are no longer competitors, producers, and investors. They are human beings who have other ideals which go beyond the realm of pure economics: ideas and sentiments of justice, honor, altruism, solidarity, beauty, and so forth. The principle of individuality, the core of the market economy, must be balanced by the principle of solidarity if the horrors of collectivism are to be avoided in the future.[23] Otherwise, the spontaneous economic order, which Hayek so brilliantly and efficaciously sustained, could easily run the danger of falling into anarchy, the first step toward a totalitarianism of either the left or the right.[24]

Few people would deny that the rights of the individual are no less mandatory than the rights of the community. But irresponsible individual freedom in its extreme form, license, is just as dangerous as an exaggeration of the rights of the community, collectivism. An unbriddled individualism is like a weed that, if left unchecked, will destroy the delicate seed of freedom. To defend freedom and the free market system from the dangers of collectivism, it is necessary to stress the need for institutional changes of an ethical nature. In the last instance, Roepke asserts, "the ultimate source of our civilization's disease is the spiritual and religious crisis which has overtaken all of us and which each must master for himself."[25]

As shown in chapter 3, Adam Smith in his famous works *The Theory of Moral Sentiments* and *The Wealth of Nations* tried to give an ethical explanation to his theory of economic liberalism. He fully realized that there was a contradiction between his concept of self-interest and the tendency of man to be greedy, as manifested in many a "successful" businessman, and a system that is supposed to lead automatically toward the welfare of society. He tried to reconcile these two concepts by introducing the notion of mutual sympathies and the idea of the invisible hand of God, a deus ex machina, that would bring about the desired results. Smith, an excellent Christian, was a Deist who did not believe in a providential God and left man to operate freely on his own without giving too much importance—if any—to objective moral principles, based on Natural Law, that ought to govern his actions. Being a firm believer in the natural goodness of man, he ignored his fallen nature. For all practical matters, the founder of the English Classical School assumed that man's exercise of individual freedom in economic matters was not a choice "as governed by principles but choice as prior to and determining our principles."[26] This choice was—and still is—often identified with the concept of liberty.

It can safely be said that the philosophical foundation of economic liberalism is quite different from the philosophical and theological principles of Aquinas. Quite another thing is to claim, as Schumpeter does, that many of the concepts that Smith uses such as competition, price determination, and so forth, were already analyzed by St. Thomas.[27] But, for example, Smith's concept of self-interest, in spite of his efforts to give it an ethical meaning, lacks the necessary ingredient if it is to be morally acceptable: self-restraint and the acceptance of a moral order which distinguishes right from wrong. This is not what normally can be interpreted from Smith's concept of self-interest. A simple belief in mutual sympathies is not enough, as history has amply demonstrated.

Nevertheless, let us not fall into the opposite error of rejecting capitalism as the source of all types of injustices and the only source of labor exploitation. In spite of its obvious deficiencies, an indiscriminate condemnation of capitalism is not justified. To set the record straight and leaving aside its philosophical foundations, a clear distinction must be made between the technical and human dimensions of capitalism. From the technical point of view, as has already been stressed, capitalism is far superior to socialism. For over two hundred years it has demonstrated its great efficiency and its productive capacity to satisfy the material needs of an ever increasing population whose needs have become more and more demanding as the years go by. Its basic economic principles of righteous self-interest, legitimate profit motivation, private property, honest competition, and so forth, have served the public extremely well. It is only the misuse of these principles that must be rejected. To capitalism's credit, it cannot be denied that it has fostered private initiative, personal savings, and the merits of work, something which socialism has been unable to do. But, at the same time, capitalism in its crude form has unmistakenly contributed to the materialistic and relativistic society that now prevails. The love of money, economic success, and an unrestrained self-interest have become the guiding principles of many a contemporary man to the detriment of his spiritual and cultural values. The efficient technological dimension of capitalism is not questioned. It fosters as no other system man's creativity and the utilization of natural resources with the minimum of waste. But in the very process of mechanization and technical development capitalism can pose serious social problems that need to be overcome.[28]

With the arrival of the new century man is beginning to realize that technology per se is not the harbinger of a new civilization free from want and the hazards of nature.[29] The Industrial Revolution, under the patronage of capitalism, placed the economic dimension at the very center of its explicit or implicit anthropology. Even John Stuart Mill, the author of the book *Principles of Political Economy* and one of the pillars of classical economic liberalism, had second thoughts about the practical consequences of liberalism's "ethical" foundations and the role of the State. Perhaps, as a result of the influence the French utopian socialists had on some of his writings.

His autobiography reflects the early attraction he felt toward the ideas of the French socialists and August Comte. However, Mill never ceased to be concerned about the excesses of the State or authoritarian intervention in the life of the individual. He remained faithful to the fundamental postulates of economic liberalism although his "final attitude was one of qualified advocacy of democracy and qualified acceptance of socialism as it was influenced by his study of de Tocqueville and the socialist program of the 1848 revolution."[30]

In spite of all the criticisms, it cannot be denied that capitalism's technological dimension together with the entrepreneur's intelligent use of practical experience were and continue to be extremely positive values. However, to believe that the free market can function efficiently and automatically with amoral economic agents selfishly looking for the greatest pleasure with a minimum of pain is an abstraction which runs counter to reality. Persons are affected by a particular ethos, a particular cultural framework, that has a decisive influence on the way the market works. A free market economy is only viable where there exists a culture of liberty and a sense of moral responsibility, an ethical discipline of self-control.[31]

Man must come to the realization that he has to respect an objective moral order founded on Natural Law and be committed to the principle of responsible freedom.[32] Unless capitalism corrects its traditional prejudice against the application of moral values in economic matters and relies exclusively on market forces, the threat of the State overstepping its boundaries and endangering personal freedom becomes a distinct reality. To avoid such an eventuality the free enterprise system must accept and apply two basic principles which are at the core of Catholic Social Doctrine and which are indispensable for the proper ordering of society: the principle of subsidiarity and the principle of solidarity.[33] To ignore them threatens to impede the harmonious relationships between individuals, in particular between capital and labor, not to mention intermediary associations such as the family.[34] The abandonment of these principles has resulted in the imposition of collectivist policies and other types of counterproductive welfare measures that have ended in failure. But first let us take a look at the fundamental issue of human work and its impact on society. To disregard the true nature of human work is counterproductive for the proper functioning of any economic system.

## NOTES

1. Elie Halévy, *The Growth of Philosophical Liberalism* (Boston: Beacon Press, 1955), 89. On this issue of egoism, as presented by Smith, Halévy comments: "If you persist in wishing to call egoism a vice, you will have to say, with Mandeville, that the vices of individuals tend to the advantage of the public. The economic

doctrine of Adam Smith is the doctrine of Mandeville set out in a form which is no longer paradoxical and literary, but rational and scientific" (90).

2. Halévy, *The Growth of Philosophical Liberalism*, 90.

3. Briefs, *Zwischen Kapitalismus und Syndicalismus*, 70.

4. See Thomas Aquinas, *Summa Theologiae* (II-II,57,1). Quoted by Joseph M. de Torre, *The Roots of Society* (Manila, Philippines: Sinag-Tala Publishers. 1977), 25–26.

5. See de Torre, *The Roots of Society*, 26.

6. For an excellent description of modern mass society, see Wilhelm Roepke, *A Humane Economy* (Chicago: Henry Regnery, 1969), chapter 2, 57–65.

7. Friedrich Engels, *L'Órigine de la Famille, de la Propriété Privée et de l'Etat*, 1884. As quoted by Andre Piettre, *Marx et Marxisme* (Paris: Presses Universitaires de France, 1959). See part 3, section 2, Communism and the Family, 158–59.

8. Engels, as quoted by Piettre, *Marx et Marxisme*, 159.

9. Engels's views on the family and marriage were not only his own. He simply expressed some of the ideas that Marx had held but was not able to express in writing because of his early death. What is considered license under capitalism is regarded as "moral" under communism. See Piettre, *Marx et Marxisme*, 158–61.

10. De Torre, *The Roots of Society*, 13–14.

11. More than thirty years ago the perceptive economist Kenneth E. Boulding wrote the following: "There are those who think that as economic development comes to fruition in a humanistic heaven on earth where war, poverty, and disease are abolished, religion will wither away. In that millennium faith will be swallowed up in knowledge, hope in fulfillment, and love in psychoanalysis and group dynamics! Such a belief seems to be naive. As power and knowledge increase, the question of the *truth* of religion—of what is the 'will of God', and how it is discovered and incorporated into the human will—becomes all-important. The feather of religious experience may then tip the great scales toward either heaven or hell on earth." See Kenneth E Boulding, *Beyond Economics* (Ann Arbor: University of Michigan Press, 1968), 210–211.

12. See de Torre, *The Roots of Society*, xi–xvii.

13. F. A. Hayek, *The Final Conceit, The Errors of Socialism* [The Collected Works of F. A. Hayek] (Chicago: University of Chicago Press, 1989).

14. Hayek, *The Final Conceit*, 9.

15. Friedrich A. Hayek, *The Road to Serfdom* (Chicago: University of Chicago Press, 1958).

16. Hayek, *The Road to Serfdom*, 8.

17. Hayek, *The Road to Serfdom*, 70.

18. Hayek, *The Road to Serfdom*, 70.

19. Hayek, *The Road to Serfdom*, 52.

20. For a brief analysis of Hayek's book, *The Fatal Conceit*, see Rafael Termes, *Antropologia del Capitalismo* (Madrid: Plaza & Janes Editores, 1992).

21. See Antonio Argandona, "Orden Espontaneo y Etica. La Moral en la Fatal Arrogancia de F. A. Hayek," *Cuadernos del Pensamiento Liberal*, no.12, Union Editorial, Madrid, 1991.

22. Wilhelm Roepke, *A Humane Economy* (Chicago: Henry Regnery, 1960), 123.

23. See Wilhelm Roepke, *Civitas Humana* (Madrid: Biblioteca de la Ciencia Economica, Revista de Occidente, 1949), 37–38.

24. This is the danger that Russia is facing today. As Ella Pamphilova, the pro-reform member of the Russian Parliament, said referring to the chaotic situation in her country: "People have lost all their faith. They don't believe in anyone. But a society without ideals, without morality, dies." *The Washington Post*, November 13, 1994, 1.

25. Roepke, *A Humane Economy*, 8.

26. See Alasdaire MacIntyre, "Theories of Natural Law in the Culture of Advanced Modernity," in *Common Truths* (Wilmington, DE: Intercollegiate Studies Institute, ISI Books, 2000), 112.

27. For an excellent analysis on the views of St. Thomas Aquinas concerning his contribution to economic thinking, see Jacob Viner, *Religious Thought and Economic Society*, ed. Jacques Melitz and Donald Winch (Durham, NC: Duke University Press, 1978).

28. The well-known historian Arnold J. Toynbee writing on the social problems posed by the process of mechanization and the development of technology under capitalism says the following: "The outstanding feature on the economic-social plane was the tug-of-war between a regimentation imposed by mechanical industry and an obstinate human reluctance to be regimented. The crux of the situation was the fact that mechanization and police were unfortunately inseparable." His criticism of certain materialistic aspects of capitalism goes as far as to say, "Western man has brought himself into danger of losing his soul through his concentration on a sensationally successful endeavour to increase his material well-being." See Arnold J. Toynbee, *A Study of History*, abridgment by D. C. Sommervell (New York: Oxford University Press, 1957), volume 2, 334, 345.

29. The scholar Patrick de Laubier, quoting from George Friedman's book *La Puissance de la Sagesse* (1970), says the following: " A la veille du XXie siècle, on prend serieusement conscience que la technique par elle même n'apporte pas la civilisation." See Patrick de Laubier, *La Pensée Socialède l'Eglise Catholique* (Fribourg, Switzerland: PREMICES, Editions Universitaires), 186–87.

30. See Iris Wessel Mueller's enlightening study of the influence the French socialists had on John Stuart Mill in her book, *John Stuart Mill and French Thought* (Urbana: University of Illinois Press, 1956), vi.

31. See José Miguel Ibañez Langlois, *Doctrina Social de la Iglesia* (Pamplona, Spain: Ediciones Universidad de Navarra, 1987), 260. See also José M. de Torre, *La Iglesia y la Cuestión Social* (Madrid: Ediciones Palabra, S.A, 1988),16.

32. John Paul II, *Dignitatis Humanae* #8.

33. For a comprehensive analysis of the social doctrine of the Catholic Church, especially the encyclical *Mater et Magistra* of Pope John XXIII, see Marcel Clement, *La Corporation Pofessionelle* (Paris: Nouvelles Editions Latines, 1958).

34. *Libertatis Consciencia* #73.

# 7

—⚏—

# The Fundamental
# Issue of Human Work

## THE TELEOLOGY OF WORK

Undoubtedly, the immediate failure of communism was the result of Marx's false concept of development; a concept that was intellectually biased from the beginning and was unable to deliver the goods and services that the communist economic planners had promised. But, above all, it was the failure of the Marxist system to recognize the dignity of man as a human person. A false understanding of the real significance of human labor and the dignity and role of human work were just as responsible, if not more, for the demise of communism, as were its obvious scarcities and inefficiencies. Without a proper recognition of the dignity and role of work, political and economic justice cannot prevail.

Work plays a crucial role in the integral development of man not only because it is indispensable for the perfection of every human being but also because it is essential for the perfection of society in its integrity. Only by accepting work, which has a very specific purpose in nature as a fundamental dimension of man's existence on earth, can development be really integral and help solve the major economic and social problems that affect modern society. In general, most modern approaches to development have rescinded from answering the question, what is the real meaning of work? Can development be approached exclusively from a purely materialistic and hedonistic point of view, looking at work solely as an input or object of production necessary for the creation of wealth? Can the goal of development be separated from the moral law and, consequently work treated as something impersonal, one more input in the production function?

No one will deny the importance of technology and capital in the development of nations. Both, together with labor, are crucial inputs in the production function and are basic coefficients in the process of economic growth. But, human work cannot be treated as any other input in the production function because it has both a subjective and an objective dimension to it.[1] Human work cannot be separated from its subject which is man. To attempt to quantify and remunerate labor's contribution to the production process exclusively and at all times in terms of a strict application of the "laws" of supply and demand and the marginal productivity theory can be risky and may even violate the virtue of justice, not to mention charity. These are thorny problems which do not have easy solutions. They go beyond pure economic theory because they have also social and ethical implications. If the ethical implications of these issues are ignored or brushed aside by economists as not pertinent to a strict application of economic theory, the 'social question' will not be solved and the entire process of development may be jeopardized. As a result, serious problems of a political and social nature, including the specter of unemployment and other ills, may ensue, endangering the entire fabric of society and, as visualized by Marx, causing further and graver antagonisms between the various social classes and, in particular, between labor and capital.

Thus, the vital function that work plays in the process of human development must be clearly understood if the social conflicts and evils that characterize the contemporary world are to be overcome and a more just socioeconomic order is to be reached. The book of Genesis as well as the books of the Old and the New Testament leave no doubt as to the significance of human work for the integral development of man and the attainment of his ultimate destiny. Concerning work and in reference to those persons who were living in idleness, St. Paul went as far as saying in his epistle to the Thessolonians, "If anyone will not work, let him not eat." In fact, it is only through work that man can reach the fullness of his being.

In spite of these basic truths, the teleological implications of work are generally overlooked. As Joseph Cardinal Hoffner has written, "Work is the conscious, serious, object related activation of the intellectual or bodily faculties of man for the appropriate realization of values that serve the divinely appointed fulfillment of man himself [his self-performance] as well as human society and, ultimately, the honor of God."[2] Although Christianity stressed through the centuries the dignity of work and its importance for man's ultimate salvation, most of the intellectual movements of the eighteenth and nineteenth centuries reduced work, as any other factor of production, to a necessary object for economic growth and development.[3] However, to abandon the Christian concept of work, as it was done by the *encyclopédistes* and a century later by Marx, had the opposite effect and led to a worsening of the class conflicts which prevailed during the Industrial Revolution.

## THE ERRONEOUS CONCEPT OF
## WORK: ITS ROOTS AND CONSEQUENCES

To attempt to integrate the various human sciences with the goal of reaching a comprehensive science of man and society was the ultimate objective of the materialistic current of thought characteristic of the Enlightenment and of modern atheism, including the philosophical and sociological systems of Comte and Marx. According to Rocco Buttiglioni, professor of political philosophy at the University of Teramo, the attempt to integrate the various human sciences with the objective of creating a comprehensive science of man and society on the basis of pure objects has been the ultimate goal of the materialistic current of thought characteristic of the Enlightenment and of modern atheism, including the philosophical and sociological systems of Comte.[4]

The reality of this approach, continues Buttiglione, is particularly exemplified in the writings of the French philosophers of the Enlightenment and later in the work of Marx. To try to build an integral science of man on a purely natural basis fails to explain man in his entirety. It was pretentious on the part of men like Diderot and D'Alembert to believe that, through the writings of an encyclopedia and leaving aside the notion of God, they could fully explain the substantial unity of human knowledge. They failed in their attempt to make the *encyclopédie* the *summa theologica* that provided the ultimate explanation of man and the world. Their failure can be explained once it is realized that in a scientific discipline the total is always something more than the simple sum of its parts.[5] Projects such as the *encyclopédie*, which lacked a sound philosophical idea of the transcendental nature of man, were at the root of many of the false interpretations of work. Without a proper definition of man, the full dimension of work cannot be understood.

Fortunately few people still believe in the weak and often erroneous philosophical foundations of the prophets of the Enlightenment. In a similar way the lack of a proper understanding of the transcendental nature of man and work by the authors of the Communist Manifesto lay at the root of the communist system's discredit and ultimate demise. Marx's misunderstanding of the nature of man and work led him to reach false conclusions about what he considered the inevitability of class conflict and the exploitative nature of private property.

Marx based his theory of development on the inevitable conflict that, according to him, exists between social classes. Marx and Engels claimed in the Communist Manifesto that "the history of all hitherto existing society is the history of class struggles. Freeman and slave, patrician and plebeian, lord and serf, guild master and journeyman, in a word, oppressor and oppressed, stood in constant opposition to one another, carried on an interrupted, now hidden, now open fight that each time ended, either in a revolutionary reconstruction of society at large, or in the common ruin of the contending classes."[6]

Buttiglione claims that Marx and Engels were following most of the contractual theories which traced the origin of human society to a social contract which was supposed to put an end to the original enmity which exists between men.[7] Conflict had to be overcome but, according to Marx, it was through the class struggle that the final liberation of man from oppression would occur. In accordance with the basic tenants of modern social science, Marx tried to give meaning to man's place in the universe using the traditional master–slave relationship. For Marx, the class struggle became the dialectical motor that set in motion the dynamics of history and the source of all progress. It would continue unabated until the final triumph of labor under communism when the dialectical process would disappear. The very dynamics of the development process would bring about the creation of a classless society free of contradictions and antagonisms, in other words, the redemption of man.

The English experience of the eighteenth century seemed to give credibility to Marx's theory of class conflict.[8] The modern bourgeois society which arose from the ruins of feudalism instead of putting an end to the class struggle seemed to have aggravated it.. By establishing a new class structure, the capitalist and the proletariat, bourgeois society created different types of antagonisms and prepared the way for new forms of struggle. The owners of the means of production, the bourgeois capitalists, were now the exploiters, the oppressors and the proletariat the exploited, the oppressed.

What probably radicalized the antinomies between capital and labor at the time of the Industrial Revolution was the economic and social practice of giving preference to the acquisition of material wealth and economic power over the respect that is due to the dignity of man and his work. Instead of wealth being placed at the service of man, the opposite frequently occurred; wealth became an end in itself and the profit motive enthroned. This gave ground to an ethically just social reaction against the unjust human practices of the Industrial Revolution. To overcome these theoretical and practical errors of early capitalism, it became necessary to make appropriate changes both in theory and practice—and to recognize both the subjective and objective reality of human work. Without accepting the intrinsic value of work and the priority and dignity of the human person over objects, it is extremely difficult if not impossible to overcome the antinomies that normally exist in any type of society.

The idea that labor served one basic purpose, the production of goods, violates the natural right of man to be treated as a human person and not as an object, a mere instrument of production. To consider human labor exclusively in accordance with its economic contribution to the productive process is what John Paul II calls "the error of economism."[9] In reality it should be called an error of materialism because it does not recognize the primacy of the spiritual over the material. Once the primacy of the spiritual is rejected, man easily falls into cross materialism. He limits his vision of life to a search for pleasure and an avoidance of pain, implicitly giving his blessing to a Utilitarian morality and Bentham's felicific calculus.[10] As the previously quoted French philosopher Elie Halévy has so adequately stated: "What is known as Utilitarianism or Philosophical Liberalism, can be defined as nothing but an attempt to apply the principles of Newton to the affairs of politics and morality."[11] Much harm would have been avoided in early capitalism if the proper nature of man and work had been properly understood.

The right to private property was the major nemesis for Marx and Engels. Here again their claim that property is based on the exploitation of the proletariat is based on a total misunderstanding of the nature of man and work. Marx in his famous book *Das Kapital* claims that the average price of wage labor is the minimum wage, that is, that quantum of the means of subsistence which is absolutely necessary to keep the laborer in bare existence. Whatever is above this amount is absorbed by the capitalists. As capital and the means of production accumulate in the hands of the capitalist exploiters the surplus laboring population increases and with it unemployment or what Marx called enforced idleness with its toll of misery and despair. Thus, according to Marx, the private ownership of the means of production is the result of exploitation.

Marx's explanation of the law of capital accumulation and the ever increasing surplus of labor has been proven to be far from true. His belief in the resulting unavoidable class struggle between the capitalist and the proletariat has proved to be another Marxian myth that can easily be discarded once a better understanding of the anthropology of man is grasped.

One of the major reasons that gave ground to Marx's hatred of private ownership was his ignorance concerning the proper role of private property within a well-ordered society. In the England of his time he only saw the cross effects on society of an unbridled individualism and an economic system where the determining factors were the impersonal rules of the market, unlimited competition, and raw self-interest. Lacking the proper institutions and void of a solid ethical foundation, the system triggered a period of unquestionable economic growth but at the expense of the laboring poor, who were defenseless in the face of the inflexible laws of supply and demand. Marx was correct in his concern for the pitiful state of the laboring poor and the abuses of child labor, both of which characterized the early stages of capitalism.

Marx, the atheist, could not accept that man through his work—whether intellectual or manual—shares in the activity of the Creator and within the limits of his own capabilities continues to develop that activity and perfects it as he advances further in the discovery of the resources and values contained in the whole of creation.[12] Capital and labor do not have to be antagonistic, as Marx proclaimed. On the contrary, they should complement each other in a joint effort conducive toward progress and the common good of society. Marx, however, did not understand the proper function and meaning of capital and labor, their respective rights and duties nor their unique contribution to the process of economic growth and development. In other words, Marx lacked a full understanding of the subjective and objective dimensions of work.

In his encyclical *Rerum Novarum*, Pope Leo XIII unequivocally maintains that given the fact that "God has given the earth to the use and enjoyment of the universal human race is not to deny that there can be private property." On the contrary, the Pope continues, "When man spends the industry of his mind and the strength of his body in procuring the fruits of nature, by that act he makes his own that portion of nature's field which he cultivates—that portion on which he leaves, as it were, the impress of his own personality. And it cannot but be just that he should possess that portion as his own, and should have a right to keep it without molestation."[13] Thus, it can rightly be said that the right to private property is in accordance with the law of nature. But, as in the process of appropriation both capital and labor participate, cooperation between them should be the norm for the benefit of society. It is totally false to assert that "the worth of labor and therefore the return to be made for it, should equal the entire value added." To claim that the wage earner has the right to the full value of the finished product is erroneous. In spite of the priority of labor in the productive process, it cannot be denied, as the Marxists do, that all the factors of production—intellect, capital, and labor—have a right to a share of their joint efforts in the production of goods and services. They all work together in a harmonious and efficient way for the common good. The inevitability of the class struggle and to consider private property as the major source of exploitation are among the major myths that should be buried in the annals of history.

To believe, as Marx and Engels did, that private property of the means of production is the major source of worker exploitation is a further proof of their misunderstanding of the concept of work. By condemning private property they seemed to have forgotten that it belongs to the teleology of work that man has the right to possess the fruits of his work or its equivalent. It is only through human work that the fullness of the relationship between man and nature is accomplished. But, Buttiglione claims that in order to do so, man must have the freedom to act, that is to say, a certain measure of control over the environment. In the language of law, "this control over ourselves and over the environment is called 'property.'"[14] Although rejecting Hegel's philosophy, Buttiglione agrees with the German philosopher's statement that property is the external sphere of realization of freedom. Marx, in his biased philosophical approach, failed to see the basic truth that the exterior dimension of freedom is property. Without the recognition of the right to private property, the whole concept of freedom is de facto rejected.

Marx did not visualize a free economic and social order where labor together with capital would play the leading roles in the economy whilst the state, respecting the principle of subsidiarity, would help set up the proper legal and institutional structure. He simply ignored the Christian concept of an *amicitia politica* developed by Aquinas, which implies the possibility of mutual aid in everyday relationships among the members of a community, city, or state. This concept was later developed by the Roman pontiffs under the name of the "principle of solidarity." Neither did he believe that capitalism would be capable of recognizing the social function of private property nor respect the dignity of work. In other words, Marx never conceived the possibility that the harsh and abusive capitalism of nineteenth century England could ever evolve into a more humane type of economic system. History has proven that he was wrong. The world did not have to fall into the horrors of a Marxist ideology which places its faith in the power of the state and, contrary to its biased theory, disregards individual freedom and the dignity of the human person.

## THE REDEMPTION OF WORK THROUGH
## THE PRACTICE OF HUMAN VIRTUES

To be just, a socioeconomic order must give prominence to the primacy of man and work in the production process. It must give priority to labor over capital; capital understood in the broad sense of the term. It is man who, through his personal work, has developed the means of production that have permitted him to reach the advanced stage of civilization that the world is witnessing at the beginning of the new millennium. But, it must be admitted also that the great accomplishments in science, technology and the arts would not have taken place without the development and practice of human virtues.

Work well done, both natural and intellectual, affects not only the economy but also, and in a very particular way, the overall well-being of society. The economy and society as a whole benefit when work is performed conscientiously and efficiently. The truth leads us to the question of human

virtues and how their development is indispensable if integral development is to take place.

It seems logical to conclude that over the long run there exists a corre-
lation between virtue and productivity. When a society becomes lax in the
area of human virtues, productivity tends to decline. This is reflected in a
tendency for workers to become sloppy and careless in their work and to
perform the jobs entrusted to them in a routine fashion without taking a
real interest and much less pride in their final product. If the human
virtues of sincerity, fraternity, loyalty, and so forth, are lacking, the manual worker will tend to do the least work possible as long as he can get
away with it. By no means can it be taken for granted that he will be inclined to fulfill as perfectly as possible the work entrusted to him.

But the need to develop human virtues does not apply to labor alone.
The lack of virtue very often found in captains of industry and other influential sectors of society can also have devastating effects on the common good of society. Lacking virtue, man's innate tendency toward greed
will impair all efforts to reach a better understanding between capital and
labor and, thus, prevent social peace. Overall morale in the working place
will then tend to fall precipitously with its concomitant decline in productive efficiency.

In ancient Greece, Aristotle had already commented on the propensity
of men to act selfishly. He warned his contemporaries that the wickedness
and avarice of man are insatiable.[15] The past abuses of capitalism seem to
give further credence to this statement. The owners of capital, led by an
unrestrained desire for profits, have often strived to acquire a greater
share of production even at the expense of labor. The teacher of Alexan-
der the Great reminds us that "the nature of desire is without limit, and it
is with a view to satisfying this that the many live."[16] Knowing the deficiencies of human nature, he was well aware of the need to stress the importance of ethics. Moral considerations, insisted Aristotle, are the only
ones that can restrain man's disordered desires and appetites. Man can
only become just and temperate through the practice of virtuous actions
and by exercising temperance.[17] Without the development and practice of
human virtues, social peace becomes an unattainable utopia.

There seems to be in man a natural tendency to apply the well-known
"law" of the least effort, to the area of moral conduct. For example, man's
effort to substitute a difficult and strict moral code by a more lenient one:
a moral code that is less demanding and requires lower ethical standards
in the accomplishment of his goals. The old moral code, often associated
with all sorts of pejorative epithets, is no longer accepted because, so the
saying goes, it runs counter to the more modern concepts of morality.

By placing reason at the service of passion, the law of the least effort
produces in the individual, with the help of man's lower instincts—

laziness, dishonesty, and so forth—the "rational conditions" that permit "reason" to elude right conscience. Once the rule of right conscience is diluted to a minimum, it is difficult, if not impossible, to expect fair play and much less a proper moral conduct from the various players in the political and economic arenas. As a result, corruption is generalized and, thus, no one should be surprised if, overall, economic efficiency is affected negatively, production suffers and there is a marked tendency for the increases in the real rate of economic growth to start declining. This is a phenomenon which characterizes all societies which are experiencing a decline in their ethical standards and virtue loses its significance. Once an objective moral code of conduct is removed from political and economic life and ethical relativism sets in, history tends to demonstrate that both democratic and free societies eventually turn into an open or thinly disguised totalitarianism.

Thus, there is a real danger that some type of neo-Marxism or national socialism could revive with all its nefarious consequences. After all, Marxism arose as a reaction against the abuses of capitalism and it is far from impossible that a continuous disregard for the dignity of man could resurrect extreme ideologies of either the left or the right under the false banner of "social justice" or some type of religious fanaticism.

The social problem of the past two centuries has become now, at the beginning of the twenty-first century, a world problem. The "class struggle" that was at the core of Marx's theory of capitalism has been transferred to the world arena where the conflict is no longer exclusively between labor and capital, not even between the "haves" and "have nots," but a war of ethnic rivalries and nationalities, not to mention the mounting threat arising from destructive drugs and uncontrolled terrorism backed and supported by fanatical religious groups.[18]

Recent events around the world—the economically more advanced nations included—clearly demonstrate that the higher standards of living and the rapid increase in consumer goods have not fulfilled man's expectations for a better world. On the contrary, as the moral fiber of society tends to break down, under the influence of insatiable egoistic tendencies, man's unfulfilled expectations not only remain but even increase, giving rise to further frustrations which can, in their turn, lead to new types of antinomies and excesses of all kinds.

However, attempts to find solutions to man's unsatisfied aspirations continue to be fruitless and are destined to fail. Not being able to find the right answer to the social problems of today's modern world, man remains dissatisfied with himself and with what he sees around him. As a result, he falls even deeper and deeper into despair or into the hands of false idols, forgetting that the solution to these problems lies within his easy reach, within his own heart.

In this new era of globalization it becomes evident that there is a great need to find better and more just solutions to the many worldwide problems of development. Previous models of development fell far below expectations. In their race toward rapid growth and higher standards of living, they often overemphasized the importance of technology to the detriment of the cultural and spiritual needs of man. It cannot be denied that some of these models contributed to the elimination of many of the prevailing antinomies of the past but, it must be recognized, in the process they created new ones, as is reflected in the many perilous crises that have developed around the world.

The social problems of a global nature that are threatening the peace and stability of many nations will be solved only when the moral fiber of mankind is strengthened and man ceases to apply the law of least effort when dealing with moral questions. The solution does not lie in watering down a moral code of behavior or in mere changes in the political and economic structures of society, as is commonly suggested. The revolutionary changes of the past should be proof enough of the futility of such endeavors. Only when man renews his faith in the transcendental, recognizes his dignity as a human person, and considers work not only as a right but also as a service can society be so thoroughly transformed that peace and justice can prevail. For man's integral development to take place, human virtues must be stressed, both at the school level and within the family. This way, the important role of work and the rights and obligations that they entail, both for capital and labor, will be better understood and, hopefully, many of the prevailing injustices disappear. In particular, emphasis must be placed in the principle of solidarity, a principle which, if observed, will help to bring people together, independently of their race, nationality or religion and avoid the appalling consequences of class warfare and other types of violent conflict.

Although Marx and Lenin were totally wrong in their predictions concerning the inevitability of the "class struggle," it must be admitted that the acute social and economic differences that separate the developed industrialized Western World from the so-called Third World countries are creating tensions of an extremely serious nature. The attractions that the high standard of living and opportunities that both Western Europe and the United States offer to the poverty-stricken peoples of the world has provoked a migratory problem of major proportions. The wealth and prosperity of the capitalist nations contrasts sharply with the deprivation and indigence which oppress a large proportion of the world population. It seems only logical that this wave of immigrants, seeking a better life for their children, should look at Western Europe and the United States as their only hope for the future. Not being able to find work in their native countries, they turn their eyes to the West hoping to find it there. The recipient countries, however, are far from satisfied with a migratory movement which is causing racial and social tensions never before witnessed in Western Europe and which threatens to become more critical in the years to come.[19] However, the crisis of poverty and deprivation affecting the less endowed nations is also affecting their counterparts in the Western World that are already burdened with their own grave unsolved problems, not the least of which are the potential cultural problems associated with these migratory movements.[20]

Ironically, the wealthier countries, especially in Europe, are also facing a major potential crisis, a crisis that is the result of the rapidly falling rates of population. The decline in the proportion of young people within the total population together with the aging of the population can have dire consequences for the development and future growth of these countries. In fact, the need for foreign workers has become imperative for many European countries in order to meet the scarcity of manpower at home. In brief, the dilemma facing the Western European nations can be reduced to the following: on the one hand the need for foreign workers and on the other the rejection of alien cultures and traditions which clash with their own and which, as mentioned earlier, are causing social and political unrest. However, leaving aside the ethical implications of migratory movements, the fact still remains that the economic needs for manpower of a continent rapidly being depopulated will force the European nations, at least in the short run, to "import" labor from abroad.

Hopefully, the cultural differences which draw Europe apart will gradually disappear and the newly arrived immigrants will be able to integrate into the European community. The world must be permeated with a fresh spirit of national and international solidarity which will bring people together independently of their race, religion, or national identity. But for that to happen a deeper and more profound understanding of the true nature of man and work must be necessary in order to avoid the antinomies not only between capital and labor but, above all, those that exist between the various cultural entities within the world community. The dangers of a too great concentration of power in the new era of globalization that is approaching represent a real challenge for contemporary man, not the least of which are the ones related to population, the family and the environment. The next two chapters will stress the ethical implications of these issues for the future well-being of humanity.

## NOTES

1. See John Paul II, *Laborem Exercens* #5 and #6.
2. Joseph Cardinal Hoffner, *Christian Social Teaching* (Cologne: Ordo Socialis, 1983), 114.

3. Christians of all denominations have always stressed the importance of work for man's ultimate salvation. As the Spanish theologian Jose Luis Llanes comments, "Luther's idea of work as service and Calvin's statements about the value of work as a sign of predestination had very widespread influence in their time. But they both set up a dualism—on the one hand, the sola fides, faith alone, which justifies together with predestination; and, on the other, work seen as a service to man, but regarded as having no value in God's sight; and this dualism led to a severe dichotomy between an individualistic pietism on the one hand and a humanism without theological roots on the other. We can hear the echo of this even today." See José Luis Llanes, *On the Theory of Work* (New Rochelle, NY: Scepter Press, 1982).

4. Rocco Buttiglione, *El Hombre y el Trabajo* (Madrid: Encuentro Ediciones, 1984), 29.

5. Buttiglione, *El Hombre y el Trabajo*, 30–31.

6. Karl Marx and Friedrich Engels, *The Communist Manifesto*, ed. Samuel H. Beer (Arlington Heights, IL: Harlan Davidson, 1955), 9.

7. Buttiglione, *El Hombre y el Trabajo*.

8. The blatant injustices of early capitalism in England were not left unnoticed to the Spanish philosopher of the mid-1850s Jaime Balmes when he wrote, "Now, surrounding a manufacturing enterprise, that by its extension and magnificence surpasses that of the feudal castles, there dwell also a large number of unfortunate people who hardly have the means of survival. Perhaps, working the entire day in the manufacture of the most exquisite tweeds, they remain covered with rags which do not even protect them from the rigors of the weather. At night, after they leave the huge hall in which they work, they bury themselves in a humid and unhealthy hovel where the tears of their wives and children await them." See Jaime Balmes, *Obras Completas* (Madrid: Biblioteca de Autores Cristianos [BAC], 1949), 591. See also his work "El Socialismo," *Obras Completas*, 561. Quoted in Vicente Rodriguez Casado, *Orígenes del Capitalismo y del Socialismo Contemporaneo* (Madrid: Espasa Calpe, S.A., 1981), 254–55.

9. John Paul II, *Laborem Exercens* #13.

10. Jeremy Bentham and his followers believed that the social problems could be solved by "applying an exact science of ethics, jurisprudence, and politics, using as its master tool a [Bentham's] 'felicific calculus' of the relative quantities of pleasure and pain to be expected as results of different public and private actions, and so the pattern of all actions require to bring about 'the greatest happiness for the greatest number.'" See Overton H. Taylor, *A History of Economic Analysis* (McGraw-Hill, 1960), 120. According to Schopenhauer, "The English Utilitarians talk about happiness but they mean money."

11. Elie Halévy, *The Growth of Philosophical Liberalism* (Boston: Beacon Press, 1955), 6.

12. The Christian recognizes that the world is good and that through his work he can transform the earth for the benefit of all humanity. That is why Christianity is a powerful force for the development of science and technology and helps foster artistic creativity. It is not sufficient to transform the world in order to make it more productive but also to make it more beautiful. See Jose M. de Torre, *La Iglesia y la Cuestión Social* (Madrid: Ediciones Palabra, S.A., 1988), 125.

13. Leo XIII, *Rerum Novarum* #7.

14. Rocco Buttiglione, "Social Justice in the Changing Economic Environment: Encounter or Conflict," *Faith and Reason* (winter 1991).

15. Aristotle, *The Politics* (Chicago: University of Chicago Press, 1984), book 2, chapter 5, 1267 al.

16. Aristotle, *The Politics*, 1267bl.

17. Aristotle, *Nichomachean Ethics*, book 2, chapter 1, 1103b.

18. Perhaps recent events in Russia, the Balkans, and the Middle East are good examples of what may happen in the future if the new political and economic freedoms are not based on solid ethical foundations. But, the specter of totalitarianism is not limited to the geographical areas mentioned. It can occur in any society where there takes place a total breakdown of moral standards.

19. In 1973, Jean Raspail wrote a well-known novel in which he narrates the peaceful invasion of the south of France by millions of refugees fleeing from the poverty and misery of their native countries. See Jean Raspail, *Le Camp des Saints* (Paris: Editions Robert Laffont, 1973).

20. Professor Jude Dougherty is well aware of some of the moral problems associated with immigration, in particular the one related to assimilation. Concerning this matter, he says the following: "The doors to immigration cannot be opened indiscriminately. The conditions of the immigrant and prospects for assimilation must be taken into account. All aspects of the culture need not be shared by the immigrant, but a respect for the traditions of the host country and a capacity for self-reliance are fundamental. Still the immigrant cannot be valued only for what he can contribute. A means test may be necessary, but it cannot be the sole criterion." See Jude Dougherty, "Moral Aspects of Immigration Policy," *Crisis*, August 8, 2000, 8.

# 8

—⁓—

# Population, the Welfare State, and the Challenge of the Environment

## THE DANGERS OF POPULATION GROWTH: MYTH OR REALITY

The basic principles of our Western heritage are being questioned and even challenged by powerful forces which either openly or surreptitiously deny the very existence of the transcendental and reduce man to the purely immanent. New values, more in accordance with "the spirit of the times," have permeated large sectors of society. An ethos based primarily on the love of wealth and material well-being has become a natural substitute for the old-fashioned spiritual and cultural values of the past. The consumer society of our post modern era, imbued with a high dose of hedonism, does not accept many of the most basic traditional values which for centuries had characterized Western societies. In particular, man's spiritual dimension apparently had drowned under a sea of material well-being.

Very often, to avoid personal responsibility man tends to place the blame for many of the problems facing our contemporary society on factors external to him. The serious effects that a deterioration of the habitat is having on the earth's natural endowments are frequently associated with overpopulation and hardly ever on the lack of personal responsibility of each individual who has the duty to preserve the beauty of creation. To consider population as the only variable that can be manipulated in order to solve the ills of society runs counter to the most recent available data.[1] As a result, governments and international organizations, falsely interpreting Malthus' theory on population, do not hesitate to recommend and even foster birth control policies, such as abortion and sterilization, that violate Natural Law and by so doing undermine the basic foundations of family life.

Even though the family is the fundamental pillar of a healthy society, it is, nevertheless, not immune from the buffeting winds of the so-called "new" and "progressive" ideas that threaten its very existence. The traditional Christian concept of the family is gradually being undermined under the pretext that it requires certain fundamental changes if it is to keep up with the modern trends of our contemporary society.

Under the banners of postmodernism and deconstructionism, the new generations are made to believe that the family has lost its significance as a major player in the moral, cultural, and economic life of nations. The very concept of the family is challenged and its role limited to a transitory arrangement between two persons who are free to terminate it whenever it suits their purpose. The traditional family is no longer considered the pivotal factor of a healthy society. The state, the community, and other collective agencies are supposed to replace the major functions that previously had been performed by the family.

Apparently, some of these collective institutions seem to know what is best for each individual. They believe that they are able to determine not only what is the optimum population in order to control it but also to decide at what age a person is no longer useful to society. Consequently, the future of the very elderly is becoming more and more uncertain, especially as life expectancy at birth increases and the concept of "mercy killing" (euthanasia) is more generalized. But even in those case where life is respected, the elderly parents are told that they no longer have to worry about their economic and social needs because when they reach the age of retirement and are unable to earn a living because the state will provide for their well-being. Government authorities will always be there to protect their interests through its extensive social and medical security plans.

The same philosophy applies to the education and the health care of children. State-run day care centers for young children will permit mothers to join the work force. This way they can earn an income which can give them a certain degree of independence. The children, meanwhile, will be under the tutelage of government specialized personnel who will take care of them physically whilst at the same time provide them with the most elementary standards of education. The state with its numerous bureaucratic institutions for the aged and the very young will see to it that all their basic needs will be taken care of. At least, so the theory goes.

Leaving aside a debate on the possible merits or serious flaws of such a philosophy which, we personally believe, has many dangerous ramifications in terms of the future moral well-being of the family, the fact still remains that population does play a significant and positive role in the economic and social development of nations. It is ironic that extensive social programs of the state, the modern deus ex machina, which supposedly were going to supplant the family as the purveyors of the needs of the old, the infirm, and the children are running into serious financial problems. It is estimated that relatively soon they will lack the necessary funds to carry out such an altruistic mission. If the social security systems and other state-run medical plans fall into bankruptcy, the state will have to rely once again on the family and private religious organizations, to take care of the pressing and increasing needs of the young and the old. This is especially true of the old who, in relative numbers, are increasing at an unprecedented rate. This can be easily verified by looking at the latest figures on population trends of the United Nations. How ironic will it be if, in the new millennium, the traditional family so belittled by certain sectors of society turns out to be the main reliable supporter of the old and the young.

The latest data on population clearly show that in Europe and the United States the ratio of the elderly with respect to the total population has increased significantly during the last few years whilst, on the other hand, the proportion of the young has decreased.[2] This trend, if it continuous, will have serious negative consequences for the future well-being of our societies, not to mention its depressive economic impact.

Without being an alarmist, it cannot be denied that the aging of the population together with the fall in the ratio of young people within the total population gives ground for serious concern. In the book *La Peste Blanche*, Professor Pierre Chaunu stated in no uncertain terms that, just as the plagues of medieval times decimated the population of Europe, in our own time the "white plague," caused by persistent radically low fertility rates, is performing the same destructive role on the European continent.[3] The delusion of overpopulation led governments to sponsor policies geared toward population control which led to low fertility rates and contributed to the present population problems.[4] Such policies became an infatuation for demographers and many Western governments.

For many years the major concern of the majority of demographers was the specter of overpopulation and its negative political, economic, and social implications for society as a whole. The United Nations and other international organizations joined the chorus of dire warnings concerning the future of mankind resulting from a global population implosion that was not far from occurring. The Malthusian theories of the dangers of an overpopulated world incapable of feeding itself gained renewed impetus in the most influential circles of contemporary society. But was this threat a myth or a reality? The most recent data available on population trends will help us verify the accuracy of these predictions.

During the 1960s official publications on population trends predicted that by the year 2000 the world population would reach 7.5 billion people and would continue growing in the future.[5] Predictions such as these proved to be incorrect, giving ample ground to doubt the soundness of certain population policies which are based on unfounded fears.[6] By the 1970s, some forecasters were already predicting the opposite, a decline in population by the year 2000, a prediction which also proved to be wrong. These flip-flops in population forecasts prove that forecasting is a dangerous subject that must be taken with a grain of salt.

In spite of the uncertain results of forecasting, data provided by some of the best demographers of our century have kept warning us once and again about the dangers of overpopulation. They claimed insistently that the world's population has been increasing at such high rates that future food crisis and the total breakdown of our civilization is close at hand. The 1966 Club of Rome's famous report with its estimates on the rapidly declining resources of our planet had a tremendous impact on world opinion and seemed to corroborate the dire predictions of the prophets of gloom and doom.[7]

More recent statistics provided by well-known demographers and international organizations have tended to minimize those scary forecast and have seriously predicted that the world population is not only showing signs that it will soon reach its peak but that there are already indications of a future steady decline in its absolute rate of growth. They clearly indicate that in the more developed countries negative rates of natural increase will occur after the year 2000. In other words, the death rate will be higher than the birth rate. This decline in natural population growth rates will be partially compensated by net immigration but only until the year 2005.

Net migration flowing into Western Europe and other developed nations might tend to taper off from the observed levels of the early 1990s. In the less developed countries, the negative natural rate increase will only appear after the year 2045. Given expected fertility rates, the latest data provided by the United Nations seem to provide ample proof of this trend.[8] Using a "medium fertility" scenario the likely future demographic trends indicate that the world population will increase from 5.7 billion in 1995 to 9.4 billion in 2150 and 10.8 billion in the year 2150. However, if the "low fertility" variant is applied, total world population will drop to 3.6 billion in 2150, a fall of 4.1 billion from the year 1995. In the case of Europe, the decrease in population would be even more significant. Applying the "low fertility" variant, which would be more appropriate for Europe given its low fertility rates, the continent's total population would fall from 728 million in 1955 to 556 million in 2050 and to the dangerously low level of 137 million in 2150.[9]

Assuming the trend toward continued low or even lower fertility rates in most areas of the world, the human population will crest around the year 2050 at about 7.7 billion people and then begin to fall dramatically to 5.6 billion in 2100 and possibly 3.6 billion in 2150.[10] This phenomenon will be accompanied by a substantial geographical shift in the world population from the more developed regions to the countries in the process of development. The share of the world population living in the currently more developed countries will shrink from 19 to 10 percent between the years 1995 and 2150.

These projections of the United Nations do not assume the possibility of future catastrophes as Malthus had done in his famous book on population published in the nineteenth century.[11] The projected global depopulation of the second century of the second millennium has not been calculated on the basis of possible famines, wars, or plagues, as Malthus had envisioned. If these calamitous events were to take place, the projected depopulation would be much greater. But, even leaving aside these catastrophic factors, projections of future demographic trends in the more developed countries do reflect persistent low fertility rates combined with higher life expectancy ratios and continued immigration flows. These projection may differ significantly depending on the database used.

According to the United Nations, the world's average fertility level in 1990–1995 was 3.0 births per woman of child-bearing age. However, this average figure does not show the disparity in rates between different areas of the world. Fertility rates for major areas and regions of the world (1990–1995) varied from a low of 1.6 in Europe to a high of 5.8 in Africa. In the other major regions of the world, fertility rates were as follows: Asia 3.0, Latin America and the Caribbean 3.1, North America 2.1, and Oceania (Australia and New Zealand) 2.5.[12]

Average fertility rates in the more developed countries fell to a low of 1.69 for the period 1990–1995. This rate is well below the 2.1 required for long-term replacement of generations. In Western Europe the following nine countries had fertility rates of 1.5 or less: Italy (1.2), Spain (1.3), Germany (1.3), Austria (1.5), Greece (1.5), and Portugal (1.5). Another six countries had fertility rates of 2 or less. They were Belgium, Denmark, France, Netherlands, Norway, and Switzerland. Given the possibility that the low fertility rates prevailing in Europe will continue into the near future, it is estimated that its population will decline to one-fifth of the one in Africa. In 1950 Europe's population was more than twice that

In Eastern Europe, fertility rate declined precipitously from 1980–1985 to 1990–1995. They fell in every single country, including the Baltic states, from 2.1 to 1.6. The decline was especially acute in the Russian Federation, from 2.1 to 1.5. These low fertility rates in Western and Eastern Europe contrast sharply with the much higher fertility rates in Asia (3.0) and Latin America and the Caribbean (3.1), not to mention its neighbors to the south in Africa (5.8).

On the other hand, during the period 1990–1995, Western Europe had an average life expectancy of 76.7 years. In Eastern Europe and the Baltic countries the average life expectancy was 72 years. The Russian Federation experienced the lowest life expectancy (66.5) and recent data tend to indicate that there has been no improvement during the last two years. The low life expectancy rate in Eastern Europe and the Baltic states was mainly the result of an extremely poor health situation which was responsible for the region's high mortality rates. However, the drastic decline in population that occurred in Eastern Europe and the Baltic states was due, in large part, to international migration which was estimated to be 1.4 million during the same period 1990–1995.[13]

The declining birth rates, resulting from the low fertility rates, together with the assumption that life expectancy at birth will rise significantly will affect drastically the age structure of the world's population. All demographers agree that the world's population is getting older whilst the young are diminishing both in absolute and relative numbers, a trend that can have serious consequences for the planet's future economic growth. The major impact of these changes will be felt in the more developed countries, in particular Western Europe, where declining birth rates have reached critical proportions.

For many years the world has been hearing about the threat posed on society by a dangerously high total dependency ratio which is defined as the population 0 to 14 and 65 and over to the population aged 15 to 64 (the economically active population). However, the dependency ratio was often understood as the ratio between the number of children aged from birth to 14 years of age and the total active population. Emphasis was always placed on the theory that the greater the number of children in relation to the economically active population, the larger would be the dependency ratio and, consequently, it was concluded that the standard of living would be higher if the birth rates were lower. There would be fewer children of an unproductive age to be taken care of by the economically active population who, as a result, would be able to enjoy a greater share of the nation's output. The argument was used to justify population control policies that would reduce the birth rate and lower the child dependency ratio. Very little, if anything, was said about the aging of the population and the elderly dependency ratio which relates the older and retired persons with the economically active population.[14]

Nevertheless, counter to the expectations of the prophets of doom and gloom, fertility rates are declining and the population is rapidly aging both in absolute and relative numbers.[15] It is ironic that it now turns out that one of the greatest dangers to the economic and social stability of the industrialized countries is not the persistence of high fertility rates but the aging of the population and the critically high elderly dependency ratios.[16] Although it may be true that simple arithmetic would give credence to the fact that, in the short run, each additional baby means less goods to go around, it is also true that as the population grows older each person in the labor force has a larger number of elderly people to support and the cost of supporting a retired person is much greater than supporting a child.

The drop in the child dependency ratio due to the fertility decline will not necessarily free resources to meet the needs of the growing older population. It has been shown that reallocating resources from children to old people is an arduous and difficult task. Serious studies have demonstrated that in the Organisation for Economic Co-operation and Development (OECD) countries public spending per old person on social services and transfers have been two to three times larger than public spending per child.[17] Public and private resources freed will be significantly less than those needed by the aging population. Furthermore, the fewer the number of children per family, the greater will be the tendency to invest in each child and as a result fewer resources will be available at the margin. Thus, both the young and the old will need increasing costly social services and financial support. To meet these needs will require a thorough reevaluation of existing social security systems.

Old age social security systems are in trouble worldwide.[18] As community- and government-based arrangements are beset by escalating costs which require high tax rates, the burden of responsibility for maintaining the ageing population will fall more and more into the hands of private individuals and families.

Furthermore, the changing values on the role of women in society has created conditions which tend to favor the gradual movement of women from the home to the workplace. Economic reasons have also forced many families to rely on both parents joining the work force. Otherwise, they would not be able to maintain a reasonable standard of living that would permit them to educate their children in a satisfactory manner. Expenditures in our contemporary consumer society have become so weighty that the average working family cannot prosper without the additional income provided by the working mother. These trends do not seem to be propitious for a reversal of the declining fertility rates in Western Europe, at least in the short run.

There is also the added problem that by the year 2050 more than 55 percent of the world's women will be outside the child-bearing age. The situation will be even worse in the industrialized nations where it is estimated that over 65 percent of all women would not fall within the reproductive range. This is in sharp contrast with the approximately 50 percent figure which demographers believe was the percentage of women of child-bearing age in the past.

The real tragedy of this hazardous trend is the fact that the number of young people, the cream and future of any healthy society, within the total population will decline in both absolute and relative terms. By the year 2050, it is estimated that adolescents and young adults will represent less than 12 percent of the world population. This constitutes a significant fall when compared with the 18 percent of 1995. The decline in the industrialized nations will be even worse, less than 9 percent.

The full realization of the economic and social consequences of the rapidly ageing process has not dawned yet on large sectors of the population. They are still not fully aware that the present demographic trends of longer lives and falling fertility rates has brought about a radical aging of the human population, a phenomenon never before experienced in the history of mankind. Europe, in particular, is exposed to the dangers of an aging population that will require ever increasing security assistance when the old are no longer able to maintain themselves. The consumer-oriented societies of our postmodern age, with their tendency to have low saving rates, do not seem to provide adequate mechanisms for a viable and satisfactory solution of this very real and threatening problem.

The gravity of the situation should not be underestimated. The figures speak for themselves. The short-term demographic outlook leaves no doubt that by the year 2030 the elderly dependency ratios will have reached 49.2 percent in Germany, 48.3 percent in Italy, and almost 40 percent in France and the United Kingdom, more than double than what they are today. Population aging is less pronounced in the United States and in Canada. Nevertheless, the elderly dependency ratios will reach almost 40 percent by the year 2030. After the year 2030, elderly dependency ratios are expected to stabilize in most countries except Japan and Italy where they will experience a further increase of ten percentage points.

By the year 2030, the projected long-term increase in the very elderly dependency ratio will reach slightly over 48 percent in France and Italy.[19] In Sweden the rate is expected to attain 52.2 percent and approximately 45 percent in Germany, the United States, the United Kingdom, and Canada. Japan will have the highest rate (56.3 percent) followed closely by Sweden (52.2 percent).[20]

The significant rise in the projected elderly dependency ratios of most countries is, to a large extent, due to the passage of the postwar baby-boom generation into retirement.[21] However, independently of the reasons for the rise in the projected elderly dependency ratios, the fact still remains that the world's population is aging rapidly.

In 1990 slightly more than 9 percent of the world's population (almost half a billion people) was 60 years or older. By the year 2030 the number will triple to 1.4 billion. In the OECD countries, the average percentage of the population over 60 year old will climb from 18.2 percent in 1990 to 30.8 percent in 2030. In Eastern Europe and the former Soviet Union the percentage rise will only be from 13.8 percent to 22.2 percent. The expected increase in North Africa and the Middle East will be from 6.2 in 1990 to 13.1 in the year 2030 whilst in sub-Sahara Africa the rise will be much smaller, from 5.2 percent to 6.8 percent in 2030. Asia and Latin America will also sustain increases, from 6.3 percent to 11.6 percent in the former and from 8.2 percent to 16.4 percent in the latter.

The need for new arrangements for old age security becomes more critical as the percentage of the population over 60 increases and that of the young decreases. By the year 2030, when the very elderly dependency ratios will have reached an average of approximately 50 percent in Western Europe, the Old Continent will face a critical stage.[22] The traditional old age security arrangements will have to be reformed and made more viable if social upheavals are to be avoided. Public and private institutions have no choice but to take the necessary measures that will help solve a rapidly deteriorating situation. A just and satisfactory solution must be found, keeping in mind the well-being of the old and the young who, at the same time, cannot disavow the serious responsibility that they have toward their elders.

As most countries can no longer afford the formal programs of old age security that, in many cases, are on the verge of bankruptcy, the need for a thorough reevaluation of existing policies is no longer a question of debate. It is an accepted fact that liberal early retirement schemes and generous benefits can no longer be maintained. The fabulous and idealistic goals of the Welfare State proved to be unattainable. The state also has its limitations as recent events have demonstrated. Can the Welfare State survive the challenges of the twenty-first century? At present it seems doubtful unless it experiences fundamental changes more in accordance with the needs of our times and the resources available.

## THE WELFARE STATE AND
## THE ROLE OF THE FAMILY

During the years following the Second World War, the trend toward the Welfare State seemed irreversible. "Freedom from Want" and the guarantee of security for everybody, together with drastic income redistribution policies, became the main objectives of the numerous economic plans introduced by many European socialist governments. The utopian promises of "Freedom from Want" and general welfare became well-known slogans in the European political scene of the sixties and seventies. It was believed by many a prominent economist and social scientist, not to mention politicians, that the Welfare State was capable of solving the most pressing problems of postmodern society. The state, with its generous distributive plans and social security schemes, was to become the deus ex machina that would eliminate poverty whilst, at the same time, posing no overwhelming macroeconomic threat to future generations. The state was to become a sort of Father Christmas in charge of the distribution of "goodies" as if that were the normal and only way of satisfying the needs of large sectors of the population. The goal of "Freedom from Want" would finally be attained through the generosity and patronage of government authorities.

The optimism and faith in the bounties of the Welfare State that characterized the 1960s and 1970s gradually turned to skepticism, even among those who had most strongly spoused its interventionist policies. After years of Welfare State initiatives many countries are beginning to realize that the utopian ideals of its sponsors—among them Freedom from Want—did not materialize. On the contrary, there are already signs of possible economic and social upheavals in the near future if present trends continue. The costs of overextended government expenditures have become too high even for the industrialized countries to afford. Governments no longer have the financial means to maintain the same level of public expenditures without running into serious economic difficulties.[23]

It is a well-known fact that the budget deficits of many European countries are at an all-time high.[24] The rise in unemployment rates complicates even more an already deteriorating budget deficit situation, threatening the political and social stability of the continent and casting a shadow on the future of the Euro. Drastic austerity measures, although unpopular, will have to be taken in order to reduce government expenditures and alleviate an already overburdened deficit. The European governments are well aware of the the great need to reevaluate their social security systems and their often abusive redistributive policies. If they are not able to cut their deficits to 3 percent of gross domestic product (GDP), the European Union may become another utopia for future historians to discuss.

France, for example, with its overextended welfare system, has no choice but to reevaluate its entire social security system.[25] The French fully realize that the time has arrived for the government to take action and inform the public about the seriousness of the problem: the near bankruptcy of the Welfare State. The government realizes that if it does not take strong measures in the areas of social security, pension plans, and so forth, France faces, at a not too distant future, a rude awakening, the consequences of which can be disastrous for the French nation. The numerous strikes that took place in November–December 1995 were already scary warnings of what might come later.[26]

It seems that for many European countries the moment of truth has finally arrived. The great Welfare State ideal of the famous Lord Beveridge has run afoul of its grandiose expectations.[27] The Beveridge Report had promoted a much larger role for the state in old-age security under the assumption that it would be able to compensate for private market failures. Beveridge saw publicly financed pensions as a way for the state to guarantee a minimum income to all older persons. They were clearly meant to provide a very generous pension to the old.[28] However, Beveridge's belief that no power less than the state "can ensure adequate total outlays at all times" has not materialized. It is time that the Europeans become aware that the state is not omnipotent and cannot solve all problems. With the below-replacement fertility rates and increasing longevity, the elderly dependency ratio has increased to such a level that the usual pay-as-you-go retirement system can no longer be sustained. The entire system is on the verge of bankruptcy. To avoid such an outcome the only viable alternatives are to increase taxes, reduce pension benefits, or increase significantly the retirement age. Alternatives which are difficult to enforce in democratic states where the retirees and older generations constitute such a large proportion of the total population.

Governments that find themselves with serious budget problems, as is the case in many European countries, will no longer be able to finance the overgenerous social security plans that were promised by the Welfare State. It is obvious that the state will no longer be able to maintain the level of expenditures that it had in the past, especially when government spending represents one half of the GDP. The tax load is already so heavy that in certain countries tax revenues represent almost 50 percent of GDP. Thus, the need for cuts in social programs which are no longer indispensable becomes imperative.

When people of working age outnumber the retirement age group (five to one), the danger of the social security system going into bankruptcy is less imminent and the much-needed revisions can be postponed, at least in the short run. However, once the ratio of the economically active population to the retirees falls and becomes two to one, as it is expected to be in the year 2050, the situation becomes really critical. Therefore, drastic revisions of the social security system must start taking place much before that date if total bankruptcy is to be avoided with its concomitant disastrous effects for the economy.

Perhaps, in order to avoid further encroachments on the private lives of the population and reduce the size of an overburdened state, the solution may lie in the privatization of social insurance.[29] The challenge consists in devising new old age security systems that are acceptable to the old but that do not hamper sustainable economic growth and the proper development of the young.

The Welfare State is no substitute for the family, as recent trends tend to indicate. Leaving aside the ethical implications of a demise of the family, purely economic considerations may find it necessary that it play a more significant role in the protection and safeguard of the material and spiritual of its members, especially of the young and the elderly. Present-day population trends in the Western World, if they continue, will not facilitate this endeavor but, on the contrary, aggravate it as the size and influence of the family diminishes.

The sharp decline in fertility rates will unavoidably affect the composition of the family. If the present subreplacement fertility rates continue, as they are expected to do according to United Nations estimates, the family will undoubtedly experience substantial changes. With fertility rates in many European countries below 1.5, the former family units composed of grandparents and aunts and uncles, not to mention cousins and so forth, will be a thing of the past. The cohesiveness and unity of the traditional large family will be replaced by a family composed of a single son or daughter, his parents and grandparents. The only child of the future "progressive" family will no longer have the benefit of enjoying the assistance and advice of relatives who in the past had often served as a fall back when the family was experiencing difficulties and had to rely on them for assistance.

On the basis of the existing estimates on population trends that we have discussed above, it is not too difficult to visualize the new typology of the family in the years to come. It is still too early to determine with certainty the economic and social consequences of such a change in the family structure. However, Nicholas Eberstadt does give us a good idea as to how family and social life will change under these new parameters. He says the following: "Throughout the remembered human experience, the family has been the primary and indispensable instrument for socializing a people. In the family, the individual found extended bonds of obligation and reciprocal resources—including emotional resources—upon which he could draw." Under the demographic projections generally accepted, he continues, "all that would change momentously. For many people, 'family' would be understood as a unit that does not include any biological contemporaries or peers."[30]

The aging of the population will only aggravate an already precarious situation. As the population grows older, there is a greater need for a secure source of income for old age. Governments have mechanisms to provide income security for the elderly as part of the social safety net to reduce inequalities and other economic needs of the poor and unemployed. But as formal programs are beset by increasing costs that require high tax rates and deter private sector growth, a viable alternative may lie in informal arrangements, especially those that are family based.

It was common in the past, and even today in large areas of the world, for informal and traditional arrangements to take care of the old, providing them with some type of income security. The elderly would receive from close relatives or extended family the necessary requirements of food and shelter. But, as the size of the families becomes smaller and smaller the burden of assistance increasingly falls on a smaller number of family members, in some cases an only grandson or granddaughter. In addition, as employment opportunities for the younger generation increase, the opportunity cost of taking care of the old increases and the young are less willing to dedicate time and effort to satisfy the needs of their progenitors. The same occurs with those women who, in order to supplement their household income, have found it necessary to find outside jobs away from the family rather than to remain at home and take care of the young and the old who need assistance. This trend has become more acute as the number of women in the labor market has increased significantly. These changing family patterns have weakened traditional arrangements for income security for the old as in the case of the extended family.

The family has always been considered the foundation on which is based the broader communion of parents and children, of brothers and sisters, and of relatives and other members of the household. The union that characterizes the interpersonal relationships of the family has constituted the inner strength that animates the family and the community. All members of the family share in the responsibility for the care of small children, the sick and the aged. But, this family communion will occur only when parents educate their children in an environment of responsible freedom and a spirit of self giving.

To avoid many and the varied forms of tension and discord that frequently appear in families, parents have the responsibility to prepare their children from early childhood for the day when they become adults and claim their rightful independence to be free from parental authority. At the same time, they must be taught to avoid selfishness and develop a spirit of sacrifice and self-giving, a difficult task in our contemporary materialistic society. This is the only way to achieve the fullness of community life within the family and its broader ramifications in society. Otherwise, societies will continue to be torn and split by tensions caused by a false understanding of freedom and unrestrained individual and group interests; societies that lack the necessary moral principles that will help curb the excesses of man's selfishness.

With the arrival of the Industrial Revolution and in the wake of disordered industrial and urban development, family bonds have been weakened and the spirit of sacrifice and service has been evaporating gradually. It is precisely the weakening of these family bonds and spirit of sacrifice, together with a decline in moral principles, what may limit the effectiveness of the role of the family as a partial substitute for the existing and nearly bankrupt public security arrangements. The family, undermined by a spirit of selfishness and guided by utilitarian principles that do not recognize the virtues of sacrifice and self-giving, will be deprived of playing the role for which it is naturally fitted: the protection and assistance of the elderly, especially those within its own extended family. What a lost opportunity this would be!

If by modernity is meant the gradual breakdown of many of the principles and values which, through the ages, constituted the foundation of our civilization, the world is on the path to self-destruction.[31] Selfishness grounded on a utilitarian philosophy that stresses the importance of the "ego" and considers all past values as "demode" cannot but lead in the end to a society that rests on the Darwinian principle "the survival of the fittest." Such a philosophy carried à outrance leaves no place for love and understanding and much less for the nonproductive infirm and the old.

In a depopulated world the family or better still the family of the future will be reduced to a minimum expression in which the very concept of close relatives will be a thing of the past. Based on purely utilitarian principles and under the influence of modernity with its new set of "morals," the value of a person will be measured almost exclusively in terms of his material contribution to society. Under those circumstances, it would not seem very probable that the younger generation, educated and formed under those set of principles, would be inclined to finance the security of its elders. The opportunity cost, measured in dollars and cents, would be too high.

In spite of the failure of the Welfare State, there are still be people who want to place on the public sector the responsibility for the care of the sick and elderly. The claim persists that, given the fact that the elderly did not take the necessary provisions for the future during their productive years, the young can not be held responsible for their needs. However, the problem remains as to how the state with a bankrupt public social security system will be able to assist in the near future the increasing number of elderly people.

A philosophy based on the principle that "in the end we will all be dead" tends to lead to a society that scorns savings and is geared toward consumption. The enjoyment of life in the present takes precedence over the virtue of saving for the future. The future will take care of itself! A rude awakening may be in store for those who still believe that there is always the State to rely on in time of need. If the young follow this philosophy, they will have to confront similar problems to the ones facing their parents and grandparents. A society ruled by such norms, where selfishness and pure egotism prevails, has no time for unremunerated sacrifice and self giving. To expect that the family will play a significant role among the informal security arrangements that are under discussion is doubtful unless there is a renewal in family values and a deeper understanding of the positive effects of human virtues.

Unfortunately, a so-called progressive society guided primarily by utilitarian principles will most certainly not nurture among the young the development of a virtuous life. Consequently, individuals and families, carried away by their materialistic and selfish interests, will not be inclined to accept generously the responsibility and burden of assisting the elderly, the sick and the infirm. On the contrary, they would still claim that the responsibility for their care, rests on a vague term called "society," whatever that may mean. As a result, the elderly will be neglected in ways that are totally unacceptable not only because of the suffering it causes them but also because of the spiritual impoverishment of many families that no longer would enjoy the love and understanding of the elderly.

Among the victims of this late twentieth century phenomenon which is characterized by declining birth rates and the aging of the population, the elderly have been especially affected. As the productive years of the old tend to be a thing of the past, they are considered no longer a useful asset for society and are liable to be easily ignored or even discarded. This danger is not to be taken lightly. The increasing demand for what is now called mercy killings or assistance to suicide cannot be ignored in a society that is gradually running the risk of becoming more depersonalized and inhuman.

However, the family still possesses sufficient energies capable of rescuing man from his dehumanizing selfishness. It has the potential of making its members aware of their personal dignity, whether young or old, and by so doing contribute also to the improvement and stability of society. Inspired and guided by the principle of self-giving, the family can serve as the perfect catalyst for performing acts of service and solidarity. No better way to demonstrate this spirit of self-giving than by assisting those family member who because of illness or old age can no longer help themselves and to whom the young generations owe an eternal debt of gratitude. The new generations of the young should always remember the contribution made by their parents and grandparents to their lives. They should not hesitate to give them the much needed security and love that they need and long for during the declining years of their lives.

Over two thousand years ago, Aesop, the great Greek writer of fables, wrote in The Frog and the Ox, "Gratitude is the sign of noble souls." It is to be hoped that the new millennium will bring to our disturbed world many noble souls that will not hesitate to meet their family obligations in a spirit of true self-giving and love. The economic needs of the population will best be served in an environment of love and mutual solidarity and this has to start within the family where parents and children learn to live in harmony and mutual assistance. The state is no substitute for the family no matter how much the defenders of collectivist policies have tried to belittle the fundamental unit of a healthy society. It has certain rights and duties which it cannot disregard.

## THE RIGHTS AND
## DUTIES OF THE STATE

No matter how important free competition is for the well functioning of an economic system, it is nevertheless true that it is not the only controlling principle in economic affairs. History has abundantly proven that when purely individualistic ideals are given free rein, the well-being of large sectors of the population have suffered the consequences and opened the door to the assaults of socialism. Economic affairs cannot be run exclusively by unrestrained self-interest and the laws of the market. The economy cannot be governed by itself, especially when the evil tendencies of man are ignored or rejected. Higher and more noble principles must be sought in order to bring about social justice and reduce the tensions and antinomies that prevail in the national and international arenas. As mentioned earlier, the more these moral principles are lacking, the greater will be the need for the state or any other external authority to intervene. To avoid falling into the trap of totalitarianism with its ruinous collectivist policies, the rights and duties of the state must be known and accepted. To apply and respect the principles of subsidiarity and solidarity in the political and economic arenas is the best guarantee against the excesses of both individualism and collectivism.

Leo XIII in his encyclical *Rerum Novarum* had already asked for a more active intervention of the state in economic matters in order to help bring about, among other things, a better understanding between capital and labor, a greater protection for the poor and destitute and the recognition of the natural right to private property.[32] But, it must be stressed also that a greater degree of government intervention (statism) is not by itself the solution to the social problem. The moral good of the economy ( justice) is not an exclusive function of the free play of market forces, but neither can it be made dependent on the arbitrary will of government authorities. Too much power placed in the hands of the state can easily lead to oppression and totalitarianism and, consequently, violate social justice and trample on the most fundamental rights of the human person. The basic rights of individual persons and groups cannot be subordinated to the collective organization of production and/or the whims of the state.[33] To do this would ultimately hamper growth and development and violate the principle of subsidiarity.

The principle of subsidiarity is "a fundamental principle of social philosophy, fixed and unchangeable, that one should not withdraw from individuals and commit to the community what they can accomplish by their own enterprise and industry. So, too, it is an injustice and at the same time a grave evil and a disturbance of right order, to transfer to the larger and higher collectivity functions which can be performed and provided for by lesser and subordinate bodies. Inasmuch as every social activity should, by its very nature, prove a help to members of the body social, it should never destroy or absorb them."[34]

The foundations of the principle of subsidiarity lie in the freedom and dignity of man as well as "in the structure and characteristic features of smaller social circles, to which tasks and rights are due that cannot be fulfilled in a meaningful way by the more comprehensive social bodies."[35] It protects individual persons and smaller social bodies from the inroads of more comprehensive entities such as the state. It also implies the concept of assistance. In brief, what the principle is telling us is that no sector of society can shy away from its obligation to assist those in need.[36]

Collectivism by stressing the role of the state beyond its legitimate functions, encroaches upon the freedom of the individual and, consequently violates the principle of subsidiarity. It would be a gross error to believe that the social nature of man can be fulfilled in the state. It can only be realized if intermediary groups such as the family and other economic, social, political, and cultural groups are respected and honored. Their autonomy is indispensable for the well-being of society and the common good.[37]

The main role of the state is to create the conditions that are necessary for the free exercise of economic activity; an economic activity that will foster employment and growth. Private initiative cannot succeed unless governments provide the proper environment for their development. But, the important role played by the government in the process of development should never blur the fact that it has no right to repress or smother private initiative. It is not the role of the government to compete with the individual, but rather to complement its efforts. On the contrary, it should strengthen individual initiative and whenever possible establish guidelines to attain the common good.

Under the guise of the "Welfare State," governments have gradually been acquiring more and more functions which traditionally have pertained to private initiative. "Freedom from Want" was the main goal of the Beveridge Report, and it was the state's function to make sure that this objective was realized.[38] Through the years, the Welfare State has increasingly tried to impose its owns set of rules with the object of helping the needy and bringing about a more equalitarian society even at the cost of personal liberties.[39]

Otto von Bismarck, the "Iron Chancellor" of the German Empire, was probably the first statesman who introduced many of the welfare measures that in later years became rather fashionable in left-wing socialist circles.[40] The German experience was quickly followed by the socialist Fabian Society in England under the leadership of Sidney and Beatrice Webb.[41] Roosevelt's policies during the New Deal clearly reflected the influence of the English Fabians.

After the Second World War, collectivism in the form of the so-called Welfare State became once again rather popular among many economists and intellectuals of left-leaning tendencies. However, the dangers to private initiative and individual freedoms inherent in such a socialist system seemed to have been overlooked by its sponsors.[42] The principle of sub-sidiarity was fundamentally ignored as too much power was placed in the hands of the state. Even in the case of the environment, contemporary man tends to forget that the solution to many of the problems related to its deterioration does not lie necessarily in more government regulations but in man himself who often lacks the proper appreciation of his re-sponsibility toward the habitat that surrounds him.

## THE ENVIRONMENT:
## THE CULTURAL FACTORS

The specter of overpopulation is very much alive when debating the problems related to the environment. Once again overpopulation is con-sidered by many experts to be the major factor contributing to the deple-tion of natural resources and the deterioration of the environment. There is no doubt that there is a real danger that the habitat in which we live may continue to decay in the years to come. But, it would be erroneous to place the blame on a planet which, according to some professional de-mographers, is heavily overpopulated.

The relationship between population dynamics and the natural envi-ronment is greatly influenced by technology, governmental policies, and the prevailing culture. The new technological advances that have taken place during the twentieth century have affected the environment espe-cially with respect to energy. The consumption of petrol, natural gas, and coal have increased dramatically and, in many instances, contributed to the deterioration of the natural environment. But, on the other hand, proper policy actions have not only ameliorated the environmental de-cline but also improved it, contrary to the opinion of some experts.[43] Per-haps the area that needs to be stressed the most is the way cultural factors, in particular education, affect the environment.

The problem does not lie in an overpopulated world but, as indicated earlier, in man himself who has not been trained to respect and love the habitat which surrounds him. Can it be really said that the earth's re-sources have reached or are rapidly reaching their absolute limits and a pe-riod of scarcities is in the making? The neo-Malthusians, basing their con-clusions on the assumption that all factors in the population-resource equation remain the same, would answer in the affirmative. However, sci-entific findings do not seem to give credence to such a position. In a pub-lic debate that took place some years ago between Lester Brown and Julien Simon, the latter presented significant data that cast serious doubts on the forecasts of the prophets of doom and gloom. These data were given fur-ther weight by the research carried out by Julien Simon.[44] The important point that needs to be stressed is that many of the gloomy arguments presented by the neo-Malthusians do have serious flaws and, as they often lack solid scientific evidence, should not be taken as absolute truths.[45]

To single out overpopulation as the main culprit for the deterioration of the environment ignores the more fundamental problem related to the ecological question: man himself. If he acts arbitrarily and uses the earth in an irresponsible manner, sooner or later he will have to pay the price for his recklessness. Man must respect everything that constitutes the natural world, which the ancient Greeks called the "cosmos." The concern for the preservation of the natural habitat has been a constant preoccupation of Pope John Paul II. In his encyclical *Sollicitudo Rei Socialis* he emphatically states that man must acquire a growing awareness of the fact that he "cannot use with impunity the different categories of beings, whether living or inanimate—animals, plants, the natural elements—simply as one wishes, according to one's own economic needs. On the contrary, one must take into account *the nature of each being* and of its *mutual connection* in an ordered system, which is precisely the 'cosmos.'"[46]

Even though the neo-Malthusian predictions on the limits of growth and development have serious shortcomings, it is nevertheless true that in the long run natural resources are limited. Man does not have absolute dominion over nature. To believe otherwise and to use natural resources as if they were inexhaustible seriously jeopardizes their availability both at present and above all for future generations.

The family, in accordance with its proper nature, is the main source from which the young will acquire the human virtues that will teach them to respect the common good and love the environment that surrounds them. It is the first and fundamental structure of human ecology and it is within its nucleus that man receives his first formative principles; principles that will help him become aware of his responsibility for the preservation of the natural habitat. Children will be taught within the family to love and respect the natural environment which surrounds them. They will discover and admire the beauty of the world that God has created for their enjoyment and that He has placed at their disposal so that, through their work, they can reap the fruits of the earth. Man, they will learn, has an obligation to protect the radical good of life in all its manifestations and love and preserve the environment for the benefit of future generations in accordance with the plan of the Creator.

The role of the state is a subsidiary one. It cannot absorb the functions that properly belong to the family and other private intermediary organizations. The principle of subsidiarity must be honored in all matters, including the relationship between state and family. To comply with this fundamental principle will have positive economic and social effects that will redound to the benefit of a free economic system. To reject it would violate social justice and open the door to abuse of power.

The destruction of the natural environment goes together with the sub-version of the human environment. If man lacks the moral conditions for the safeguard of an authentic "human ecology," he will not be able to use the earth with the respect for the original good purpose for which it was given to him by his Creator.[47] A well-ordered society is conditioned by the social structure on which it is based.

Population growth is not the real cause behind the break in the har-mony of man's relations with nature, as some "experts" believe. There-fore, it is misleading to claim that in order to protect the environment it is necessary to curtail population growth. Population cannot be made the scapegoat for man's personal deficiencies. The real culprit for the deterio-ration and devastation of the earth's habitat lies primarily in man himself who, because of his selfishness and lack of social virtues, very often has little if any regard for the common good.

Undoubtedly, the environment with all of its economic and political ef-fects presents a challenge to contemporary man. He must accept the chal-lenge and do whatever is necessary to protect the natural environment which is so crucial for the future well-being of humanity. This must be done through increased research and the development of improved attitudes that teach the young to respect wildlife and the beauty of the natural habitat. Governments have an important role to play in this worthwhile effort but in order to limit their level of intervention people in general—businessmen and private citizens—must take seriously their re-sponsibility toward the common good and, as much as possible, avoid highly polluting production processes. The less government the better, if political and economic freedoms are among man's most cherished goals. Once again the principle of subsidiarity must be respected.

The new millennium has brought with it new challenges. The most important legacy of the last decades has been the challenge of global-ization. The narrow economic prism of viewing the world, a character-istic of previous centuries, is a thing of the past. The international system is becoming more and more unified; economic factors playing an ever-increasing role. How this challenge can be met is the subject of the next chapter.

## NOTES

1. See an excellent study prepared by Dr. Sophia Aguirre entitled *Population, Resources and Environment* (Washington, DC: The Catholic University of America Press, 2000).

2. The well-known French demographer Alfred Sauvy a number of years ago was already warning his countrymen of the dangers posed by declining fertility

rates. He unequivocally mentions that governments have tended to ignore the negative consequences of such a trend, in particular with respect to the aging of the population and the continuous decline in the relative number of young people. As far back as 1987 he went as far as to say that the aging of the population can be just as dangerous for France as the spread of AIDS. He claimed, "Bien moins connu, bien moins redouté que le SIDA, le vieillissement de la population. Il reste a savoir lequel est le plus dangereux pour la nation. Édifiant serait un sondage sur cette question, suivi d'une étude sérieuse." See Alfred Sauvy, *L'Europe Submergée* (Paris: Dunod, 1987), 128.

3. When asked how he would define the white plague, Chaunu answered, "Qu'est-ce que la peste blanche? La désesperance generalisée. L'indifférance à la vie, le réfus de tout système de valeurs, l'égoisme presenté comme le plus raffiné des beaux-arts." See Pierre Chaunu and Georges Suffert, *La Peste Blanche, Comment éviter le suicide de l'Occident* (Paris: Editions Gallimard, 1976), 8.

4. See Paul R. Ehrlich, *The Population Bomb* (New York: Ballantine Books, 1971), chapters 1 and 5. See also Donella H. Meadows, Dennis L. Meadows, Jorgen Randers, and William W. Behrens III, *The Limits of Growth* (New York: Universe Books, 1972).

5. According to the latest data from the United Nations, total world population in the year 2000 was 6,057 million, a reduction of approximately 1,000 million from earlier forecasts. See United Nations, *World Population Prospects: The 2000 Revision* (New York: United Nations, 2001). See also United Nations, *World Population Prospects, as Assessed in 1963* (New York: United Nations, 1966). See also U.S. Department of State Bulletin, Washington, DC, 1969. Data taken from Julian L. Simon, *The Ultimate Resource* (Princeton, NJ: Princeton University Press, 1981), 169.

6. In the 1930s the fear was exactly the opposite. A large number of countries were concerned with the expected decline in population growth. This was particularly true in the case of France. Many prominent economists were predicting stagnation as one of the most important dynamic variables of growth, population, was expected to decline. See, among others, Alvin Hansen, *Business Cycle Theory* (Boston: Ginn & Company, 1927), *Full Recovery or Stagnation?* (New York: McGraw-Hill, 1938), and *Fiscal Policy and Business Cycle* (New York: Norton, 1941).

7. Among the better known prophets of gloom and doom during the 1960s and 1970s the following can be mentioned: Meadows et al., *The Limits to Growth*. See also Paul R. Ehrlich, *The Population Bomb* (New York: A Sierra Club/Ballantine Book, 1968); René Dumont and Bernard Rosier, *The Hungry Future* (New York: Praeger, 1969); and William Paddock and Paul Paddock, *Famine 1975! America's Decision: Who Will Survive?* (Boston: Little, Brown, 1967). On the other hand, there were prominent economists during that same period who challenged their pessimistic views on the future of the world. See Colin Clark, "World Population (1958)" in *Population*, ed. Edward Pohlman (New York: New American Library, 1973); Julian Simon, "Science Does Not Show that There Is Overpopulation in the U.S.—or Elsewhere" in *Population*, ed. Edward Pohlman (New York: New American Library, 1973); and Simon Kuznets, *Population, Capital and Growth* (New York: Norton, 1973).

8. The United Nations data on fertility rates present different fertility scenarios, ranging from high fertility to low fertility. Medium fertility rates which lie at the center of the projection scenario imply that each woman of child-bearing age will have 2.2 children. The fertility gap between the high (more than two) and the low fertility (less than two) scenarios is about one child. The average fertility rate in Europe was approximately 1.4 in 1997 while in Africa it was well above 2.5. See United Nations, *World Population Projections to 2150* (New York: United Nations, 1998).

9. See United Nations, *World Population Projections to 2150* (New York: United Nations, 1998). For the most recent data, see also United Nations, *World Population Prospects, the 2000 Revision*, Highlights, 1.

10. United Nations, *World Population Projections to 2150*, 2.

11. Thomas Malthus, *On Population* (New York: Random House, 1960).

12. See United Nations, Population Division, Department of Economic and Social Information and Policy Analysis, *World Population Prospects*, 1995. The most recent data show a further drop in fertility rates in Europe. The average for the period 1995–2000 was 1.41. See *World Population Prospects, the 2000 Revision*, 4.

13. Expectation of life at birth for the world will probably rise from 65.0 in 1995–2000 to 76.0 in 2000–2050. See United Nations, *World Population Prospects, the 2000 Revision*, 4.

14. See Alberto Martínez Piedra, "The Welfare State and Its Ethical Implications: A Viable Alternative for Post-Castro Cuba?" *Cuba in Transition*, vol. 6, (Springfield, MD: ASCE Books, 1997), 352–72.

15. Conscious of the fact that the aging of the world's population represents an unparalleled, but urgent, challenge to governments, nongovernmental organizations and private groups, the United Nations General Assembly (resolution 47/5) decided that the year 1999 be observed as the "International Year of Older Persons." See "The Ageing of the World's Population," United Nations, Department of Public Information, DPI/1858/AGE, October 1996.

16. Elderly dependency ratios are defined as "the ratio of the population aged 65 and over to the population aged 15 to 64." International Monetary Fund, *Aging Population and Public Pension Schemes* (Washington, DC: International Monetary Fund, 1996), 4.

17. OECD (1998) cited in Palmer, Smeeding, and Torrey (1998).

18. See Peter Heller, "Aging in the Asian Tigers: Challenges for Fiscal Policy," Occasional Paper Series (Washington, DC: International Monetary Fund, 1997). See also Chand, Sheetal, and Jaeger, "Aging Populations and Public Pension Schemes," Occasional Paper Series (Washington, DC: International Monetary Fund, 1996), and Maria Sophia Aguirre, "Aging Population: Paying the Consequences," *World and I*, April 2000, 66–71.

19. The very elderly ratio is defined as the population aged 75 and over as a percent of the population aged 65 and over. International Monetary Fund, *Aging Population and Public Pension Schemes*, 4.

20. International Monetary Fund, *Aging Population and Public Pension Schemes*, 4.

21. International Monetary Fund, *Aging Population and Public Pension Schemes*, 3.

22. International Monetary Fund, *Aging Population and Public Pension Schemes*, 3–4.

23. Alberto Martínez Piedra, "The Welfare State and Its Ethical Implications," 157.

24. For a very good analysis of the implications of the prospective aging of the U.S. population for the security system, see Liam Ebrill, *Social Security, Demographic Trends, and the Federal Budget,* unpublished manuscript.

25. The cases of France, Germany, and Sweeden are well documented in Maria Sophia Aguirres' article "Sustainable Development: Why the Focus on an Aging Population." See *International Journal of Social Economics,* 29:3, 2002.

26. For an excellent summary of the many problems facing the Welfare State in France, see Patrice Bourdelais, Xavier Gaullier, Marie Jose Imbault-Huart, Denis Olivennes, Jean-Marie Poursin, and François Stasse, *Etat-Providence, Arguments pour une Réforme* (Paris: Editions Gallimard, 1996). It is in this book that the authors ask the pertinent question: "Qui l'ignore? La réforme de l'Etat-providence constitue l'horizon indépassable de nos prochaînes années. Probablement les grèves de novembre-décembre 1995 ont-elles marqué un tournant a cet égard, l'entreé dans une phase de turbulances durables."

27. William H. Beveridge, *Full Employment in a Free Society* (New York: Norton, 1945), 36.

28. A. Atkinson, *State Pensions, Taxation and Retirement Income: 1981–2031* (London: Simon and Schuster International, 1989).

29. For an excellent study of the Chilean alternative to public pension and health insurance system and its intention to replace the old system with a private sector security system, see G. A. Mackenzie, *Social Security Issues in Developing Countries: The Latin American Experience,* unpublished document.

30. Nicholas Eberstadt, "World Population Implosion?" *The Public Interest,* no. 129, fall 1997.

31. Among the many writers who have written about the crisis of our age, special mention should be made of Sorokin. See Pitirim A. Sorokin, *The Crisis of Our Age* (New York: E. P. Dutton, 1941). Wilhelm Roepke's well-known book *The Social Crisis of Our Time* has already been mentioned in previous chapters.

32. Leo XIII, *Rerum Novarum* #49.

33. "Growth must not be allowed merely to follow a kind of automatic course resulting from the economic activity of the individuals. Nor must it be entrusted solely to the authority of government. Hence, theories which obstruct the necessary reforms in the name of a false liberty must be branded as erroneous. The same is true of those theories which subordinate the basic rights of the individual persons and groups to the collective organization of production." See "Pastoral Constitution on the Church in the Modern World (Gaudiem et Spes)" #65 in *The Documents of Vatican II* (New York: Guild Press, 1966), 273–74.

34. Pius XI, *Quadragesimo Anno* #79.

35. See Joseph Cardinal Hoffner, *Christian Social Teaching* (Cologne: Ordo Socialis), 52. Translated from the German *Christliche Gesselschaptslehre* (8.erw. Auflage. Butzon und Bercker, 1983), 52.

36. Etymological the term proceeds from the Latin word *subsidium,* which means help or assistance.

37. John Paul II, *Centesimus Anno* #13.

38. The English economist Lord Beveridge left no doubt as to the role of the state in economic matters when he wrote, "Full employment cannot be won

and held without a great extension of the responsibilities and powers of the State exercised through organs of the central Government." See William H. Beveridge, *Full Employment in a Free Society*. (New York: Nortion, 1945), 36. See also pages 17 and 38. For an in depth defense of the "Welfare State," see A. C. Pigou, *The Economics of Welfare* (London: Macmillan, 1952).

39. With reference to the "Welfare State," Roepke says the following: "Its essential purpose is no longer to help the weak and needy, whose shoulders are not strong enough for the burden of life and its vicissitudes. This purpose is receding and, indeed, frequently to the detriment of the neediest. Today's welfare state is not simply an improved version of the old institutions of social insurance and public assistance. In an increasing number of countries it has become the tool of social revolution aiming at the greatest possible equality of income and wealth. The dominating motive is no longer compassion but envy." See Wilhelm Roepke, *A Humane Economy*, 156. See also Ludwig von Mises' brief but provocative book, *The Anti-Capitalist Mentality* (New York: D. Van Nostrand, 1956).

40. Bismarck's sponsored Welfare State was not financed by the state but by employers and employees—quite different from a Welfare State that relies heavily on government-financed assistance. See Brian Reading, *The Fourth Reich* (London: Weidenfeld and Nicolson, 1955), 36. See also Alberto Martínez Piedra, "The Welfare State and Its Ethical Implications: A Viable Alternative for Post-Castro Cuba?" in *Cuba in Transition*, volume 7 (Washington, DC: Association for the Study of the Cuban Economy, 1997).

41. See Sidney and Beatrice Webb, *History of Trade Unionism*, 1894.

42. The well-known economist Milton Friedman has the following to say concerning the adverse effects of the Welfare State: "The waste is distressing, but it is the least of the evils of the paternalistic programs that have grown to such massive size. Their major evil is their effect on the fabric of our society. They weaken the family; reduce the incentive to work, save, and innovate; reduce the accumulation of capital; and limit our freedom. These are the fundamental standards by which they should be judged." See Milton Friedman and Rose Friedman, *Free to Choose* (New York: Harcourt Brace Jovanovich, 1979), 17.

43. For an excellent study of this subject matter, see Sophia Aguirre, *Population, Resources and Environment* (Washington, DC: The Catholic University of America Press, 2000).

44. See Julien I. Simon, *The Ultimate Resource II* (Princeton, NJ: Princeton University Press, 1996).

45. Sophia Aguirre, *Population, Resources and Environment*.

46. John Paul II, *Sollicitudo Rei Socialis* #34.

47. John Paul II, *Centesimus Anno* #38.

# 9

—⚡—

# The Challenge
# of Globalization

## DIVERSITY WITHIN UNITY

The remarkable technological changes that have taken place during the last fifty years would have surprised even such a pioneering and inventive mind as that of Jules Verne in the nineteenth century. There is no doubt that the world is changing rapidly in many areas of scientific research. These innovative technological and scientific changes, which have had such positive results on the standards of living of the Western World, once again have raised expectations as to the inevitability of man's continuous economic and material progress. It is genuinely believed that the process of globalization which is taking place will bring about a new world order of peace and prosperity.[1]

Overall with minor periods of recession, the Western economies have experienced rapid and continuous rates of economic growth; a phenomenon which has led some experts to believe that business cycles are a thing of the past. Business Cycle Theory has been relegated to the bookshelves of libraries to be studied by historians and researchers. In the new age of continual progress, the study of business cycles is no longer a "must" in academic circles. The "magnificent performance" of the economy during the last decades has convinced some experts that the contemporary world has nothing to fear from the Kondratieff cycles. According to the late Professor Joseph Schumpeter of Harvard University, these long wave cycles, when they coincide at any time with the corresponding phases of other cycles of lesser magnitude (called Juglar and Kitchin), produce phenomena of unusual intensity, especially if the phases that coincide are those of prosperity and depression. Since the industrial revolution, the phase of prolonged prosperity (lasting approximately fifty years) which results from the innovative spirit of capitalism, is followed by periods of deep and long depressions.[2] Using Schumpeter's familiar terminology, can it be said that the gale of continuous innovations, that was responsible for the growth of capitalism, not only has not diminished in force but on the contrary has increased unabatedly in intensity as new and better products are continuously coming into the market place? Has this optimistic view of the continuous growth of capitalism and economic prosperity been strengthened with the fall of the Soviet Empire? Will the process of globalization reenforce these beliefs in the continual advancement of economic growth and development? Has man's renewed faith in the continuity of human progress forgotten that he is still subject to the many weaknesses and frailties of his fallen human nature and, thus, subject to serious lapses?

The possibilities and opportunities for continuous expansion seem to be even more limitless as the process of globalization becomes more and more a distinct reality. In the new world order that is developing discrete national economies tend to be a thing of the past. A new world order is in the making in which developed and less developed countries are becoming more and more politically and economically integrated under, what some experts believe, might very well turn out to be a super national state. There are great expectations that this process of globalization will bring about ever increasing levels of economic prosperity for the human family. However, in our opinion, the risks involved in such a process, both at the level of national and individual freedoms, are enormous.

Some experts are convinced that the world is on the brink of the most dramatic changes that have taken place since the Industrial Revolution.[3] They claim that the process of globalization that has occurred during the past decades is irreversible, bringing with it, not only economic growth and greater prosperity but also a better understanding between the various countries and cultures of the world.[4] Political, economic, and social barriers will tend to fall and be replaced by a gradual process of unification which will do away with "old-fashioned" divergences. In the field of finance, the process of globalization (unification) is already occurring in the capital markets where they are on the verge of being fused into a single global capital market. Capitalism, with the support of a global economy, seems to be at the crest of a wave that is heading toward unmitigated prosperity. However, the process of globalization is not limited to the economy. It is also bringing about a gradual but progressive unification of culture and society.

As the world becomes more unified (globalized) and differences tend to disappear, a new world order, under the aegis of powerful international organizations, may very well come into existence. The cry for unity could easily overshadow the notion of diversity. As a result, there is a real danger of misunderstanding the very concept of globalization and, consequently, to lose sight of the positive aspects of diversity. A healthy multiplicity of cultural heritages may be sacrificed on the altar of a false unity.

Although cultural differences must be respected it is true that in the past cultural differences have been a source of misunderstanding between peoples and the cause of conflicts. It is equally true that it is dangerous to foster or even accept a slavish conformity of cultures and submit them to cultural models derived from, for example, the Western World. It is particularly alarming to see how some of these models are inspired almost exclusively on purely secular values founded on a radical individualism with a total disrespect for the authenticity of each human culture and the soundness of its underlying ethos.

This attempt to adopt long established cultures to external models is a phenomenon, very often supported by powerful media campaigns, which tries to impose lifestyles, and social and economic programmes which run counter to the traditional principles of other laudable cultures and civilizations. This is particularly true in the case of Western cultural models which, because of their scientific and cultural appeal, attract the attention of countries in the process of development.

A healthy cultural diversity should be respected. But, this diversity "should be understood within the broader horizon of the unity of the human race, this unity constitutes the primordial historical and ontological datum in the light of which the profound meaning of cultural diversity can be grasped. In fact, only an overall vision of both the elements of unity and the elements of diversity makes it possible to understand and interpret the full truth of every human culture."[5]

Cultural differences should never be a source of misunderstanding between peoples and the cause of conflicts and wars. Much less should they be used as a pretext for aggressive claims of some cultures against others which, in the end, will only lead to increased hatreds and further tensions. All pathological manifestations leading to a false sense of patriotism, to self-exaltation and/or excessive forms of nationalism must be avoided if a perdurable and just peace is to be maintained. Otherwise, the road is wide open for conflict and, as a result, the ethnic and cultural minorities are the ones that will suffer the most.

Even though it is essential to respect the principles that characterize a given culture, it is also important to recognize the intrinsic value of other cultures and their contribution to the history of humanity. A cultural diversity which expresses the creative and unique contribution of each member of the human family must be respected but without losing sight of their underlying unity. This distinctness of cultures, understood within the broader horizon of the unity of the human race, should be fostered by means of well-structured programs in education and a constructive dialogue between peoples. A positive and functional dialogue can help maintain peace and avoid the tensions that have led to conflict and war.

The new century that has just begun has opened an era of global communications in which distances are no longer an obstacle to the flow of what in economic terms are called the factors of production. Persons, capital, and know-how can move with increasing facility from country to country and from continent to continent. This process of globalization is affecting not only political and economic relations between peoples but also man's understanding of the world. This in turn can help both the young and old to look beyond their own immediate personal experience and discover the richness to be found in other people's history and their values. Education, especially of the young, should play the leading role in building a more unified and peaceful world by helping people understand the existence of a patrimony that is common to the entire human race.

It is important to point out that without some basic ethical principles, accepted both in theory and practice as a base of reference by all nations, any process of globalization or internationalism is doomed to failure. History is replete with examples where attempts have been made to reach some type of international cooperation leading to a greater degree of unification but which, nevertheless, have failed. Perhaps, one of the best examples can be found in the disappointing results of the League of Nations, the brain child of the allied powers after the First World War. The high expectations and hopes that its founders placed on international institutions were quickly shattered by extreme nationalisms which led to the Second World War. As the late German Professor Wilhem Roepke has so correctly expressed, "If such internationalism places too optimistic hopes upon international institutions, it is again liable to unjustified pessimism as soon as these hopes are inevitably disappointed. It is then very ready to put the blame upon the international institutions instead of upon the lack of preparedness on the part of nations and governments to use such institutions and keep them going."[6]

A false globalization that limits itself to condemning old international institutions (i.e, the League of Nations) and places its hopes on the creation of new structures without analyzing the reasons for the lack of success of their predecessors will also end up in failure. What is needed is an international order respectful of the wide diversity of nationalities and cultures; cultures that in their turn are willing to accept this international order that reflects humanity's most authentic and distinctive features. These characteristics must be based upon generally accepted principles, grounded on Natural Law, that binds together the peoples of all nationalities and cultures in order to better serve the cause of peace and the common good of the human family.

Very often, the causes of international crisis do not always lie at the top levels of international organizations but rather deep down at the national level or even at the individual level. After all, global or international organizations are merely reflections of the members that form part of it. Without a unified acceptance of a basic rule of law, all efforts directed toward a greater degree of globalization and the creation of new international organizations will eventually breakdown under the weight of their proper antinomies and contradictions.[7] All nationalities and cultures must agree upon a common denominator which reflects a unified recognition of a generalized ethical code founded on Natural Law. Without such a recognition, the fundamental rights of the human person are placed in jeopardy. Any process of globalization, whether in the area of economics or otherwise, which does not include as its prime goal the protection of man's human dignity cannot be accepted at face value because, by so doing, man is jeopardizing the essence of our Western cultural heritage.

## THE RIGHTS OF MAN AT THE DAWN
## OF A NEW INTERNATIONAL ORDER

The phrase "human rights" has become so popularized in contemporary literature that very often it has lost its true meaning. In international fora rights have often been understood as what is good, or humane, or socially useful to concede to man. They are considered the result of concessions given to man. But, Sheed reminds us that "concessions, however liberal, are not rights. Rights are what man is entitled to, not what society is willing to let him have. They belong to man because he is man and are valid even against society. Unless they are this, they are not rights at all, but only a more or less hopeful expectation of society's kindness. But *has* man rights? Obviously the answer depends on what man is." As a result, man will be treated in accordance with the way he is conceived.

As the world becomes more unified, it becomes even more imperative to have a proper understanding of man's true nature. The concept of man as a human being must be clearly understood if he is to be treated justly and with the respect that his dignity demands. Without such an understanding, globalization can become a divisive source instead of a unifying one—a source that pulls people apart.

In international relations man cannot shy away from the realization that he is a particular kind of being created by God and that he has real rights rooted in the very nature God has given him. They are not granted to him by society. Unless man is aware of this, he will not be able to grasp fully his obligation to treat others the same way that he treats himself, with all the dignity which, according to their nature, they deserve.[8]

Natural Law cannot be violated with impunity. One way in which human beings tend to go wrong is "when they drift apart from one another or else collide with one another and do one another harm."[9] To respect man's inalienable rights as a human being and to maintain fair play and harmony between individuals falls within the realm of Natural Law. This applies not only at the individual and national levels but also at the international level. Any violation of these precepts of Natural Law can only have negative consequences for society.

When morality comes to mind it is quite natural to think of social relations because, as Lewis points out, the results of bad morality for society are so obvious that everybody can see them: war and poverty and graft and lies and shoddy work.[10] To believe that these evils can be offset by the development of improved social, political, and social institutions is not totally correct. Contrary to popular opinion, it must be stressed once and again that the solution to these evils does not lie exclusively on legislation or the reform of public and private institutions. No matter how excellent these institutions might be in theory, in practice they can be a total failure if man ceases to have those internal qualities of righteousness which are the result of a virtuous life. Again quoting from Lewis: "You cannot make men good by law: and without good men you cannot have a good society."[11]

International organizations are going to play an ever increasing role in this coming historical stage of globalization.[12] Given the trust that "conventional wisdom" is placing on these supranational institutions, it is important to recall that they are what you might call "value neutral." Their success will depend on the righteousness and good intentions of the member countries and the men and women who represent them. If, for example, countries disagree on such a basic principle as human rights, violations will continue to occur. It would be wrong to place the blame on the international organization. The blame falls primarily on those individual states which reject or ignore the existence of a Natural Law, the acceptance of which is the best guarantee for the protection of man's dignity as a human being. No matter how "perfect" the institution might be in theory, in practice it will fail if there is a lack of good faith, rectitude, and honesty.

History has demonstrated that to place a blind faith on international organizations, in spite of their good intentions, can be the source of major disappointments. In the particular area of human rights it can hardly be said that the United Nations has been very successful. To begin with no common agreement exists among the member states as to how the term "human rights" is interpreted and much less defined. For China it has a totally different meaning than it does for the Western democracies. What is a violation of human rights in the United Kingdom is not considered a violation in China. The same applies to other concepts, such as slave labor and so forth, including the idea of democracy. They are interpreted differently depending on the prevailing economic and political regimes that prevail in the member countries.

Although human rights are universal, they do not seem to be always self-evident even though, as mentioned earlier, they are common to all cultures because they are rooted in the nature of every human being. In cases where an unhealthy cultural exceptionalism prevails and there is no common rule of law, agreement on some of these issues is extremely difficult if not impossible.[13] Even the most self-evident inalienable human rights such as self-preservation and the right to procreate may be challenged and become the source of future conflicts.

However, this should not invalidate the need to nurture the intrinsically universal soil of goodwill which makes for fruitful and constructive dialogue. Ideological and selfish interests should not be an obstruction to the process of globalization. It would be erroneous to assume, as a given fact, that globalization is nefarious or that it is being necessarily manipulated by the Western World to foster its own self-interests. Such an assumption is not conducive to a peaceful and constructive solution to the world's major problems. Given these parameters it is utopian to believe that positive and lasting international agreements can be reached on issues that are of basic importance for the peace and well-being of humanity.

Any process of globalization which is not based upon the recognition of certain fundamental values, common to all cultures and nationalities, and rooted in the nature of man, is doomed to failure. Even today, when many academicians and politicians talk in an exhilarating way about the benefits to be derived from globalization, the harsh reality shows that agreements are difficult to reach, even on issues which are vital to the well-being of humanity. The World Economic Forum which took place in Davos, Switzerland, demonstrated once again the difficulty of reaching a consensus on vital issues when there is so much pressure placed on the delegates by powerful interest groups and/or a well-organized "popular" opposition. The World Trade Organization meeting in Seattle, which took place in November 1999, and the World Bank–International Monetary Fund meeting in Washington, D.C., in April 2000, not to mention the protests in Quebec, Gothenberg, and Genoa, are further examples of this lack of agreement on vital issues. Even the European Union is experiencing fundamental disagreements which openly came out between France and Germany at the meeting held in Nice, the famous resort at the French Riviera.

In the absence of a belief in a universal human nature, international cooperation will be difficult to attain no matter how much it night be needed to deal with modern social, economic, and political problems. Global environmental problems not to mention the ones related to nuclear proliferation require substantial international cooperation. The same can be said of the need for international action to promote economic development and to protect human rights.[14] There is even talk of creating, for the common good of society, a universal public authority or world government.

However, the road toward globalization does not necessarily mean the establishment of a world government although there are some scholars, as in the case of Robert George, who believe that Natural Law theory, given the problems of today, envisions the institution of such a world government.[15] However, realizing the risks involved in such an endeavor, George does subject it to certain qualifications. According to him, "Such authority would be justified, as is political authority generally, by its capacity efficiently to generate and implement fair and otherwise reasonable solutions to the community's coordination problems. At the same time, it must observed that concentrating power, and particularly the force of arms, in a central government that is not subject to effective countervailing power is obviously risky."[16]

Roepke, agrees that a supranational organization is a necessity but he argues, "The idea of an international organization which would degrade the individual nations to mere administrative areas is still more insufferable than the previous side by side existence of sovereign nations."[17] His wish is that no *civitas maxima* of a global nature be created but that consideration be given to both the individual life of nations as well as to the community.[18]

If history has alerted us about such dangers, it would be wise to be cautious in the path toward a greater degree of centralization of power. It is true that ideally the institution of a world government could foster the common good and protect the rights of man but, in practice, reality does not seem to confirm such an outcome. If this ideal did not materialize in the past, when man had a clearer concept of the true nature of man, it is doubtful that it can be attained in our age: an age, the product of a secular Enlightenment, where the fundamental principles of Western tradition and culture have been challenged.

In our contemporary world where Natural Law is for all practical purposes denied and where virtue has lost its innocence, we find it very difficult to believe that an international order based on a powerful centralized government can operate with equanimity and justice without abusing its power. The need for an effective countervailing power becomes a necessity if a proper balance is to be restored between the centralized world government and the various national entities that form part of it. One way of lessening the risks of abuse of power would be through the establishment of "constitutional schemes that divide, check and limit governmental powers."[19] Roepke suggests that the best solution would be to establish a federal structure where the weight of political power would be split between the smaller and larger units within the state. The larger units would perform those tasks that are too universal for the smaller. This type of structure "preserves the individual rights of each member unit, without endangering the necessary combination in the respective overall associations."[20]

Only by a general acceptance of the earlier mentioned principle of subsidiarity can the power of a centralized government be peacefully checked. Power tends to corrupt and absolute power tends to corrupt absolutely as we already know and Lord Acton warned us many years ago. History should have taught us that power tends to be abusive if it is not decentralized. This is confirmed if we take a profound look into the fallen nature of man and his often unrestrained desire and abuse of power. Consequently, it is perfectly logical to mistrust the accumulation of power, whether it is in the hands of a national, regional, or international organization.

The best and, ultimately, the only way to solve peacefully many of the problems that result from this growing interdependence among nationalities and cultures lies in the need to instill among all peoples a greater consciousness of the prime values of the principles of subsidiarity and solidarity. As John Paul II has so explicitly stated, "The present reality of global interdependence makes it easier to appreciate the common destiny of the entire human family, and makes all thoughtful people increasingly appreciate the virtue of solidarity."[21]

A better understanding among peoples cannot be separated from the realization that flagrant social inequalities do exist both at the international level and within nations. Thus, at the heart of a true culture of solidarity lies the promotion of justice. And this will require a change of lifestyles, of models of production and consumption and, if necessary, of some of the established structures of power which today govern societies. It is unacceptable that the more affluent world, in spite of the huge technological innovations that are taking place, keeps its eyes closed to the degradation and misery that exists around it. A deeper awareness of the values and limitations within one's culture can only come about though a constructive dialogue between nations in a spirit of solidarity and always within a solid ethical framework.

## MAN AT THE
## CROSSROADS OF HISTORY

The world is at a crossroads of history. The way is open to the future. Man is free to choose the path that can lead him toward a new age of peace and prosperity for all or, on the contrary, he may choose the road that is conducive to his own destruction. Globalization is not to be feared. It can be a great catalyst for the development of a more just and prosperous international socioeconomic order. If used properly, with due respect for the dignity of the human person, it can serve to unite a culturally diverse human family and be the proper channel for the establishment of a new millennium of greater peace and justice for all.

In our materialistic postmodern society there is always the temptation of falling into a new Machiavellism with its philosophy of political amorality.[22] The Florentine statesman seems to justify that in the sphere of politics a good end justifies what is morally wrong. To accept such a principle in the field of politics can be applied easily in economics where the search for power and wealth overrides the intrinsic value of justice. To follow Machiavellian moral principles at the international level under the mantle of scientific positivism would de facto deny actions that are considered morally wrong by Christian standards. But, to do justice to the great Florentine thinker, at the sight of all the corruption that surrounded him, he writes the following in defense of what he calls "our religion" (Christianity): "Though it looks as if the world were to become effeminate and as if heaven were powerless, this undoubtedly is due rather to the pusillanimity of those who have interpreted our religion in terms of *laissez faire (l'ozio)* not in terms of valour *(virtu)*. For, had they borne in mind that religion permits us to exalt and defend the fatherland, they would have seen that it also wishes us to love and honour it, and to train ourselves to be such that we may defend it."[23]

Even though perfection will never be attained in this life, man does have the obligation to struggle to achieve it. He can never justify what is intrinsically evil, as Machiavelli seemed to justify. Historically, utopian dreams of perfect societies have clashed with the reality of human frailties and ended in total failures. The experience of Marxism with its promises of the ideal state is only the latest example of this false belief in the construction of the perfect society. The supporters of globalization must guard against raising expectations that also go beyond the realities of past human experiences. Man must accept his own limitations and avoid being carried away by a false pride in his own accomplishments that can only lead to his perdition.

The belief in the inevitability of continuous progress, very often the result of man's *exclusive* reliance on the power of reason and his innovative mind, is the perfect manifestation of his pride and rejection of the transcendental. Progress, whether economic or otherwise, is not guaranteed by the immanent development of history and much less by a blind reliance on the virtues of globalization. It is wrong to optimistically join the movement of history and oppose the Christian attitude toward the historical future. As the eminent philosopher Dietrich von Hildebrand wrote over thirty years ago, "A shallow, optimistic, 'progressive' ideology of history will have replaced the holy sobriety and supernatural strength born of hope that we witness in the saints."[24]

Globalization can be a marvelous instrument for the good of humanity but, as with all instruments and/or means, it can be used for good or for evil. As long as man is fully aware of his own deficiencies and is not carried away by his own pride and forgets his reliance on the transcendental there is little danger of his making the same mistake as the Hebrews made when they tried to build the Tower of Babel which, they thought, would lead them to paradise.

The ancient Greeks can teach us a lesson about the dangers of an unfounded pride and the rejection of a transcendental divinity. The city of Thebes, well known in the ancient world for its loose living and excessive materialism, provides a good example of arrogant pride together with a dire contempt for what the citizens of Thebes considered their culturally inferior neighbors.

The citizens of Thebes were so engrossed with themselves that they lost sight of their own deficiencies. They were convinced that, because of their righteousness and honesty, they could dictate their own way of life and moral codes to their less-enlightened neighbors. Euripides in his famous tragedy *Bacchae* warns the Greeks about the dangers of self-deception in particular the Thebans' when they attempted to put limits on divinity. He asserts the reality of divinity in a world that, by becoming so hedonistic and foolish in its customs, had denied its reality in favor of an accomodating ideology. Pride comes before fall and this is what Euripides was trying to tell the people of Thebes when he wrote, "When mind runs mad, / dishonours God, / And worships self and senseless pride, / Then Law eternal wields the rod."

It is to be hoped that these famous verses of Euripides expressed in his tragedy *Bacchae* do not have to be applied to our contemporary society in this postmodernist age, where pride, utilitarianism, materialism, and positivism play such important roles and are responsible for an unfounded faith in the inevitability of human progress. To misunderstand the concept of globalization, and to give it a reality which denies the legitimate diversity of national cultures and customs is an error which can only be the source of future conflicts. Much worse is to try to impose upon the less endowed nations of the world certain patterns or models of utilitarian and hedonistic behavior which prevail in the more affluent societies of the Western World and which run counter to their own basic principles. Globalization is not necessarily the panacea for the deficiencies and evils afflicting the modern world. Neither is it the deus ex machina that will automatically guarantee continuous and unprecedented rates of economic growth and development. But, if properly used, globalization can become an important factor in restoring faith in the progress of mankind which suffered such a severe blow during the turbulent twentieth century.

Man must have faith in the progress of the human family. St. Augustine praised the genius of man and paid tribute to man's own achievements on earth. But, for the great Bishop of Hippo, progress cannot take place if it is not grounded on theistic assumptions. Immanent developmentalism cannot ignore the transcendental, as modern Western social and political thought has tended to do since the eighteenth century.

In his masterpiece, *The City of God*, St. Augustine contrasts the growth and development of mankind to a river or torrent that has carried man's virtues as well as his vices through all periods of history. For globalization to be successful, all peoples of good will should follow his advice and concentrate their efforts in the development of human virtues so that the new era of globalization may really contribute to the progress of mankind.[25]

## NOTES

1. For a good analysis of the history of the idea of progress, see Robert Nisbet, *History of the Idea of Progress* (New York: Basic Books, 1970). See also Thomas Molnar, *Utopia: The Perennial Heresy* (New York: Sheed & Ward, 1957).

2. According to Schumpeter, "The three deepest and longest 'depressions' within the epoch covered by our material—1852–1830, 1873–1878 and 1928–1934—all display that characteristic." See Joseph Schumpeter, *Business Cycles* (New York: McGraw-Hill, 1939), 173. See also Joseph Schumpeter, *Capitalism, Socialism and Democracy* (London: Allen & Unwin 1952), chapter 7, 81–86.

3. See Francis Fukuyama, *The End of History and the Last Man* (New York: The Free Press, 1992) and Samuel Huntington, *The Clash of Civilizations and the Remaking of World Order* (New York: Simon and Schuster, 1996).

4. For an excellent and rather optimistic analysis of the process of globalization, see Lowell Bryan, *Market Unbound, Unleashing Global Capitalism* (New York: John Wiley and Sons, 1966). See also Lowell Bryan and Jane Fraser, *Race for the World: Strategies to Build a Great Global Firm* (Boston: Harvard Business School Press, 1999) and a paper presented by Lord Brian Griffiths, Vice-Chairman of Goldman Sachs Europe, "The Challenge of Global Capitalism, A Christian Perspective."

5. "Dialogue between Cultures for a Civilization of Love and Peace," Pope John Paul II's message for World Day of Peace, January 1, 2001.

6. Wilhelm Roepke, *International Order and International Integration* (St. Louis, MO: Eden, 1959), 18.

7. Reinhold Niebuhr reminds us that in the process of building international societies we must not fall into the error, often found in business, of following the "Law of the Jungle—dog eats dog," where the strong exterminate the weak, instead of the Law of Christ. If an international order is built that way, "we find inevitably that violence or force of arms brings mutual distrust; mistrust turns into hate; hatred leads to murder. We need a state of society where people are going to

stop this business of exterminating the weak and establish some kind of society free from chaos." See *Young Reinhold Niebuhr, His Early Writings 1911–1931*, ed. William G. Chrystal (St. Louis, MO: Eden, 1977), 11.

8. Chrystal, *Young Reinhold Niebuhr*, 32.

9. C. S. Lewis, *Mere Christianity* (New York: Macmillan, 1975), 70.

10. Lewis, *Mere Christianity*, 72.

11. Lewis, *Mere Christianity*, 72.

12. Toynbee had already foreseen the advent of a supernational order in the mid-fifties. See Arnold J. Toynbee, *A Study of History* (New York: Oxford University Press, 1957), chapter 42.

13. For an interesting article on this topic, see Thomas M. Franck, "Are Human Rights Universal," *Foreign Affairs*, January/February 2001.

14. For an excellent analysis of Natural Law and the International Order, see Robert George, *In Defense of Natural Law* (New York: Oxford University Press, 1999), 228–36.

15. George, *In Defense of Natural Law*, 236.

16. George, *In Defense of Natural Law*, 236.

17. Roepke, *International Order and Economic Integration*, 44.

18. Roepke, *International Order and Economic Integration*, 44.

19. George, *In Defense of Natural Law*, 236.

20. Roepke, *International Order and Economic Integration*, 45.

21. John Paul II, "Dialogue between Cultures for a Civilization of Love and Peace."

22. Writing about the best form of government, Machiavelli says the following: "It is a sound maxim that reprehensible actions ay be justified by their effects, and that when the effect is good, as it was in the case of Romulus, it always justifies the action. For it is the man who uses violence to spoil things, not to mend them, that is blameworthy." See Niccolo Machiavelli, *The Discourses* (New York: Penguin Classics, 1983), book I, I.9, 132.

23. Machiavelli, *The Discourses*, book II, II.2, 278.

24. Dietrich von Hildebrand, *Trojan Horse in the City of God* (Chicago: Franciscan Press, 1967), 72.

25. The importance of virtue for the well-being of society is highlighted by Gertrude Himmelfarb when she claims that the classical and Christian concept of virtue was subverted by the secular philosophers: "All of them insisted upon the importance of virtues not only for the good life of individuals but for the well-being of society and the state. And all of them believed in the intimate relationship between the character of the people and the health of the polity. Even Montesquieu who assigned different virtues to different regimes and different *moeurs* to different societies, did not denigrate or deny the idea of virtue itself." See: Gertrude Himmelfarb, *The De-Moralization of Society, From Victorian Virtues to Modern Values* (New York: Alfred Knopf, 1955), 5.

—⁓—

# Epilogue

Throughout the pages of this book we have attempted to show how important it is for man to become aware of his intrinsic value as a human person. Without such an awareness, all attempts to construct ideal political and/or economic systems will turn out to be futile. Man must realize that he is a finite being created by God in his image and likeness and is endowed with free will. As a result, he cannot shy away from accepting the responsibility for his free actions. For man to claim that he has an autonomous will not subject to any higher authority runs counter to the very concept of a created being. Being free, he is not the product of circumstances or the forces of nature. On the contrary, man has the power of choice. Within his own limitations, he has the potential to control nature and the environment for better or for worse. Romano Guardini expresses this concept very well when he writes that the ordinary man must understand that ". . . the fate of the *res publica*, the common cause of human existence in freedom and dignity, lies in his hands."[1] The future success of political and economic systems will depend on man's hunger and thirst for justice and for that he must "recover the will to see the essence of things and to do 'the right' that it demands."[2] Unless man has a clear comprehension of Natural Law, and the responsibility that such an understanding entails, the fate of the res publica and freedom itself is endangered.

All along the different chapters we have emphasized that man is a rational human being and, given his fallen nature, cannot act in a totally autonomous way. For his own good, safety, and protection, he must submit himself to some sort of rules and regulations. These norms form part of a body of laws created by a legislator and constitute the basis of what is called positive law. However, positive law is a human creation and subject to error. It is not universal and immutable and, thus, subject to change. Only Natural Law, the participation of the Eternal Law in the rational creature, has the characteristics of immutability, universality, and is unchangeable. It is the source of morality and the foundation of an objective moral order which measures the goodness or wickedness of all free human acts. Man cannot ignore it he wants to preserve and foster the well-being of society. The same applies to all political and economic systems, whether crass capitalism or a debasing socialism. To rebuff or ignore the fundamental principles of Natural Law can only lead to eventual disaster.

Since the fall of the Soviet empire, capitalism is often hailed, not only as the heir to the collectivist policies of a discredited socialism but as the harbinger of a new era of prosperity and well-being. However, in spite of its undeniable material accomplishments and statements about justice and the common good, the fact still remains that its economic doctrine has its roots in a false individualistic principle, a principle which distorts the very nature of man. Capitalism, in its crude form, has a tendency to promote a type of man that is guided exclusively by his instinctive self-interest. The metaphysical dimension of man is largely ignored and, for all practical purposes, reason and conscience are no longer considered as pivotal factors in man's decision-making process. The crass capitalism of the nineteenth century encouraged a type of individual that stressed his selfish individuality to the detriment of the common good. Man's social dimension was dismissed as an unimportant factor in a naturally harmonious world where the greatest happiness for all would be reached as long as each individual followed his own self-interest.

A capitalism that accepts unconditional competition and profit making, and is based on pure utilitarian principles, bestows value only on those things that can serve economic ends. Under such conditions man is regarded as one more input in the production process and subject to the same laws of supply and demand as any other factor of production. The human dimension of man is lost and his worth is measured exclusively in terms of his productive capacity. The principle of the priority of labor over capital is de facto denied, forgetting that in the process of production labour is the primary *efficient cause* and capital is nothing more than an *instrument* or instrumental cause. To give primary importance to the objective over the subjective dimension of labor is a clear characteristic of all one sided materialistic civilizations.

The crucial question that we have tried to bring to the attention of the reader is that, under raw capitalism and in accordance with the basic rationalistic postulates of the French Enlightenment, man considers himself the final arbiter of what is right and what is wrong. The existence of an objective moral order, founded on Natural Law, is either ignored or rejected. The "natural ethics" of the eighteenth century moral philosophers replaces the traditional Christian concept of Natural Law. Consequently, individualistic freedom becomes the sole "moral" standard under which banner the interests of the individual are carried out. Self-interest becomes the only regulating principle in economic matters. All external—transcendental or otherwise—is rejected and denied the right to assert norms of conduct that oppose or contradict man's "omnipotent" right to distinguish good from evil. The role of the state or, for that matter, any other form of regulating authority becomes superfluous. Its authority is limited to the prevention of infringements on the free activity of all economic agents. Individual transactions are no longer related to a higher ethical point of reference. As considerations of an ethical nature withdraw into the background, morality becomes increasingly relativized. Lacking a strong moral foundation based on Natural Law, freedom gradually turns into license and with it the most reprehensible excesses tend to follow. Sooner or later, chaos cries for order. Society cannot exist without it. From there, only a short step will lead to totalitarianism and the eventual loss of both economic and political freedoms.

Many critics of capitalism have clamored for its demise. They base their criticism on the undeniable abuses that took place during the Industrial Revolution. For them, the solution to the ills of early capitalism lies in the construction of a socialist society that will fulfill man's expectations of "equality," "justice," and "prosperity" for all. It is believed that under the aegis of a powerful centralized government, these objectives can be reached. Contrary to these outright condemnations of capitalism we have tried to show during the course of this book its positive contributions to the material progress and advancement of mankind, something that can hardly be said of the accomplishments of socialism.

For centuries socialism, in a wide variety of forms, has been considered the solution to the many social and economic problems affecting society. But, Marx claimed, all socialist movements prior to the enactment of the Communist Manifesto had been utopian. It was only with the advent of Marxism-Leninism in Russia that socialism passed from a theoretical "scientific" doctrine to the practical application of its basic principles. It no longer limited itself to the criticism of the prevailing political and socioeconomic systems but to the creation and application by violent means of a series of radical political and economic measures which were supposed to bring about a happier and more just society. *Das Kapital* became the "bible" of socialist economics and Russia the example of its achievements.

Ironically, in spite of the violent and criminal actions of the Marxist takeover of Russia in the fateful year of 1917, politicians, intellectuals, and many well-intentioned people in the West believed that the revolution marked the beginning of a new era of freedom, democracy, and economic development for Russia.[3] Contrary to these naïve expectations, the October Revolution, led by Lenin and his Bolshevik allies, did away with any hope of freedom and democracy for Holy Russia. Reality has amply demonstrated that the Marxist-Leninist revolution, through terror and deceit, replaced the Romanov dynasty with the most ruthless and totalitarian regime that the world has ever known. A revolution that not only created chaos and brought misery and despair to the people of Russia but threatened the peace and stability of the rest of the world. Socialist economics and its bedrock *Das Kapital* became the quagmire into which the Russian people fell during the long and fateful years of Marxism-socialism.

Given the political experience and the disastrous socioeconomic policies of the Soviet regime, it is difficult to believe that socialism can be seen as a viable substitute for capitalism. Socialist policies have demonstrated once and again the inefficiencies of a system which tries to stamp out man's individuality and make him a tool of the state. There is no need to reiterate that socialism, by ruling out the possibility of legitimate gain, destroys not only the motivation for work but also the incentive for economic activity. In the name of a utopian equality it has attempted to destroy man's right to individual uniqueness and by so doing limited his freedom. Equality carried to its extreme is the enemy of freedom. Such was the case in the former Soviet Union and other socialist experiments.

The greatest danger for the future well-being of humanity would be the establishment of a socialist regime that crushes man's unique individuality and ends up destroying him as a human person. For man, everything that gives meaning to life is tied in with his personality. If man's personality is crushed under the weight of the state he ceases to be a human person and becomes a slave at the service of the governing power. The Russian mathematician Igor Chafarevich clearly saw this danger and gives a clear and tragic picture of humanity if it should ever fall into this type of collectivist system. According to him, if socialism should ever triumph and put into practice the principles that it proclaims, depriving individuality of its irreplaceable role, it would purge with the stroke of the pen all that gives meaning to life.[4]

Sufficient evidence accumulated through the years have proven that socialism has not been able to deliver its promises of equality and justice for all. If anything, it has brought poverty and misery to the great majority of the population. Marxism-Leninism is the best example of the system's economic failures. However, it is important to emphasize that even the more benign types of socialism have shown fundamental economic and philosophical weaknesses. It may be true that the more moderate types of socialism have given up the class struggle and the collectivization of property, but they still promote the creation of a fundamentally material-istic society. They reject the transcendental and limit man's and society's goals to the acquisition of material goods, sacrificing their greater cultural and spiritual ends even at the cost of freedom. The omnipresence of the state and the diminished role of the individuality of man and the family, not to mention the persistent myth of equalitarianism, are sufficient rea-sons to mistrust the "good intentions" of socialism. With such a scenario, it is difficult to believe that this type of benign socialism can be the proper substitute for Marxism-Leninism in the post-Soviet era.

Another issue that needed to be asserted is that, independently of the flagrant errors of socialism's economic theory and practice, the greatest danger for man's cultural and spiritual development lies in the power of the state to control the family. This is often overlooked when the criticism of socialism is limited to its economic failures. It is within the family en-vironment that the child develops his personality and acquires the cul-tural and spiritual values that are needed for his integral development. State-run institutions are no substitute for the uniqueness of the learning experience that the family provides. The close psychological ties which exist within the family, between parents and children, cannot be replaced by an anonymous government employed bureaucratic staff. They can never supplant the love and understanding which exists within the fam-ily environment. To do so, as Chafarevich reminds us, would threaten to provoke the *slow death* of all those who follow the directives of socialism, that is to say of the entire human race.

Neither are the Western capitalist countries exempt from their respon-sibility in carrying out population policies which threaten the well-being of the family and disregard their moral and economic implications for so-ciety. Overpopulation is being blamed for many of the problems facing contemporary man, including the deterioration of the environment. In the process of applying neo-Malthusian policies to curtail population growth, the family also comes under attack. As a result, the traditional concept of the family is being undermined and the basic nucleus of a healthy society made vulnerable to the preconceived notions of those "experts" who know best what the the "optimum population" should be. To destroy the family, or to reduce it to a mere tool of the state or to the whims of other nongovernment organization, is equivalent to the gradual subversion of the moral fiber of any nation. To do so is not only contrary to the basic ten-ants of morality but it is also uneconomic. As the years go by and the re-sources of the state are slowly depleted, because of overextended expen-ditures on welfare policies and untenable social security systems, the government will have to rely more on the family for the care of the aging and the young. The exceedingly low fertility rates that now prevail in most industrialized countries is not going to be helpful. On the contrary, they constitute a serious threat to their future political and economic stability.

The cry for globalization, which is being heard at the highest levels of government and in intellectual and academic circles, needs to be analyzed with care. A gradual process of unification is to be welcomed. International organizations have an important role to play in this new era of rapid technological advances. The information revolution is changing the mentality and habits of large sectors of the globe. Distances have been shortened to such an extent that migratory movements are putting in close contact peoples of different races and cultures, a phenomenon which had never been seen before in the history of mankind. There is nothing wrong with this process of globalization. It can foster better relationships among the various members of the human family and help them in their needs. However, cultural differences must be respected and the inalienable rights of man honored. A healthy diversity must not be sacrificed in the name of a deceptive unity. The danger is that too great a concentration of political and economic power in the hands of an international bureaucratic "elite" can easily lead to abuse and be the source of future conflicts.

We hope that we have made it clear that capitalism, in spite of its well known historical deficiencies, has demonstrated a greater degree of flexibility for change than most types of socialism. It has the further advantage that it has proclaimed more eloquently the concept of freedom and the independent role of the individual vis-à-vis the all encompassing power of the state. It is also worth repeating that its technological dimension is far more efficient and productive than socialism in any of its forms. What it needs is to reinforce its technological dimension with a strong ethical foundation. It must become more human and more aware that physical well-being and the worldly possession of material goods are not the greatest good in life.

A panoramic view of the world in the post-Soviet era tends to indicate that the great majority of countries are adopting economic policies more in accordance with the basic principles of economic liberalism. The process of privatization has expanded and greater weight is being given to the private sector. The importance of free trade as an independent variable in the process of development is more amply recognized. Protectionist policies that played such an important role in the development plans of the 1950s and 1960s have been replaced by a greater reliance on the virtues of competition both at the national and international levels.

This process of economic liberalization is healthy and very much in accordance with the democratic principles that are spreading with great enthusiasm and optimism around the globe. Nevertheless, it would be wrong to conclude from the failures of the Soviet economy and the collapse of communism that, under the aegis of a free market system, the path is necessarily open to a new era of prosperity and progress. No matter how strong is contemporary man's euphoria for political and economic freedoms, he cannot take them for granted and believe that totalitarianism has definitely been defeated.

Political and economic liberalism may have won a decisive battle over totalitarian collectivism, but can it be ascertained that it has also won the war against the forces of materialism and relativism? Has the Soviet experience been sufficiently tragic to have inoculated the West against all types of collectivism and earned it the title of defender of true freedom? Is a capitalism, focused exclusively on worldly concerns and the search for material gain, a true defender of authentic freedom and a proper substitute for the evils of socialism? These are some of the questions that we have tried to answer along the pages of this book.

There is no doubt that the attraction for collectivism has diminished but this does not mean that the danger of its recurrence has been dispelled. A quick look at the gradual encroachment of individual rights by the state, that is taking place in many Western countries, will quickly dissipate any false expectations as to the permanentness of freedom or the inevitability of human progress. Neither can it be said that a liberal economic system is free from the perils of a crass materialism that pays little, if any, attention to Natural Law and the transcendental nature of man. It has even been suggested in certain Western intellectual circles that contemporary man no longer needs to be guided by objective conceptions of what is right and what is wrong.[5]

The renaissance of economic liberalism with its renewed emphasis on a free market system, based on personal self-interest, private initiative, and competition, is not free from sliding into the excesses of the past. It is still liable to fall prey to the same exacerbated individualism and ravages of an egotistic self-interest that excludes the common good of society. This is the case of a capitalism void of a human dimension that either explicitly or implicitly denies the transcendental nature of man. It would be ironical that individual freedom, so crucial for the efficient functioning of economic liberalism, if misused, would turn into a Damocles sword that would destroy not only capitalism but freedom itself.

To avoid this possibility from occurring, it is essential that capitalism be socially adjusted in order to better meet the needs of the common good and avoid the evils of a "super-development" grounded on a false philosophy of a self-centered "consumerism." But, above all, it must be grounded in a solid ethical foundation that protects it from both the evils of an excessive individualism and the threat of an overpowering state. The late economist von Hayek was right in stressing that all activities of the state must be limited by a set of fixed rules—what he calls the Rule of Law—so as to avoid the abuses of concentrated power.[6] But the Rule of Law must be grounded on an objective system of moral values that sets the limits on an unrestrained individualism. Otherwise, the abuses of unrestrained individualism will serve as a pretext for the government to step in and establish its own rules and regulations. Loss of freedom is the price that has to be paid every time that the government is "forced" to intervene. Very often it is precisely a misunderstood individualism that opens the door to totalitarianism.

The science of economics must not be reduced to simple techniques which have as their only objective the attainment of optimum economic conditions. In fact, the notion of optimum, so much used in economics, is unquestionably normative. It is based on a conscientious decision of what an "expert" considers to be the best for man's development. When "optimum population," "optimum production," and so forth, are set as goals of economic activity, as is often the case, a given set of normative criteria lies behind the decision of the "experts." For example, the decision as to what is the "optimum population" is generally based on a predetermined goal, measured in quantitative terms. This obviously implies the acceptance by the "expert" of some specific normative criteria which serve him as a guideline for policy action.[7]

Economics cannot be circumscribed to a mere analysis of economic data and the construction and application of simple mathematical models which juggle around with quantifiable inputs that very often have little significance in the real world. No matter how important mathematical calculations may be in certain areas of economic analysis, they do not and cannot reflect man's innermost expectations for a better life. Man cannot be reduced to a mere number, measured and valued exclusively in terms of his contribution to a nation's economic output. He has other aspirations of a cultural and spiritual nature that fall beyond the boundaries of mathematical calculations. Contemporary economists should be cautious and avoid falling into the trap of concentrating too much of their efforts in the construction of certain complicated and seldom understood mathematical models which do not meet the real needs of the average person. As Roepke quite correctly wrote in the 1950s: "When one tries to read an economic journal nowadays, often enough one wonders whether one has not inadvertently picked a journal of chemistry or hydraulics."[8] The human dimension of man is often lost in the midst of a generalized passion for measurable quantities and mathematical formulae.

Professor Gerard Debreu in his presidential address delivered at the meeting of the American Economic Association on December 25, 1990, in Washington, D.C., discussed the impact of the mathematization of economic theory. He mentioned both the advances and serious problems caused by the continuous process of mathematization of economic theory. Professor Debreu emphasized the impenetrability to the overwhelming majority of economists of the work done by their mathematical colleagues. The rigor of the assumptions and logical structure of mathematization, which results from the need for simplicity, unfortunately cannot be satisfied by all economic observations. This brings about a continuing weakening process of the applicability of mathematical solutions to the reality of life situations. Professor Debreu believes that in their endeavors to make their field into a science, economists must renounce a favorite mode of thinking—wishful thinking.[9]

The reality of man's development requires that it be integral. It cannot be reduced to the simplicity of a set of given mathematical equations. It must be ordered not only in terms of man's economic needs—as a consumer and a producer—that are easer to quantify but also in terms of his spiritual, cultural, and moral needs. The idea that man is purely an *homo oeconomicus* cannot be accepted. Man as a human being is a moral person with certain specific requirements which go beyond his economic needs. The essential goal of social life is the conservation, development and the perfection of the human person. Man, the person, cannot be considered as a mere object of economics. He is primarily, and above all, the subject of economics and, consequently, must be treated with all the respect that he deserves.

It is true that the formal object of economics is concerned with the dynamics of change and the production of goods and services. But economics, being a social science, is also concerned with the knowledge of means and results in relation to a desired goal. If the economic process rests on free actions of men which are not "naturally" determined, then, as Pesch would say, economic science cannot renounce the prerogative of being a practical science oriented by a scientifically established and founded norm, and to this extent of being normative. This approach to economic science is in direct opposition to a method in economics which would exclude from economic theory every consideration of an end, every value judgment. It would restore to economics the concept of what ought to be and not only what is. Thus, economics, dealing with both theory and practice, must subordinate its formal object to a higher norm: the principle of a moral and spiritual finality.

Economics, as John Paul II reminds us in his encyclical *Sollicitudo Rei Socialis*, must be defined in terms of man's final end and should not cast aside ethics and teleology. It must include the cultural, transcendental, and religious dimensions of man and society and attempt to direct its efforts toward that goal. Not to do so would violate the inalienable rights of man, endanger the very foundations of a free society, and make a mockery of the common good. The higher values of man as a person, the family and political society cannot be subordinated to the exclusive attainment of material wealth. Material goods are not the ultimate goal of individual and social well-being. Such a goal cannot be in opposition to man's spiritual and moral welfare.[10]

Thus, economic theory cannot be totally disassociated from ethics. Man, the free agent of economic activity, cannot ignore the moral law. The moral law has general validity at all times and places and, therefore, is applicable to man's actions in all of his economic activities. However, this does not mean that economics is not an independent science with its own formal object which is different from the formal object of ethics which deals with the goodness or wickedness of an act. Economics is not supposed to teach us about the beauty of virtue or the malice of vice. This falls within the realm of ethics. However, the economist cannot ignore the ethics of an economic action even though, as an economist, it is not his job to establish the rules of morality. This job belongs to the theologians.[11] As the French philosopher Etienne Gilson has said, "To demand that science and philosophy regulate themselves under theology is first of all to ask them to agree to recognize their limits, to be content to be a science or a philosophy without pretending to transform themselves, as they are constantly doing, into a theology."[12]

The Western world cannot be lured into believing that, because of the failures of collectivist policies, capitalism is necessarily the answer to the economic challenges of the twenty-first century. The triumph of technology and know-how over inefficiency and wastefulness is no guarantee of a bright future for humanity. Unless capitalism carries out appropriate changes in the system, the optimism that followed the collapse of the Soviet experiment can easily turn into disappointment. As mentioned above, economics does have its own formal object independent from philosophy or theology but man, being the agent of economic activity, cannot shy away from accepting the responsibility for his free actions. To avoid the excesses of his fallen nature, he must accept the existence of the transcendental and of an objective moral order based on Natural Law. Otherwise, disappointment can turn into direct and violent opposition to the abuses of economic liberalism with dire consequences for freedom itself and the healthy development of society.

Let us hope that the Western World will be able to overcome the lethargy in which it finds itself, a lethargy that is crippling its traditional spirit of initiative as champion and promoter of the fundamental cultural and spiritual values of its Christian heritage. It must become aware of the grave dangers that threaten its very existence. Otherwise, we run the risk that it could be said of our civilization what the perceptive Spanish writer Donoso Cortés said about imperial Rome over a hundred years ago. He warned the Europe of his time that once nations reach a critical level of decay, it becomes necessary for a dreadful revolution to take place in order to purify them of their collective crimes and permit man to follow the path that Providence planned for him. The revolution brought ruin to Imperial Rome but it was necessary for the future progress of society. Barbarian cruelty, continues Cortes, suspended progress for a while but the persistence of a degraded people would have choked it forever.

Donoso Cortés was right in alerting the Europeans of his time of the fate that befell imperial Rome when its citizens became corrupt and abandoned the traditional values of its founders. Our Western World is also threatened by the grave moral problems that are besieging our civilization and culture. At the birth of the new century the West seems to have been anesthetized with a deleterious state of acedia which manifests itself in the indifference, if not open rejection, of its cultural and spiritual heritage. This lamentable state of affairs, which persists in refusing to accept Natural Law and the transcendental, are not good omens for the future wellbeing of our civilization. It would be spurious to deny such a possibility under the cover of a false optimism.

In our opinion, there is ample reason to share the pessimism of many a prominent historian. But, a true Christian believer cannot fall into the trap of letting himself be carried away by the transient events of history. Pessimism must never stifle the virtue of hope and the joy of knowing that, in the end, the good always triumphs over evil. The great Chesterton in his brilliant manner brings this out quite clearly when he writes, "Man is more himself, man is more manlike, when joy is the fundamental thing in him, and grief the superficial. Melancholy should be an innocent interlude, a tender and fugitive frame of mind; praise should be the permanent pulsation of the soul. Pessimism is at best an emotional half-holiday; joy is the uproarious labour by which all things live."[13]

In writing this book, it has been far from our desire to strike a note of pessimism in the hearts and minds of its readers, especially the young. Far from it. Our intention has merely been to reemphasize some of the grave dangers that threaten the very core of our Western culture and to stress that their solution cannot be limited to changes in political and/or economic structures. No matter how much we advocate political and economic freedoms, as expressed in democratic and liberal economic systems, they will not thrive and flourish if they lack the mandatory moral foundation based on Natural Law. The cure for the ills of contemporary society lies in the hearts of men and much less in the political and economic structures that surround them.

Modern man has the capability and the means to avoid falling into the errors of Imperial Rome but to do so he must not only contribute to the construction of better and more efficient political and economic structures but, above all, he must reevaluate his whole attitude toward life and accept his own limitations. He must convince himself of his own dignity and worth as a human being. This way man will be able to understand that all men are entitled to the same dignity and respect that he expects from others. To accept these truths is the best guarantee for the success of any political or economic system and for freedom to survive. Only then can it be rightly said that the twenty-first century has the potential to usher in a new era of justice, prosperity and peace. This is the message of confidence and hope that the author has attempted to convey throughout the pages of this book.

## NOTES

1. Romano Guardini, *The End of the Modern World* (Wilmington, DE: ISI Books, 1998), 194.

2. Guardini, *The End of the Modern World*, 192.

3. Even such a knowledgeable economist as Gunnar Myrdal gave the Soviet Union as an example of an economic system that cannot only compete with the United States in rates of economic growth but even surpass it. In the early 1960s, he wrote the following: "At present the rate of economic growth is considerably higher in the Soviet Union than in the United States, by at least double and perhaps more and particularly so in the case of heavy industry and of the facilities for education, research and health protection. Even though the level of national product in the Soviet Union is still much lower than in the United States, the power of the principle of compound interest implies that if the United States should not soon succeed in overcoming its relative economic stagnation, the Soviet Union would within a not too distant future approach, reach and eventually surpass the United States in important fields." See Gunnar Myrdal, *Challenge to Affluence* (New York: Pantheon Books, 1962), 120–21.

4. Igor Chafarevich was a well-known Russian mathematician who had received the first prize Lenin award when a member of the Soviet Academy of Sciences. See Igor Chafarevich, *Le Phénomène Socialiste* (Paris: Editions du Seuil, 1977). See part III, chapter IV.

5. "The ultimate implication of the idea of moral freedom is not that people are created in the image of a higher authority. It is that any form of higher authority has to tailor its commandments to the needs of real people." See Alan Wolfe, "The Final Freedom," *New York Times Magazine*, March 18, 2001, 48, 50, 51.

6. Hayek, *The Road to Serfdom*, 72.

7. The German Christian economist Johannes Haessle used the terms maximum and minimum when discussing the two fundamental rules governing the relationship between the acquisition of economic goods and ethics. In his book *Le Travail*, published in Paris in 1933, he wrote the following two rules: (1) the maximum of material goods is always an optimum if he who possesses them believes that they have a relative value and (2) the maximum of material goods is morally a minimum if he who possesses them believes they have an absolute value. The quotation is taken from A. Dauphin-Meunier, *La Doctrina Económica de la Iglesia* (Valencia, Spain: Fomento de Cultura, 1952).

8. Roepke, *A Humane Economy*, 247.

9. Gerard Debreu, "The Mathematics of Economic Theory," *The American Economic Review*, March 1991, 1–7.

10. For an interesting approach to economics and social justice, see Shigeto Tsuru, "L'éxperience Japonaise: Croissance Économique Accelere et Justice Sociale" in *Economie et Société Humaine*. Rencontres internationales du ministère de l'economie et des finances, présentation de Lionel Stoleru, Paris, 1972. Tsuru, a former professor of economics and business in Tokyo, concluded his presentation the following way: "A new era of men of heart will prevail eventually in this world. Because if we keep encouraging the criteria of force and wealth I cannot avoid but think that this world will no longer be an appropriate place for human beings to live in" (378). See also Jacques Austruy, *Le Scandale du Développement* (Paris: Editions Marcel Rivière et Cie., 1965). The French professor stresses in the book that economics is at the same time a culture, a technique, and a perspective. It goes far beyond economic considerations no matter how important these may be. Professor Adrien Taymans of the University of Louvain also emphasizes the importance of man as a human person in the process of development, in particular the efficacy of his free will. Referring to Schumpeter's theory of development, he says the following: "Comme on le voit, cette histoire de l'entrepreneur 'révolutionaire' fait entièrement credit a la personne humaine et l'efficacite de l'action libre personelle, que celle-ci soit individuelle ou cooperative. Ceci n'est pas un faible mérite pour une ère qui menace de 'mécaniser' l'âme humaine." See Adrian Taymans, S.J., *L'Homme l'Agent du Développement Économique* (Louvain, France: Institut de Recherches Économiques et Sociales de l'Université de Louvain, 1951), xi.

11. This is clearly stated by Pesch when he writes that the economist must "not oppose the demands of moral theology , but neither must he lose sight of the fact that economics has become an autonomous science, which treats of the economic life of nations from a viewpoint different from that of moral theology." As quoted by Richard Mulcahy, *The Economics of Heinrich Pesch*, (New York: Holt, 1952), 40.

12. See Etienne Gilson, *Christianity and Philosophy* (New York: Sheed & Ward, 1939), 103–25.

13. G. K. Chesterton, *Orthodoxy* (Garden City, NY: Image Books, 1959), 159.

—⸎—

# Bibliography

Acton [Lord]. *The History of Freedom and Other Essays*. London: Macmillan, 1907.

Aguirre, Sophia. "The Wealth of the Nations, Sympathy and Their Relation to Economic Behavior." *Economics and Philosophy* 8, no. 2 (October 1992), 259–71.

———. *Population, Resources and Environment*. Washington, DC: The Catholic University of America Press, 2000.

Aristotle. *The Politics*. Chicago: University of Chicago Press, 1984.

———. *Nicomachean Ethics*. Indianapolis, IN: Hackett, 1985.

Atkinson, A. *State Pensions, Taxation and Retirement Income: 1981–2031*. London: Simon & Schuster, 1989.

Austruy, Jacques. *Le Scandale du Développement*. Paris: Editions Marcel Rivière et Cie., 1965.

"The Balance of Payments of the United States." *The Economic Journal*, Vol. LVI, no. 222 (June 1946), 185–86.

Balmes, Jaime. *Obras Completas*. Madrid: Biblioteca de Autores Cristianos (BAC), 1949.

Baran, Paul. *The Political Economy of Growth*. New York: Monthly Review Press, 1957.

Bauer, P. T. *Dissent on Development*. Cambridge, MA: Harvard University Press, 1972.

Beveridge, William. *Full Employment in a Free Society*. New York: Norton, 1945.

Boulding, Kenneth E. *Beyond Economics*. Ann Arbor: University of Michigan Press, 1968.

———. "A New Look at Institutionalism." *American Economic Review*, Vol. 48 (May 1957).

Bourdelais, Xavier Gaullier, Marie Jose Imbault-Huart, Denis Olivennes, Jean-Marie Poursin, and François Stasse. *Etat-Providence. Arguments pour une Réforme*. Paris: Editions Gallimard, 1996.

Briefs, Goetz. *Zwischen Kapitalismus und Syndicalismus*. Bern: Franclie Ag. Verlag, 1952.

Bryan, Lowell. *Market Unbound, Unleashing Global Capitalism*. New York: John Wiley and Sons, 1966.

Burke, Edmund. *Reflections on the Revolution in France*. New York: Dolphin Books, 1961.

Buttiglione, Rocco. *El Hombre y el Trabajo*. Madrid: Encuentro Ediciones, 1984.

Buttiglione, Rocco. "Social Justice in the Changing Economic Environment: Encounter or Conflict." *Faith and Reason* (winter 1991).

Cardona, Carlos. *René Descartes, Discurso del Método*. Madrid: Editorial Magisterio Espanol, E.M.S.A., 1975.

Casado, Vicente Rodriguez. *Orígenes del Capitalismo y del Socialismo Contemporáneo*. Madrid: Espasa-Calpe, S.A., 1981.

Chafarevich, Igor. *Le Phénomène Socialiste*. Paris: Editions du Seuil, 1977.

Chamberlin, Edward H. *The Theory of Monopolistic Competition*. Cambridge, MA: Harvard University Press, 1950.

de Châteaubriand [François René]. *Mémoires d'Outre-Tombe*. Paris: Gallimard, 1952

Chaunu, Pierre, and Georges Suffert. *La Peste Blanche, Comment Éviter le Suicide de l'Occident*. Paris: Editions Gallimard, 1976.

Chesterton, G. K. *Orthodoxy*. Garden City, NY: Image Books, 1959.

Chrystal, William, G., ed. *Young Reinhold Niebuhr, His Early Writings 1911–1931*. St. Louis, MO: Eden, 1977.

Clark, Colin. "World Population." In *Population*, Edward Pohlman, ed. New York: New American Library, 1973.

Clark, Paul A. *Hobbes and the Enlightenment*. Ph.D. dissertation, School of Philosophy, The Catholic University of America, Washington, DC, 1996.

Clement, Marcel. *La Corporation Professionelle*. Paris: Nouvelles Editions Latines, 1958.

Comte, Auguste. *Cours de philosophie positive*. Paris: Hermann, 1998.

Courtois, Stephane, Nicolas Werth, Jean-Lois Panne, Andrzej Paczkowski, Karel Bartosek, and Jean-Louis Margolin. *Le Livre Noir du Communisme, Crimes, Terreur, Repression*. Paris: Robert Laffront, 1997.

Courtois, Stephane, Nicolas Werth, Jean-Lois Panne, Andrzej Paczkowski, Karel Bartosek, and Maurrice Cranston. *The Romantic Movement*. Oxford: Blackwell, 1994.

Cranston, Maurrice. *The Romantic Movement*. Oxford: Blackwell, 1994.

Daniel-Rops, H. *The Church in the Dark Ages*. London: J. M. Dent & Sons, 1959.

Dauphin-Meunier, A. *La Doctrina Económica de la Iglesia*. Valencia, Spain: Fomento de Cultura, 1952.

Dawson, Christopher. *The Dividing of Christendom*. New York: Image Books, 1967.

Debreu, Gerard. "The Mathematics of Economic Theory." *The American Economic Review* (March 1991), 1–7.

De Laubier, Patrick. *La Pensée Sociale de l'Eglise Catholique*. Fribourg, Switzerland: Editions universitaires, 1984.

De Lubac, Henri. *The Drama of Atheistic Humanism*. San Francisco: Ignatius Press, 1995.

De Maistre (Comte), Joseph. *Les Soirées de St. Petersbourg*. Paris: 1821.

Descartes, René. *Discours de la Méthod, Texte et Commentaires*, 4th ed. Paris: Librairie Philosophique, Vrin, 1967.

De Torre, Jose M. *La Iglesia y la Cuestión Social*. Madrid: Ediciones Palabra, S.A., 1988.

———. *Christian Philosophy*. Manila, Philippines: Vera-Reyes, 1989.

———. *The Roots of Society*. Manila, Philippines: Sinag-Tala, 1977.

Dos Santos, Theotonio. "Socialismo o Fascismo, Dilemma dell America Latina." *Il Nuovo Marxismo Latino Americano*. Milan: Feltinello Editore, 1970.

Dougherty, Jude. "Moral Aspects of Immigration Policy." *Crisis*, August 8, 2000.

———. *Western Creed, Western Identity: Essays in Legal and Social Philosophy*. Washington, DC: The Catholic University of America Press, 2000.

Dumont, René, and Bernard Rosier. *The Hungry Future*. New York: Praeger, 1969.

Eberstadt, Nicholas. "World Population Implosion?" *The Public Interest*, no. 129, fall 1997.

Ehrlich, Paul R. *The Population Bomb*. New York: Ballantine, 1971.

Ekelund, Jr., Robert B. and Robert E. Hebert. *A History of Economic Theory and Method*. New York: McGraw-Hill, 1997.

Feuerbach, Ludwig. *Essence of Christianity*.

Finnis, John. *Natural Law and Natural Rights*. Oxford: The Clarendon Press, 1996.

Franck, Thomas M. "Are Human Rights Universal." *Foreign Affairs* (January/February 2001).

Frank, Gunder. *Latin America: Underdevelopment or Revolution?* New York: Monthly Review Press, 1959.

Friedman, Milton and Rose Friedman. *Free to Choose*. New York: Harcourt Brace Jovanovich, 1979.

Fukuyama, Francis. *The End of History and the Last Man*. New York: Free Press, 1992.

Furtado, Celso. *Economic Development of Latin America: A Survey from Colonial Times to the Cuban Revolution*. Cambridge, UK: Cambridge University Press, 1970.

Galbraith, John Kenneth. *American Capitalism: The Concept of Countervailing Power*. Boston: Houghton Mifflin, 1952.

Gaxotte, Pierre. *La Révolution Française*. Paris: Historiques Éditions Complexe, 1988.

George, Robert. *In Defense of Natural Law*. New York: Oxford University Press, 1999.

Gide, Charles and Charles Rist. *Historia de las Doctrinas Económicas*. Madrid: Editorial Reus S.A., 1927.

Gilson, Etienne. *The Philosophy of St. Thomas Aquinas*. New York: Barnes & Noble, 1993.

———. *De Aristóteles a Darwin (y Vuelta)*. Pamplona, Spain: Ediciones Universidad de Navarra EUNSA, 1976.

———. *Christianity and Philosophy*. New York: Sheed & Ward, 1939.

*Globaphobia: Confronting Fears about Open Trade*. Washington, DC: The Brookings Institution, 1998.

Guardini, Romano. *The End of the Modern World*. Wilmington, DE: ISI Books, 1998.

Haberle, Gottfried. *The Theory of International Trade*. London: William Hodge & Co., 1954.

Halévy, Elie. *The Growth of Philosophical Liberalism*. Boston: Beacon Press, 1955.
Hall, A. R. *The Scientific Revolution*. London: Longmans Green, 1934.
Hansen, Alvin. *Business Cycle Theory*. Boston: Ginn, 1927.
Hayek, F. A. *Full Recovery or Stagnation?* New York: McGraw-Hill, 1938.
———. *Fiscal Policy and Business Cycle*. New York: Norton, 1941.
———. *The Road to Serfdom*. Chicago: University of Chicago Press, 1958.
———. *The Constitution of Liberty*. South Bend, IN: Gateway, 1960.
———. *The Final Conceit, The Errors of Socialism* [The Collected Works of F. A. Hayek]. Chicago: University of Chicago Press, 1989.
———. *Cuadernos del Pensamiento Liberal*, no. 12. Madrid: Union Editorial, 1991.
Hazard, Paul. *La Pensée Européenne au XVIIIe Siècle*. Paris: Librarie Arthème Fayard, 1963.
Heimann, Eduard. *History of Economic Doctrines*. New York: Oxford University Press, 1956.
Hervada, Javier. *Introducción Crítica al Derecho Natural*. Pamplona, Spain: Ediciones Universidad de Navarra, S.A., 1994.
Hildebrand, Dietrich von. *Trojan Horse in the City of God*. Chicago: Franciscan Press, 1967.
Himmelfarb, Gertrude. *The De-Moralization of Society, From Victorian Virtues to Modern Values*. New York: Alfred Knopf, 1955.
Hobbes, Thomas. *Leviathan or the Matter, Forme and Power of a Commonwealth Ecclesiastical and Civil*. New York: Collier Books, 1973.
Hobsbawn, E. J. *The Age of Capital, 1848–1875*. New York: Penguin, 1979.
Hoffner, Joseph. *Christian Social Teaching*. Cologne: Ordo Socialis, 1983.
———. *Christliche Gesllshatslehre*. Kevalaer de Renania: Verlag Butzon, 1974.
Hume, David. *Treatise on Human Nature*. London: Penguin Books, 1985.
Huntington, Samuel. *The Clash of Civilizations and the Remaking of the World Order*. New York: Simon and Schuster, 1996.
Hutcheson, Francis. *A System of Moral Philosophy*. New York: A. M. Kelley, 1968.
———. *An Inquiry into the Origins of Our Ideas of Beauty and Virtue*. New York: Garland, 1971.
Illanes, José Luis. *On the Theology of Work*. New Rochelle, NY: Scepter Press, 1982.
International Monetary Fund. *Aging Population and Public Pension Schemes*. Washington, DC: International Monetary Fund, 1996.
John Paul II. *Centesimus Anno*. Papal Encyclical.
———. "Dialogue between Cultures for a Civilization of Love and Peace." Message for World Day of Peace, January 1, 2001.
———. *Dignitatis Humanae*. Papal Encyclical.
———. *Fides et Ratio*. Papal Encyclical.
———. *Laborem Exercens*. Papal Encyclical.
———. *Sollicitudo Rei Socialis*. Papal Encyclical.
———. *Tercio Millennio Adveniente*. Papal Encyclical.
———. *Veritatis Splendor*. Papal Encyclical.
Keynes, John Maynard. *Essays in Biography*. New York: Harcourt, Brace, 1933.
———. *The General Theory of Employment, Interest and Money*. London: Macmillan, 1951.
Knight, Frank H. *Risk, Uncertainty and Profit*. Chicago: Hart, Schaffne & Marx, 1946.

——. *On the History and Methods of Economics.* Chicago: University of Chicago Press, 1956.

Kuznets, Simon. *Population, Capital and Growth.* New York: Norton, 1973.

Landreth, Harry and David C. Colander. *History of Economic Thought.* Boston: Houghton Mifflin, 1994.

Langlois, José Miguel Ibañez. *Doctrina Social de la Iglesia.* Pamplona, Spain: Ediciones Universidad de Navarra, S. A., 1987.

——. *El Marxismo: Visión Crítica.* Madrid: Rialp, 1973.

Lassman, Peter and Ronald Speirs, eds. *Max Weber: Political Writings.* New York: Cambridge University Press, 1994.

Lenin, V. I. *State and Revolution.* New York: International Publishers, 1939.

Leo XIII. *Rerum Novarum.* Papal Encyclical.

Lewis, C. S. *Mere Christianity.* New York: Macmillan, 1952 and 1975.

Llanes, José Luis. *On the Theory of Work.* New Rochelle, NY: Scepter Press, 1982.

Locke, John. *Second Treatise of Government,* ed. with an introduction by C. B. Macpherson. Indianapolis, IN: Hackett, 1980.

Lustiger, Jean-Marie. *Devenez Dignes de la Condition Humaine.* Paris: Flammarion/ Saint Maurice, Switzerland: Saint-Augustin, 1995.

Machiavelli, Niccolo. *The Discourses.* New York: Penguin Classics, 1983.

MacIntyre, Alasdaire. "Theories of Natural Law in the Culture of Advanced Modernity." In *Common Truths.* Wilmington, DE: ISI Books, 2000.

——. *After Virtue.* Notre Dame, IN: University of Notre Dame Press, 1984.

——. *A Short History of Ethics.* New York: Touchstone, 1966.

Macpherson, C. B. *The Political Theory of Possessive Individualism: Hobbes to Locke.* Oxford: Clarendon Press, 1962.

Malthus, Thomas. *On Population.* New York: Random House, 1960.

Manent, Pierre. *The City of Man.* Princeton, NJ: Princeton University Press, 1998.

Mantoux, Paul. *The Industrial Revolution in the Eighteenth Century.* New York: Macmillan, 1961.

Mao Tse-Tung. "On the Relation between Knowledge and Practice." In *Selected Readings from the Works of Mao Tse-Tung.* Peking: Foreign Language Press, 1971.

Margolin, Jean-Louis. *Le Livre Noir du Communisme, Crimes, Terreur, Répression.* Paris: Robert Laffont, 1997.

——. *A Contribution to the Critique of Political Economy.* Moscow: Progress, 1970.

Marx, Karl. *Capital.* New York: Modern Library, 1906.

Maritain, Jacques. *Man and the State.* Chicago: University of Chicago Press, 1951.

Marx, Karl and Friedrich Engels. *Manifesto of the Communist Party.* Ed. Samuel H. Beer. Arlington Heights, IL: Harlan Davidson, 1955.

Meadows, Donella H., Dennis L. Meadows, Jorgen Randers, and William W. Behrens. *The Limits of Growth.* New York: Universe Books, 1972.

Mitchell, Wesley Clair, ed. *What Veblen Taught.* New York: Viking, 1936.

Molnar, Thomas. *The Perennial Utopia.* New York: Sheed & Ward, 1967.

——. *Utopia: The Perennial Heresy.* New York: Sheed & Ward, 1967.

Mueller, Iris Wessel. *John Stuart Mill and French Thought.* Urbana: University of Illinois Press, 1956.

Mulcahy, Richard. *The Economics of Heinrich Pesch.* New York: Holt, 1952.

Myrdal, Gunnar. *Challenge to Affluence.* New York: Pantheon, 1962.
——. "Development and Underdevelopment." National Bank of Egypt, Fiftieth Anniversary Commeration Lectures, Cairo, Egypt, 1956.
——. *An International Economy.* New York: Harper & Brothers, 1956.
Neill, Thomas. *Weapons for Peace.* Milwaukee, WI: Bruce Publishing, 1945.
Neuhaus, Richard John. *Doing Well and Doing Good.* New York: Doubleday, 1992.
Nisbet, Robert A. *History of the Idea of Progress.* New York: Basic Books, 1970.
Novak, Michael. *The Catholic Ethic and the Spirit of Capitalism.* New York: The Free Press, 1993.
Ocariz-Braña, José. *Historia Sencilla del Pensamiento Político.* Madrid: Ediciones Rialp, S.A., 1988.
Ohlin, Bertil. *Interregional and International Trade.* Cambridge, MA: Harvard University Press, 1933.
Ortega y Gasset, José. *La Rebelión de las Masas, Epilogo a los Ingleses.* Madrid: Revista de Occidente en Alianza Editorial, 1983.
Paddock, William and Paul Paddock. *Famine 1975! America's Decision: Who Will Survive?* Boston: Little, Brown, 1967.
Pascal, Blaise. *Pensées.* Paris: Librairie Générale Française, 1972.
"Pastoral Constitution on the Church in the Modern World" (Gaudiem et Spes). *The Documents of Vatican II.* New York: Guild Press, 1966.
Piedra, Alberto M. "The Welfare State and Its Ethical Implications: A Viable Alternative for Post-Castro Cuba?" *Cuba in Transition,* Vol. 6. Springfield, MD: ASCE Books, 1997.
Pieper, Joseph. *Faith, Hope, Love.* San Francisco: Ignatius Press, 1997.
——. *Scholasticism: Personalities and Problems of Medieval Philosophy.* New York: McGraw-Hill, 1964.
Piettre, André. *Marx et Marxisme.* Paris: Presses Universitaires de France, 1959.
Pigou, A. C. *The Economics of Welfare.* London: Macmillan, 1952.
Pius XI. *On Atheistic Communism.* Papal Encyclical.
——. *Quadragesimo Anno.* Papal Encyclical.
Prebisch, Raul. *Towards a Dynamic Development Policy for Latin America.* New York: United Nations, 1963.
——. *Change and Development: Latin America's Great Task.* Washington, DC: Inter-American Development Bank, 1970.
Randall, John Herman. *The Making of the Modern Mind.* Boston: Houghton Mifflin, 1940.
Raspail, Jean. *Le Camp des Saints.* Paris: Editions Robert Laffont, 1973.
Rauscher, Anton. *Kirche in der Welt.* Wurzburg, Germany: Echter, Erster Band, 1988.
Reading, Brian. *The Fourth Reich.* London: Weidenfeld and Nicholson, 1955.
Riasanovsky, Nicholas V. *The Emergence of Romanticism.* New York: Oxford University Press, 1992.
Robbins, Lionel. *The Evolution of Modern Economic Theory.* Chicago: Aldine, 1970.
Robinson, Joan. *The Economics of Imperfect Competition.* London: Macmillan, 1954.
Roepke, Wilhelm. *La Crisis Social de Nuestro Tiempo.* Madrid: Biblioteca de la Ciencia Económica, 1942.

———. *Civitas Humana*. Madrid: Biblioteca de la Ciencia Económica, Revista de Occidente, 1949.

———. *International Order and International Integration*. St. Louis, MO: Eden, 1959.

———. *A Humane Economy*. Chicago: Henry Regnery, 1960.

Roll, Eric. *History of Economic Thought*. London: Faber & Faber, 1953.

Rommen, Heinrich A. *The Natural Law, A Study in Legal and Social History and Philosophy*. Indianapolis, IN: Liberty Fund, 1998.

Rousseau, Jean-Jacques. *Émile*, Book 1. Paris: Garnier-Flammarion, 1966.

Sauvy, Alfred. *L'Europe Submergée*. Paris: Dunod, 1987.

Schumpeter, Joseph. *Business Cycles*. New York: McGraw-Hill, 1939.

———. *The Great Economists*. London: Allen & Unwin, 1951.

———. *Capitalism, Socialism and Democracy*. London: Allen & Unwin, 1952.

———. *History of Economic Analysis*. New York: Oxford University Press, 1963.

Screpanti, Ernesto, and Stefano Zamagni. *An Outline of the History of Economic Thought*. New York: Oxford University Press, 1993.

See, Henri. *La France Économique et Sociale au XVIIIe Siècle*. Paris: Librairie Armand Colin, 1952.

Sen, Amartya, *On Ethics and Economics*. Oxford: Basil Blackwell, 1987.

Sheed, F. J. *Society and Sanity*. New York: Sheed & Ward, 1953.

Sigmund, Paul E., ed. *St. Thomas Aquinas in Politics and Ethics*. New York: Norton, 1988.

Simeon, J.-P. *La Démocratie selon Rousseau*. Paris: Editions du Seuil, 1977.

Simon, Julian. "Science Does Not Show that There Is Overpopulation in the U.S.— or Elsewhere." In *Population*, ed. Edward Pohlman. New York: New American Library, 1973.

———. *The Ultimate Resource*. Princeton, NJ: Princeton University Press, 1981.

Smith, Adam. *An Inquiry into the Nature and Causes of the Wealth of Nations*. Indianapolis, IN: Liberty Classics, 1981.

———. *The Theory of Moral Sentiments*. Indianapolis, IN: Liberty, 1982.

Sorokin, Pitirim A. *The Crisis of Our Age*. New York: E. P. Dutton, 1941.

Spengler, Oswald. *The Decline of the West*. New York: Knopf, 1999.

Stalin, Joseph. *Foundations of Leninism*. New York: International Publishers, 1939.

Sunkel, Oswaldo. *El Subdesarrollo Latinoamericano y la Teoría del Desarrollo*. Mexico: Siglo Veintiuno Editores, 1970.

Talmon, J. L. *Romanticism and Revolt*. New York: Norton, 1967.

Tawney, R. H. *Religion and the Rise of Capitalism*. New York: New American Library, 1953.

Taylor, Overton H. *A History of Economic Thought*. New York: McGraw-Hill, 1960.

Taymans, Adrian, S. J. *L'homme l'Agent du Développement Économique*. Louvain, France: Institut de Recherches Economiques et Sociales de l'Universite de Louvain, 1951.

Termes, Rafael. *Antropologia del Capitalismo*. Madrid: Plaza & Janes Editores, 1992.

de Tocqueville, Alexis. *The Old Regime and the French Revolution*. New York: Doubleday Anchor Books, 1955.

Torre, Joseph de. *The Roots of Society*. Manila: Sinag-Tala Publishers, 1977.

Toynbee, Arnold J. *A Study of History*. New York: Oxford University Press, 1957.

Tsuru, Shigeto. "L'Expérience Japonaise: Croissance Économique Acceleré et Justice Sociale." *Économie et societe humaine*. Rencontres Internationales du ministere de l'économie et des finances, présentation de Lionel Stoleru, Paris, 1972.

Tucker, Robert C., ed. *The Marx-Engels Reader*. 2nd ed. New York: Norton, 1978.

United Nations. Population Division, Department of Economic and Social Affairs. *World Population Prospects: The 2000 Revision*. New York: United Nations, 2001.

———. *World Population Prospects, The 2000 Revision*. New York: United Nations, Population Division, Department of Economic and Social Affairs, 1995.

———. "The Ageing of the World's Population." New York: United Nations, Department of Public Information, DPI/1858/AGE, October 1996.

———. *World Population Projections to 2150*. New York: Department of Economic and Social Affairs, U.N. Secretariat, Population Division, 1998.

U.S. Department of State. *Bulletin*. Washington, DC: U.S. Government Printing Office, 1969.

Vaughn, Karen Iversen. *John Locke, Economist and Social Scientist*. London: Athlone Press, 1980.

Veblen, Thorstein. *The Theory of the Leisure Class*. New York: Mentor, 1953.

Viner, Jacob. *International Trade and Economic Development*. Glencoe, IL: The Free Press, 1952.

———. *Religious Thought and Economic Society*. Ed. by Jacques Melitz and Donald Winch. Durham, NC: Duke University Press, 1978.

Webb, Sidney, and Beatrice Webb. *History of Trade Unionism*. London: Longmans, Green, 1894.

Von Mises, Ludwig. *The Anti-Capitalist Mentality*. New York: D. Van Nostrand, 1956.

*Washington Post*. November 13, 1994, 1.

Whittaker, Edmund. *A History of Economic Ideas*. New York: Longmans, Green, 1940.

Wolfe, Alan. "The Final Freedom." *New York Times Magazine*, March 18, 2001, 48, 50, 51.

# Index

Mill, John Stuart, 30, 55, 71–72, 103,
125–26
Mitchell, Wesley C., 102n50,
modernism, 94, 144, 155–56, 177
Montesquieu, Baron de, 179n25
moral law, 3, 5, 18–20, 22–23, 25–26,
28–29, 42, 56–57, 59, 62, 64–65, 74,
110, 121, 123, 126, 129, 133, 136–38,
172, 182–85, 188, 190
moral philosophers, 6, 13–15, 25, 28,
42, 58, 61, 67, 71
morality. *See* moral law
Moslems, 2
mutual sympathies, 58–61, 64–65, 67,
68, 115, 124–25
Myrdal, Gunnar, 192n3

"natural ethics," 6, 22, 27, 30–31, 57, 115
natural harmony, 15, 19, 22, 27, 30, 31,
58–60, 63, 68, 73, 96, 112, 115
Natural Law, 2–3, 5–7, 9–11, 13, 18–19,
21–26, 28–29, 31, 40–42, 44–46,
50–51, 124, 126, 171–72, 174–75,
181–83, 187, 190–91; on economics,
46
natural law of harmony, 15, 22, 58
natural law of nature, 20
"natural laws," 14–15, 20, 26
"natural" moral law, 22
natural rights. *See* human rights
natural theology, 18, 29
neoclassicism, 7, 103–4, 112n1, 116
Newton, Isaac, 12, 14, 19, 133
Niebuhr, Reinhold, 178n7
Nisbet, Robert, 17, 99n16
Novak, Michael, 78n55

Ohlin-Heckscher theory of trade, 71
optimism, 4, 27, 64, 68–69, 144, 188
original sin, 17, 63, 168, 181
Ortega y Gasset, José, 44, 52n15

Pascal, Blaise, 50, 65
Pesch, Heinrich, 193n11
physiocrats, 74n2
Pieper, Joseph, 79n57
Pigou, Arthur C., 55
Pius XI (pope), 91

population, 7, 139, 143–51, 185; aging
of the population, 145, 149–51, 154;
Club of Rome, 146; dependency
ratio, 148–50; family, 144–45, 149,
154–57; fertility rates, 146–47, 154;
life expectancy, 147–48; optimum
population, 144, 185, 188; security
systems, 149–51, 154, 156; sick and
elderly, 156; UN data, 145–47
positive law, 6, 9–10, 41, 43, 50, 182
Positivism. *See* Comte, August
Prebisch, Raul, 77n45
private property, 69, 93, 118, 121, 125,
133–35, 158, 184–85
profits, 63, 78n53, 95, 104, 109, 125,
132, 136
progress, 17–18, 21, 29, 68, 86, 90, 95,
167–68, 176–78, 187, 191
prophets of gloom and doom, 146, 148,
163n7
Protestant Reformation, 17

Randall, John Herman, 17, 19
Raspail, Jean, 141n19
rationalism, 9–13, 16–17, 19, 24–25, 27,
30–31, 44–46, 56, 65–66, 74, 81, 90,
94, 110, 121–23, 136–37
Rauscher, Anton, 84
reason. *See* rationalism
Reign of Terror, 17
relativism, 23, 31, 74, 187
religion, 3, 7, 16–18, 22–23, 49, 86,
91–92, 124, 137–38, 139, 176; Marx's
interpretation of, 91–92
Ricardo, David, 55, 70–71, 85
rights of man. *See* human rights
Robbins, Lionel, 113n8
Robinson, Joan, 106–7
Rodriguez Casado, Vicente, 11
Roepke, Wilhelm, 66–67, 123–24,
166n39, 170, 174–75
Roll, Eric, 83–84
romanticism, 81–82, 98n3
Rommen, Heinrich A., 43
Roscher, Wilhelm, 83
Rousseau, Jean Jacques, 15, 16, 34n34,
56, 119
Ruskin, John, 83

Sauvy, Alfred, 162n2
Say's Law, 113n10. *See also* Keynes,
    John Maynard
Schmoller, Gustav von, 83
scholasticism. *See* Aquinas, St. Thomas
Schumpeter, Joseph, 15, 18, 34, 59, 69,
    72, 74, 78n54, 79n59, 83, 98n2, 111,
    167, 178n2; comments on Keynes,
    113n11, 167–68
Screpanti, Ernesto, 86, 104
secularism, 22, 24, 68–69, 84–85, 91–92,
    94, 123
security systems. *See* population
Sen, Amartya, 62, 67
Shaftesbury, Earl of, 56–57, 75n4
Shakespeare, 1
Sheed, F. J., 43, 44, 171
Simon, Julien, 140, 160–61
Sismondi, Leonard Simonde de, 85–86
Smith, Adam, 4, 6, 51, 55–56, 58, 60–69,
    74, 76n28, 115, 119–20, 124–25
social justice, 137
social security plans, 86, 145, 153
socialism, 4, 6, 7, 84–87, 94, 106, 112,
    116–18, 120, 123, 125, 158, 182–86
solidarity, 124, 135, 138–39, 157–58, 175
Spann, Othmar, 83
Spinoza, Baruch, 33n27
Stalin, Joseph, 89
subsidiarity, 121, 126, 135, 158–61, 175
*Summa Theologiae. See* Aquinas, St.
    Thomas
surplus value. *See* labor theory of
    value

Talmon, J. L., 81
Taylor, Overton, 15, 17, 30, 33, 64, 107,
    109
teleology, 7, 25, 28, 30, 96, 123, 130. *See*

*also* Aquinas, St. Thomas
theocentric approach, 64
Thünen, J. H. von, 113n2
Tocqueville, Alexis de, 16, 126
Torre, Joseph M. de, 10, 117, 119
totalitarianism, 5, 158
Toynbee, Arnold, 92, 128n28, 179n12
transcendentalism, 2–4, 11, 29, 31, 50,
    68, 74, 123, 138, 143, 177, 183, 185,
    187, 191

United Nations, 44, 145, 147, 154,
    163n5, 164n8, 164n12, 172
United Nations Conference on Trade
    and Development (UNCTAD), 71
unity, 162, 169–71
utilitarianism, 4, 6, 14, 33n25, 58,
    60–61, 71–72, 77n48, 85–86, 104,
    113n2, 123, 133, 156, 177;
    diminishing marginal utility, 113n2
Utopian socialists, 85–86, 100n20, 125
utopianism, 17–18, 85, 87, 93–94, 120,
    151, 173, 184

Vaugn, Karen Iversen, 20
Veblen, Thorstein, 7, 95–96
virtue, 2–3, 7, 30, 57–59, 63, 66, 73–74,
    79n57, 135–38, 161, 172, 174, 176,
    179n25, 190–91
Voltaire, 15, 33n29

Weber, Max, 77n59
Weimar Republic, 84
Welfare State, 7, 106, 112, 120, 151–57,
    159, 165n26, 166nn38–40, 166n42, 185
Wells, H. G., 93–94
work, 5, 7, 129–30

Zamagni, Stephano, 86, 104

—∿∿—

# About the Author

Alberto M. Piedra is the Donald E. Bently Professor of Political Economy at the Institute of World Politics. He is the former Chairman of the Department of Economics and Business and Director of the Latin American Institute at the Catholic University of America. He has served in numerous diplomatic positions, including Senior Area Adviser for Latin America, U.S. Mission to the United Nations (1987–1988); U.S. Ambassador to Guatemala (1984–1987); U.S. Representative to the Economic and Social Council of the Organization of American States; and Senior Adviser, Bureau of Inter-American Affairs, Department of State (1982–1984).